Jennie Taylor

The People's Cook Book

Being a collection of nearly one thousand valuable cooking recipes

Jennie Taylor

The People's Cook Book
Being a collection of nearly one thousand valuable cooking recipes

ISBN/EAN: 9783744788816

Printed in Europe, USA, Canada, Australia, Japan

Cover: Foto ©Lupo / pixelio.de

More available books at **www.hansebooks.com**

Price Thirty Cents.

THE PEOPLES COOK BOOK

NEW YORK:
J. S. OGILVIE & COMPANY,
31 Rose Street.

BOOKS THAT WILL PLEASE.

Mailed free, to any address, post-paid, on receipt of advertised price, by J. S. Ogilvie & Co., Publishers.

The Album Writer's Friend. By J. S. Ogilvie. 16mo, 64 pages. Paper cover, 15 cents; cloth.................... $0.30
This is a new and choice collection of gems of Prose and Poetry, comprising over three hundred selections suitable for writing in Autograph Albums.

Amber the Adopted. By Mrs. Harriet Lewis. 12mo, 400 pp. 1.50

American Temperance Speaker. 12mo, 96 pages. Compiled by J. S. Ogilvie. Paper cover...................... .25

A Bad Boy's Diary. 12mo, 280 pages. Paper cover, 50 cents; cloth, with handsome gold side stamp................ 1.00
It creates roars of laughter wherever it is read, and has been pronounced the most acceptable book of wit and humor which has ever been issued from the American Press.

Bede's Charity. By Hesba Stretton. 12mo, 200 pages..... .75

The Blunders of a Bashful Man. By the author of "A Bad Boy's Diary." 12mo, 160 pages, paper cover, 25 cents; cloth .60

Buckskin Joe; or, The Trapper Guide. By Maurice Sillingsby. 12mo, 300 pages 1.25

Bushel of Fun (A). Gathered from the writings of the leading and most successful humorists of the day.................. .10

Case's (Dr.) New Recipe Book. By Prof. A. L. Case, M.D. 12mo, 160 pages, heavy paper cover, 50 cents; handsomely bound in cloth.... .... 1.00

Carlyle, Thomas (Life of). A history of the first forty years of his life. By James Anthony Froude, M.A. Two volumes in one. 12mo, 700 pages, neatly bound in English silk cloth... ... 1.00

Cobwebs and Cables. 12mo, 454 pages. By Hesba Stretton 1.00

Concert Exercises. 5 cents each; 50 cents per dozen.
    No. 1. *The Christian's Journey.* By Mrs. E. H. Thompson.
    No. 2. *The Story of Redeeming Love* By Mrs. E. H. Thompson. (For Christmas.)
    No. 3. *Christ is Risen.* By Thomas R. Thompson. (Appropriate for Easter.)
    No. 4. *Welcome Greeting.* By J. S. Ogilvie. (Appropriate for Children's Day.)
    No. 5. *Good Tidings.* By J. S. Ogilvie. (Appropriate for Anniversaries and Celebrations.)

THE
People's Cook Book.

BEING A COLLECTION OF NEARLY ONE THOUSAND VALUABLE COOKING RECIPES, BESIDES INVALUABLE HINTS AND INSTRUCTIONS IN REFERENCE TO THE HOME FOR ALL HOUSEKEEPERS.

Compiled by
MRS. JENNIE TAYLOR.

NEW YORK:
J. S. OGILVIE & COMPANY,
31 Rose Street.

Copyright, 1882,
By J. S. Ogilvie

INDEX.

SOUPS.	Page.
Stock for Soup	13
To Make Soup of the Liquor	13
Force Meat Balls for Soup	13
Stock for Sauces and Gravies	13
Bean Soup	14
Beef Soup	14
Beef Soup with Okra	14
Corned Beef Soup	14
Corn Soup	14
Chicken Soup	15
Clam Soup	15
Celery Soup	15
Egg Balls	15
Egg Soup	15
Fish Chowder	16
Tomato Chowder	16
Fish Soup	16
French Vegetable Soup	16
Green Pea Soup	16
Gumbo Soup	17
Plain Gumbo **Soup**	17
Giblet Soup	17
Game Soup	17
German Pea Soup	17
Julienne Soup	18
Lobster Soup	18
Macaroni Soup	18
Mock Turtle Soup	18
Mutton Soup	19
Mutton Broth	19
Noodles for Soup	19
Okra Gumbo	19
Onion Soup	19
Ox Tail Soup	19
Potato Soup	20
Pot-au-feu	20
Tomato Soup	20
Turkey Soup	20
Veal Broth	20
Vegetable Soup	21
Spring Vegetable Soup	21
Vermicelli Soup	21
FISH.	
To Fry, Broil, or Bake	22
Baked Fish	22
To Boil Fish	22
Boiled Fish	22
Pickling Fish	23
Bread Stuffing for Fish	23
Baked Black Fish	23
Brook Trout	23
Cream Baked Trout	23
Baked White Fish	23
Baked Cod Fish	23
Baked Fish	24
Broiled Salmon	24
To Broil Salmon	24
Boiled Salmon	24

	Page.
Cod Fish, Stewed	24
Cod Fish on Toast	24
Cod Fish Balls	24
Baked Cod Fish	24
Croquettes of Fish	25
Frogs, Fried	25
Fish Chowder	25
Fried Halibut	25
Fish Scallop	25
Fried Eels	25
Potted Shad	26
Pickled Salmon	26
To Fry Shad	26
To Fry Smelts	26
Spiced Shad	26
Salt Salmon	26
Salt Mackerel, Broiled	26
Turbot a la Creme	26
SHELL FISH.	
Lobster Croquettes	27
Lobster Cutlets	27
Lobster Rissoles	27
Broiled Oysters	27
Oyster Chowder	27
Oyster Croquettes	27
Fried Oysters	28
Oyster Pies	28
Oyster **Pot Pie**	28
Pickled Oysters	28
Spiced or Pickled Oysters	29
Roasted Oysters	29
Oysters, Fancy Roast	29
Oyster Stew	29
Stewed Oysters	29
Maryland Stewed Oysters	29
Oysters with Toast	29
Oyster Soup	30
Oyster Short Cake	30
Steamed Oysters	30
Oyster Omelet	30
Scalloped Oysters	30
Soft Shell Crabs	30
Deviled Clams	30
Hot Crab	30
Stewed Clams	31
MEATS.	
Rules for Selecting Meat	31
Rules for Boiling Meat	31
Rules for Broiling Meat	31
Rules for Roasting Meat	31
Beefsteak	31
Boiled Tongue	32
Broiled Ham and Eggs	32
Beef Hash	32
Beef Stew	32
Beef a-la-Mode	32
Boileau	33
Breakfast Dish	33

INDEX.

	Page.		Page.
Croquettes	33	Ham Balls	43
Corned Beef	33	Ham Toast	43
Deviled Beef	33	Pigs' Feet Hash	43
Dried Beef in Cream	34	Pigs' Head	43
Frizzled Beef	34	Pork and Beans	44
Pressed Beef	34	Boston Baked Beans	44
Beef Tongue	34	To Fry Apples and Pork Chops	44
Savory Beef	34	Spare Ribs, Boiled	44
Scrambled Eggs with Beef	34	Roast Lamb	44
Yorkshire Pudding to Roast Beef	34	Mutton a-la-Venison	44
Beefsteak Smothered with onions	34	Boiled Leg of Mutton	45
Chopped Steak	35	Breast of Mutton and Green Peas	45
Stuffed Beefsteak	35	Sweetbreads	45
Beefsteak with Oysters	35	Sweetbreads, Broiled	45
Steak and Oysters	35	Sweetbreads, Fried	45
Broiled Beefsteak	35	Sweetbreads, Stewed	45
Mock Duck	35	Traveling Lunch	46
Roast Veal	36	Sweetbread Fritters	46
Fillet of Veal	36	To Broil Sweetbreads	46
Veal Cutlets	36	Stewed Tripe	46
Veal Cutlets Broiled	36	Beef Heart	46
Veal	36	Meat Croquettes	46
Veal Cutlets Baked	36	Beef Omelet	46
Veal Cutlets	36	Pounded Beef	46
Pate de Veau	37	Mutton Pie	47
Veal Scallop	37	Pot Pie	47
Veal Steaks	37	Tomato Stew	47
Stewed Veal	37	GAME.	
Marbled Veal	37	Broiled Quail	47
Preparation of Veal	38	Broiled Prairie Chicken	47
Pressed Veal or Chicken	38	Broiled Pigeons	47
Sandwiches	38	Partridge Pie	48
Minced Liver	38	Roast Quail or Prairie Chickens	48
Veal Croquettes	38	Wild Duck	48
Veal Cheese	39	Venison Stewed	48
Veal Hash	39	Broiled Venison Steak	48
Calf's Liver, Stewed	39	To Cook Venison	48
To Dress Calf's Head	39	Pigeon Compote	48
Mock Terrapin	39	Roast Wild Fowl	49
Broiled Calves' Liver, with Bacon	39	Roast Partridges, Pheasants, or Quails	49
Sweetbreads with Mushrooms	39		
Sweetbreads with Tomatoes	40	To Broil Quail or Woodcock	49
Fried Tripe	40	To Roast Wild Duck or Teal	49
Spiced Tripe	40	Pigeon Pie	49
Baltimore Meat Pie	40	Roast Pigeons	49
Croquette	40	To Roast Pigeons	49
Meat Rissoles	40	Fried Rabbit	49
Breaded Lamb Chops	41	Stewed Rabbit	50
Cutlets a-la-Duchesse	41	Roast Rabbit	50
To Fry Lamb Steaks	41	Rabbit Pie	50
Spiced Lamb (cold)	41	Snipe	50
Stewed Lamb Chops	41	POULTRY.	
Mutton Chops	41	How to Choose Poultry	50
Haricot Mutton	42	Plain Stuffing	51
Capt. Chiraz Ragout	42	Potato Stuffing	51
Irish Stew	42	Apple Stuffing	51
Ragout	42	Chestnut Stuffing	51
Ragout of Cold Veal	42	Roast Turkey	51
Baked Ham	43	Boiled Turkey	51
Pork Steaks Broiled	43	Turkey Dressed with Oysters	52
Roast Pork	43	Turkey Scallop	52
Ham and Eggs	43	Curried Chicken	52
Boiled Ham	43	Stewed Chicken with Oysters	52

INDEX.

	Page		Page
Chicken Pie	53	Celery Sauce	63
Fried Chicken	53	Cream Dressing	63
Pressed Chicken or Veal	53	Horse Radish	63
Jellied Chicken or Veal	53	Mayonnaise Sauce	63
Chicken Pot Pie	53	Mustard for Table	63
Broiled Chicken	53	Onion Sauce	64
Chicken Croquettes	54	Tomato Sauce	64
Baked Chicken	54	Parsley Sauce	64
Nice Way to Cook Chicken	54	Melted or Drawn Butter	64
Chicken Pudding	54	Apple Sauce	64
Sculloped Chicken	54	Cranberry Sauce	64
Broiled Chicken	54	Egg Sauce	64
Croquettes	55	White Sauce	64
Fricasseed Chicken	55	Oyster Sauce	65
Poultry Croquette	55	Mint Sauce	65
Minced Fowls	55	Cream Sauce	65
Roast Duck	55	Gravy for Roast Beef	65
Roast Goose	55	Piquante Sauce	65
Boned Turkey	55	Sauce for Boiled Turkey or Chicken	65
Chickens Fried with Rice	56		
Chicken Sandwiches	56	Vegetable Sauce	65
Giblet Pie	56	**VEGETABLES.**	
Pickled Chicken	56	Lima Beans	66
Smothered Chicken	56	Cabbage a-la-Cauliflower	66
Spring Chicken	56	Cream Cabbage	66
Stewed Pigeons	56	Stewed Celery	66
Jugged Pigeon	57	Green Corn on the Cob	66
Stewed Giblets	57	Corn Fritters	66
SALADS.		Green Corn Pudding	66
Mayonnaise Salad Dressing	57	French Mushrooms Canned	67
Simple Dressing for Salads	57	Mushrooms Broiled	67
Chicken Salad Dressing	57	Baked Onions	67
Chicken Salad	58	Succotash	67
Lobster Salad	58	Tomatoes a-la-Creme	67
Lettuce Salad	58	Browned Tomatoes	67
Potato Salad	59	Broiled Tomatoes	67
Cucumber Salad	59	Baked Tomatoes	68
Sweet Bread Salad	59	Scalloped Tomatoes	68
Salmon Salad	59	Sweet Potatoes	68
Cold Slaw	60	Mash Potatoes	68
Kohl-Slaw	60	Browned Potatoes	68
Hot Slaw	60	Quirled Potatoes	68
Beef Salad	60	Potato Puff	68
Cabbage Salad	60	Saratoga Potatoes	69
Celery Salad	60	Potato Cakes	69
Chicken Celery	61	Mashed Potatoes	69
Cabbage Salad	61	Broiled Potatoes	69
Fish Salad	61	Potatoes a-la-Delmonico	69
Salad Dressing	61	Fried Potatoes with Eggs	69
Salad Dressing for Lettuce	61	Potato Balls or Croquettes	69
Salmon Salad	61	Stewed Potatoes	70
Tomato Salad	61	Lyonnaise Potatoes	70
SAUCES.		Fried Oyster Plant	70
Anchovy	62	Salsify or Vegetable Oysters	70
Butter Sauce	62	Baked Egg Plant	70
Brown Butter Sauce	62	Fried Egg Plant	70
Drawn Butter Sauce	62	Egg Plant Baked	70
Caper Sauce	62	Egg Plant	71
Substitute for Caper Sauce	62	Stuffed Cabbage	71
Boiled Egg Sauce	62	To Boil Asparagus	71
Pickle Sauce	62	Baked Beats	71
Tomato Sauce	62	Beans	71
Mushroom Sauce	63	Baked Beans	71

INDEX.

	Page.
Greens	72
Lima Beans	72
Macaroni	72
Macaroni as a Vegetable	72
Macaroni with Cheese	72
Macaroni with Oysters	72
Macaroni Stewed	72
Macaroni with Tomatoes	73
Boiled Onions	73
Escalloped Onions	73
Scotch Escallops	73
Turnips	73
Fried Parsnips	73
Asparagus	73
Spinach	73
Fresh Corn Mush	74
Parsnip Fritters	74
Parsnip Stew	74
Green Peas	74
Boiled Hominy	74
Cauliflower	74
To Fry Parsley	74
Stewed Mushrooms	74
Tomato Toast	75
Stuffed Tomatoes	75
An Excellent Dish	75
Parsnip Fritters	75
Potato Cake	75
Baked Potatoes	75
Potato Cheese Puff	75
Potato Puff	75
Carrots Stewed	76
Cauliflower with Cheese	76
Cabbage a-la-Creme	76
EGGS AND OMELETS.	
Proper Way to Cook Eggs	76
To Preserve Eggs	76
A Nice Cheese Relish	76
Scrambled Eggs with Ham	76
To Poach Eggs	77
Stuffed Eggs	77
Egg Toast	77
Cheese Omelet	77
Omelet with Oysters	77
Tomato Omelet	77
Bread Omelet	77
Baked Omelet	78
Omelet	78
Apple Omelet	78
Oyster Omelet	78
Omelet Souffle	78
French Omelet	78
Omelet with Ham	78
Boiled Eggs with Sauce	79
Baked Eggs	79
Hominy Fritters	79
Baked Cabbage	79
Beets	79
Egg a-la-Mode	79
Egg Baskets	79
French Egg Cake	80
BREAD, BISCUIT, ETC.	
Rules for Making Bread, etc.	80

	Page.
Hop Yeast	80
Potato Yeast	81
Yeast	81
Yeast and Bread	81
Yeast for the Bread	81
Vienna Bread	81
Bread	82
Steamed Brown Bread	82
Buckwheat Cakes	82
Bread Pancakes	82
Cornmeal Pancakes	82
Rice Pancakes	83
Tomato Pancakes	83
Yeast Waffles	83
Waffles	83
Brown Bread	83
Biscuits	83
Corn Bread	83
Cornmeal Gems	84
Graham Puffs	84
Graham Muffins	84
Graham Crackers	84
Graham Biscuits	84
German Puffs	85
Graham Gems	85
Brown Bread	85
Boston Brown Bread	85
Corn Bread	85
Boiled Indian Bread	85
Corn Cake (delicious)	85
Corn Bread without Eggs	85
Cornmeal Muffins	85
Corn Bread	86
Corn Griddle Cakes	86
Steamed Corn Bread	86
Miss Plater's Corn Mush	86
Drop Biscuits	86
Soda Biscuits	86
Newport Breakfast Cakes	86
Crumpets	86
English Rolls	86
How to Make Rolls	87
Rusks	87
Sweet Rusk	87
French Rolls	87
Cinnamon Rolls	87
Breakfast Rolls	87
Potato Rolls	88
Vienna Rolls	88
English Tea Cake	88
Brown Loaf	88
Steamed Graham Bread	88
Mrs. M.'s Brown Bread	88
Graham Muffins	88
Graham Breakfast Rolls	89
Graham Biscuit	89
Boston Brown Bread	89
To Freshen Stale Bread	89
Milk Sponge Bread	89
Salt Rising Bread	89
Baking Powder Biscuit	90
Soda Biscuits	90
Tremont House Rolls	90

INDEX.

	Page.
Light Biscuit	90
French Rolls	91
Rolls	91
Wheat Muffins	91
White Muffins	91
Popovers	91
Cream Puffs	91
Puffets	92
Rosettes	92
Sally Lunn	92
Strawberry Short Cake	92
Lemon Short Cake	92
Yeast Waffles	92
Waffles	93
Cream Waffles	93
Lemon Turnovers	93
Varieties	93
Drop Biscuit	93
Milk Toast	93
Mock Cream Toast	93
Oatmeal Porridge	93
Oatmeal Gems	93
Fried Corn Bread	94
French Toast	94
Graham Muffins	94
Lizzie's Cream Muffins	94
Parker House Rolls	94
Rolls	95
Rusk	95
Delicious Rice Waffles	95
Snow Balls	95
Fritters	95
Fritter Batter	95
Hominy Fritters	96
Oatmeal Gruel	96
Savory Biscuits	96
Dyspepsia Bread	96
Puffets	96
Rice Muffins	96
Rice Bread	96
Rice Croquettes	97
Apple Pancakes	97
Spanish Puffs	97
Corn Starch Puffs	97
Breakfast Puffs	97
Flannel Cakes	97
Oyster Fritters	97
Fritters	97
Apple Fritters	98
Cream Fritters	98
Egg Waffles	98
How to Cook Oatmeal	98
Oatmeal Mush	98
PUDDINGS.	
Rules for Making Pudding	99
Apple Dumplings	99
Apple Roll	99
Brown Top Pudding	99
Blackberry Pudding	99
Batter Fruit Pudding	100
Charles Pudding	100
Dyspeptic's Pudding	100
Delicious Pudding	100

	Page.
Indian Pudding	100
Aunt Kittie's Suet Pudding	100
Lemon Pudding	101
Poverty Pudding	101
English Plum Pudding	101
Plum Pudding	102
Pine Apple Pudding	102
Queen of Puddings	102
Rye Minute Pudding	102
Batter Pudding	103
Baked Indian Pudding	103
Boiled Indian Pudding	103
Brown Betty	103
Hen's Nest	103
Gooseberry Cream	103
Liquid Sauce for Puddings	104
Cracked Wheat	104
Roley-Poley	104
Snow Pudding	104
Suet Pudding	104
Mrs. Ellis' English Plum Pudding	104
Mock Strawberries	104
Extra Nice Dessert Dish	105
Strawberry Sauce	105
Foam Sauce	105
Lemon Sauce	105
Cream Pudding Sauce	105
Cocoa Sauce	105
Apple Trifle	105
Apple Cream	106
Apple Floating Island	106
Charlotte Russe	106
Dried Peach Sauce	106
Orange Float	106
Raspberry Blanc Mange	106
Chocolate Ice Cream	106
Lemon Custard	107
Lemon Ice Cream	107
Lemon Ice	107
Orange Ice	107
Peaches and Cream Frozen	107
Cream Tapioca	107
Pineapple Pudding	107
Snow Balls	107
Rice Charlotte	108
Rice Cream	108
Lemon Custard	108
Lemon Jelly	108
Jellied Grapes	108
Apple Custard	108
Cottage Pudding	108
Chocolate Pudding	109
Corn Starch Pudding	109
Cracker Pudding	109
Pudding Sauce	109
Lemon Sauce	109
Strawberry Sauce	109
Hard Sauce for Puddings	109
English Plum Pudding	110
Imitation Plum Pudding	110
Baked Apple Pudding	110
Excellent Baked Apples	110
Apple or Peach Pudding	110

INDEX.

	Page.
Apple or Peach Dumplings	110
Baked Apple Dumplings	111
Apple Batter Pudding	111
Apple Coddle	111
Steamed Dumpling	111
Apple Pudding	111
Almond Pudding	111
Delicious Pudding	112
Delmonico Pudding	112
Fig Pudding	112
Florentine Pudding	112
Gelatine Pudding	112
Bread Pudding	112
Bread and Apple Pudding	112
Cabinet Pudding	113
Cracker Pudding	113
Sauce for Cracker Pudding	113
Cocoanut Pudding	113
Chocolate Pudding	113
Cottage Pudding	114
Cherry Pudding	114
Snow Pudding	115
Sauce for Snow Pudding	115
Cream Tapioca Pudding	115
Tapioca Pudding	115
Transparent Pudding	116
Macaroni Pudding	116
Molasses Pudding	116
Orange Pudding	116
Peach Meringue	116
Peach Pudding	117
Palace Pudding	117
Printers' Pudding	117
Plain Pudding	117
Jellied Rice	117
Royal Pudding	117
Rice Pudding	118
Cream Rice	118
Sago Pudding	118
Sago Jelly	118
Suet Pudding	118
Steamed Suet Pudding	119
Plain Boiled Pudding	119
Velvet Pudding	119
Vermicelli Pudding	119

PASTRY.

Rules for Making Pastry	120
Puff Paste	120
Apple Tarts	120
Sliced Apple Pie	120
Lemon Custard Pie	121
Two-Crust Lemon Pie	121
Lemon Pie	121
Mock Mince Pie	122
Mince Meat	122
Cream Pie	122
Cocoanut Pie	123
Cream Puffs	123
French Puffs	123
Cream Tartlets	123
Delicate Pie	123
Fruit Pie	123
Good Pie Crust for Dyspeptics	124

	Page.
Mother's Lemon Pie	124
Apple Pie	124
Apple Custard Pie	124
Apples	124
Washington Pie	124
Cocoanut Pie	124
Ripe Currant Pie	124
Green Currant Pie	125
Hurry Pie	125
Summer Mince Pie	125
Orange Short Cake	125
Pineapple Pie	125
Pie-Plant Charlotte	125
Pumpkin Pie	125
Rhubarb Pie	126
Strawberry Short Cake	126
Tarts	126
Chocolate Drops	126
Lemon Taffy	126
Chocolate Caramels	126
A Pretty Tea Dish	127
Raisin Pie	127
Sweet Potato Pie	127
Orange Pie	127
Oyster Patties	127
Malborough Pie	127
Peach Pie	128

CUSTARD AND CREAMS.

Apple Meringue	128
Apple Snow	128
Apple Puffets	128
Velvet Blanc-Mange	128
Fruit Blanc-Mange	128
Chocolate Blanc-Mange	129
Rice Blanc-Mange	129
Lemon Ice	129
Ice Cream	129
Chocolate Ice Cream	129
Strawberry Ice Cream	130
Floating Island	130
Velvet Cream	130
Chocolate Custard	130
Persian Cream	130
Pink Cream	130
Russian Cream	130
Lemon Cream	131
Souffee de Russe	131
Spanish Charlotte	131
Chocolate Cream Custard	131
Boiled Custard	131
Baked Custard	131
Lemon Custard	131
Coffee Custard	132
Floating Island	132
Almond Custard	132
Indian Custard	132
Irish Moss	132
Lemon Jelly	132
A Dish of Snow	132
Apple Float	133
Strawberry Charlotte	133
Lemon Butter	133
Apple Butter	133

INDEX.

	Page.
Orange Dessert	133
Frozen Peaches and Cream	133
Ambrosia	133
Frozen Peaches	134
Frozen Strawberries	134
Chartreuse d'Oranges	134
Baked Pears	134
Charlotte Russe	134
Tutti Frutti	134
CAKES.	
Materials for Cakes	135
Soft Frosting	135
Sutti Fruitti Frosting	135
Chocolate Frosting	135
Almond Frosting	135
Gelatine Frosting	136
Hickory Nut Frosting	136
Apple Cake	136
Almond Cookies	136
Boiled Icing	136
Chocolate Icing	136
Icing	136
Icing for Cake	136
Black Cake	137
Bread Cake	137
Coffee Cakes	137
Breakfast Coffee Cakes	137
Corn Starch Cake	138
Cream Puffs	138
Citron Cake	138
Chocolate Cake	138
Cake without Eggs	139
Cream Cake	139
Cookies	139
Mrs. Caldwell's Cookies	140
Cocoa-Nut Cookies	140
Corn Gems	140
Cocoa-Nut Cake	140
Ice Cream Cake	141
Cup Cake	141
Cottage Cake	141
Cinnamon Cake	141
Cocoa-Nut Jumbles	141
Drop Cookies	141
Cocoa-Nut Biscuits	142
Delicate Cake	142
Plain Doughnuts	142
Doughnuts	142
Raised Doughnuts	142
Dolly Varden Cake	143
Fruit Cake from Dough	143
Fig Cake	143
Fried Cakes	143
Fruit Cake, par excellence	143
Gingerbread	143
Soft Gingerbread	144
Sponge Gingerbread	144
Hard Gingerbread	144
Ginger Drops	144
Ginger Pound Cake with Fruit	144
Gold and Silver Cake	145
Ginger Snaps	145
Ginger Cookies of Attrition Flour	145

	Page.
Graham Cookies	145
Ginger Cookies	146
Gold Cake	146
Gentleman's Favorite	146
Soft Ginger Cookies	146
Cheap Ginger Cookies	146
Hickory Nut Cookies	146
Hickory Nut Cakes	146
Honey Cake	146
Honey Cakes	146
Imperial Cake	147
Ice Cream Cake	147
Jelly Roll	147
Jumbles	147
Lady Fingers	147
Lemon Jelly Cake	148
Lemon Cream Cake	148
Lemon Cream for Cake	148
Molasses Fruit Cake	148
Mary's Sponge Cake	148
White Sponge Cake	148
Maccaroons	148
White and Yellow Mountain Cake	149
Marble Cake	149
Marble Spice Cake	149
Nut Cake	149
Orange Cake	150
Pine Apple Cake	150
Peach Cake	150
Porcupine Cake	150
Puff Cake	150
Pound Cake	150
Ribbon Cake	151
Ribbon Fig Cake	151
Short Cake	151
Spice Cake	151
Silver Cake	151
Snow Cake	152
Sponge Gingerbread	152
Spanish Buns	152
Sponge Cake	152
Easy Sponge Cake	152
Sea Foam	153
Scotch Short Cake	153
Strawberry Short Cake	153
Seed Cakes	153
Watermelon Cake	153
Wedding Cake	153
White Cake	154
White Pound Cake	154
TEA, COFFE, CHOCOLATE.	
Tea	154
Vienna Coffee	154
Coffee	154
Chocolate	155
Mock Cream for Tea or Coffee	155
FRESH FRUITS.	
To Crystalize Fruit	155
Pineapples	155
Oranges	155
Melons	156
Bananas and Cream	156

INDEX.

JELLIES, JAMS, PRESERVES, ETC.

	Page.
General Hints	156
Jellied Apples	156
Apple Jelly	156
Crab Apple Jelly	157
Currant Jelly	157
Currant Jelly without cooking	158
Grape Jelly	158
Apple Jam	158
Apple Preserves	158
Cherry Jam	158
Damson Preserves	158
Green Gage Preserves	159
Citron Preserves	159
Grape Preserves	159
Nonpariel Preserves	159
Pineapple Preserves	159
Pineapple Jam	160
Plum Butter	160
Pear Preserves	160
Peach Preserves	160
Plum Preserves	160
Quince Preserves	160
Strawberry or Raspberry Jam	160
Raspberry Jam	160
To Preserve Watermelon Rinds	161
Apple Marmalade	161
Orange Marmalade	161
Peach Marmalade	161
Quince Marmalade	161
Creamated Apples	162
Jellied Oranges	162
Pie Plant	162
Apple Butter	162
Lemon Butter	163
Peach Butter	163

CANNED FRUIT, VEGETABLES, ETC.

General Hints	163
Cherries	163
Black Raspberries and Blackberries	163
Green Gage Plums	163
Grapes	164
To Can Peaches	164
Rich Canned Peaches	164
Canned Peaches	164
Quinces	164
Strawberries	165
Canned Strawberries	165
Corn	165
Canned Tomatoes	165
String Beans	165

PICKLES.

Cucumbers	165
Cucumber Pickles	166
Pickled Peppers	166
Pickling Cauliflower	166
Radish Pod Pickles	166
French Pickles (delicious)	166
Pickled Onions	167
Spanish Pickled Onions	167
Chow Chow	167
English Chow Chow	167

	Page.
Red Cabbage and Cauliflower	167
Pickled Cabbage	168
Tomato Chow Chow	168
Chopped Tomatoes	168
Stuffed Peppers	168
Hayes Pickles	168
Higdom	168
Piccalilli	168
Sweet Piccalilli	169
Mixed Pickles	169
Martinoes	169
Yellow Pickle	169
Nasturtiums	170
Spiced Apples	170
Spiced Currants	170
Spiced Cherries	170
Spiced Grapes	170
Spiced Fruit	170
Spiced Peaches	170
Spiced Pears or Peaches	171
Spiced Plums	171
Pickled Cherries	171
Pickled Peaches	171
Sweet Pickled Peaches	171
Pickled Plums	171
Pickled Cantaloupes	171
Sweet Cantaloupe Pickle	172
Sweet Pickles	172
Musk Melon Pickle	172
Sweet Pickled Watermelon Rinds	172
Mock Olives	172
Tomato Figs	172
Spiced Grapes	172
Pickled Pears	173
Gooseberry Sauce	173
Green Tomato Sauce	173
Currant Sauce	173
Spiced Currants	173
Cucumber Ketchup	173
Tomato Ketchup	173
Chili Sauce	173
Oude Sauce	174
Cucumber Ketchup	174
Gooseberry Ketchup	174
Grape Ketchup	174
Tomato Ketchup	175

COOKERY FOR THE SICK.

Beef Tea	175
Veal or Mutton Broth	175
Chicken Broth	175
Scraped Beef	175
To Prepare an Egg	175
Milk Porridge	176
Panada	176
Oatmeal Gruel	176
Port Wine Jelly	176
Barley Water	176
Rice Milk	176
Flaxseed Tea	176
Appleade	176
Blackberry Syrup	176
Toast Water	176
Toast	176

	Page.		Page.
Blackberry Wine	176	**CANDIES.**	
Wine Whey	177	Cocoa-Nut Candy	178
Arrowroot Custards	177	Almond Candy	178
Cracked Wheat	177	To Candy Nuts	178
Raw Egg	177	Chocolate Caramels	178
Fine Hominy	177	Sugar Candy	179
Oatmeal Mush	177	Cream Candy	179
Blackberry Cordial	177	Maple Candy	179
Dried Flour for Infants	177	Butter Scotch	179
Oyster Toast	177		
Egg Gruel	177	Antidotes for Poisons	179-180
Mulled Jelly	178	**MISCELLANEOUS.**	
Irish Moss Blanc Mange	178	Receipts for House-keepers	180, 181, 182, 183, 184, 185
Chicken Jelly	178		

THE PEOPLE'S COOK BOOK.

SOUPS.

The base of soup should be made of good lean fresh meat and bones—two ounces of bone to a pound of meat; allow one quart of water to a pound of meat; put it on a good fire, and when it boils skim well and set back where it will simmer for five hours; add a little pepper and salt, and then strain into a stone jar and place where it can cool quickly. In cold weather this stock will keep several days, and from it can be made a variety of soups, according to flavorings or materials used. Vegetables, tapioca, rice, etc., should be cooked before being added, as too much boiling spoils the flavor of the broth.

It is best to make the broth or stock the day before it is to be used, so that all the grease may be removed.

Onions are nicer if fried until brown in hot butter before being added to the soup.

Yolks of hard-boiled eggs, poached eggs, lemon slices, or *croutons* are simple additions used with soup. Place in the tureen one for each person, and pour the soup over them.

STOCK FOR SAUCES AND GRAVIES.—Place in a saucepan fresh bones of beef, mutton, lamb, veal, or poultry, of either or all; also bones of the same meats from roasted pieces or trimmings; with one quart of cold water to every pound of meat or bones, add vegetables and seasonings, and simmer six hours; then skim off all the fat, pass through a strainer, and set aside for use.

TO MAKE A SOUP OF THE LIQUOR.—Remove the fat and put two quarts, or more if required, of the liquor into a saucepan, and put on the fire to boil; when boiling, sprinkle in two ounces of tapioca or sago, and boil fifteen minutes, stirring occasionally.

FORCE MEAT BALLS FOR SOUP.—Take cooked-meat or fowl and chop fine; season with pepper, salt, and herbs, and a little lemon; mix together with an egg; roll in crumbs, and fry in hot lard.

STOCK FOR SOUP.—Have a large pot on the back of the stove. Put in lean beef, either after having been cooked or before, in the proportion of one pound of beef to one quart of water. Add pork rinds with all the fat taken off. This may cook slowly two or three days. When cold, skim off all the fat and put into another vessel. This stock may be used for all soups in which meat broth is required. By adding for thickening either barley, rice, sago, macaroni or vermicelli, it will make any of these soups.

BEAN SOUP.

1. Boil the beans and put them first through a colander and then through a sieve; season with butter, pepper and salt.

2. Soak one and a half pints of beans in cold water over night. In the morning drain off the water, wash the beans in fresh water, and put into soup kettle, with four quarts of good beef stock, from which all the fat has been removed. Set it where it will boil slowly but steadily till dinner, or three hours at the least. Two hours before dinner slice in an onion and a carrot. Some think it improved by adding a little tomato. If the beans are not liked whole, strain through a colander and send to the table hot.

BEEF SOUP.

Boil a soup bone about four hours, then take out meat into a chopping bowl; put the bones back into the kettle. Slice very thin one small onion, six potatoes and three turnips into the soup. Boil until all are tender. Have at least one gallon of soup when done. It is improved by adding crackers rolled, or noodles, just before taking off. Take the meat that has been cut from the bones, chop fine while warm, season with salt and pepper, and one teacup of soup saved out before putting in the vegetables. Pack in a dish, and slice down for tea or lunch, when cold.

BEEF SOUP WITH OKRA.

Cut a round steak in small pieces and fry three tablespoonfuls of butter, together with one sliced onion, until very brown; put into a soup kettle with four quarts of cold water, and boil slowly an hour; add salt, pepper and one pint of sliced okra, and simmer three and one-half hours longer. Strain before serving.

CORNED BEEF SOUP.

When the liquid in which the beef and vegetables were boiled is cold, remove all the grease that has risen and hardened on top, and add tomatoes and tomato ketchup and boil half an hour—thus making an excellent tomato soup; or add to it rice or sago, or pearl barley, or turn it into a vegetable soup by boiling in the liquor any vegetables that are fancied; several varieties of soup may have this "stock" for a basis, and be agreeable and nutritious.

CORN SOUP.

1. Cut the corn from the cob, and to a pint of corn allow one quart of hot water; boil an hour and pass through a colander; put into a saucepan an ounce of butter and a tablespoonful of flour, being careful to stir well to prevent it being lumpy; then add the corn pulp, a little cayenne pepper, salt, and a pint of boiling milk, and half a pint of cream.

2. Twelve ears of corn scraped and the cob boiled twenty minutes in one quart of water. Remove the cobs and put in the corn and boil fifteen minutes, then add two quarts of rich milk. Season with salt, pepper and butter, and thicken with two tablespoonfuls of flour. Boil the whole ten minutes and turn into a tureen on which the yolks of three eggs have been well beaten.

CHICKEN SOUP.

1. To the broth in which chickens have been boiled for salad, etc., add one onion and eight or ten tomatoes, season with pepper and salt; boil thirty minutes; add two well beaten eggs just before sending to the table.

2. Roast or bake a chicken until turning brown; put it in a soup kettle with three pints of water, and set on a slow fire; skim off the scum; add a middling-sized onion, a little celery, and simmer about three hours; take out the chicken and vegetables, strain and use; the chicken may be used for salad.

3. Boil a pair of chickens with great care, skimming constantly and keeping them covered with water. When tender, take out the chicken, and remove the bone. Put a large lump of butter into a spider, dredge the chicken meat well with flour, and lay in the hot pan; fry a nice brown, and keep hot and dry. Take a pint of the chicken water, and stir in two large teaspoonfuls of curry powder, two of butter and one of flour, one teaspoonful of salt and a little cayenne; stir until smooth, then mix it with the broth in the pot. When well mixed, simmer five minutes, then add the brown chicken. Serve with rice.

CLAM SOUP.

Select five large plump clams, and after chopping them finely add the liquor to the meat. To every dozen allow a quart of cold water, and putting meat, liquor and water into a clean vessel allow them to simmer gently, but not boil, about one-and-a-half hours. Every particle of meat should be so well cooked that you seem to have only a thick broth. Season to taste and pour into a tureen in which a few slices of well-browned toast have been placed. If desired, to every two dozen of clams allow a teacupful of new milk and one egg. Beat the latter very light, add slowly the milk, beat hard a minute or so, and when the soup is removed from the fire stir the egg and milk into it.

CELERY SOUP.

One shank of beef, one large bunch of celery, one cup of rich cream. Make a good broth of a shank of beef, skim off the fat and thicken the broth with a little flour mixed with water. Cut into small pieces one large bunch of celery, or two small ones, boiling them in the soup till tender. Add a cup of rich cream with pepper and salt.

EGG BALLS.

Two hard-boiled yolks of eggs; mix with the raw yolk of one egg a little flour; roll the size of a hazel-nut.

EGG SOUP.

Boil a leg of lamb about two hours in water enough to cover it. After it has boiled about an hour and when carefully skimmed, add one half-cup of rice, and pepper and salt to taste. Have ready in your tureen two eggs well-beaten; add the boiling soup, a little at a time, stirring constantly. Serve the lamb with drawn butter, garnished with parsley and hard-boiled eggs cut into slices.

FISH CHOWDER.

1. Take a fresh haddock, of three or four pounds, clean it well, and cut in pieces of three inches square. Place in the bottom of your dinner-pot five or six slices of salt pork, fry brown, then add three onions sliced thin, and fry those brown. Remove the kettle from the fire, and place on the onions and pork a layer of fish; sprinkle over a little pepper and salt, then a layer of pared and sliced potatoes, a layer of fish and potatoes, till the fish is used up. Cover with water, and let it boil for half an hour. Pound six biscuits or crackers fine as meal, and pour into the pot; and, lastly, add a quart or pint of milk; let it scald well, and serve.

2. Take a small piece of pork, cut into squares, and put it into the bottom of a kettle. Then take your fish (about three pounds would make a good-sized chowder), cut it into pieces (larger squares than the pork), lay enough of this on the pork to cover well, then a layer of potatoes, next a layer of Boston crackers split, on this pepper and salt. Above this put a layer of pork, and repeat the order given above until the materials are all exhausted; let the top layer be buttered crackers. Pour on boiling water until covered, and cover the kettle; keep boiling half an hour. Five minutes before dinner, dredge well with flour, and pour on a pint of milk. This will make the genuine Ryebeach fish chowder.

TOMATO CHOWDER.

Slice a peck of green tomatoes, six green peppers, and four onions; strew a teacup of salt over them. In the morning turn off the water, and put them in a kettle with vinegar enough to cover them, a teacup of sugar, one of grated horseradish, a tablespoonful of cloves, allspice, and cinnamon, each. Boil until soft.

FISH SOUP.

Slice three middling-sized onions and fry them with one ounce of butter till turning yellow; add three or four pounds of fish—bass, pike, trout, salmon, or any fish having a firm flesh; add, also, two carrots, two onions sliced, a little parsley, thyme, one clove of garlic, a bay leaf, one clove, six pepper corns, and salt; cover the whole with cold water and boil gently for two hours; add more water, if needed; strain and use.

FRENCH VEGETABLE SOUP.

To a leg of lamb of moderate size take four quarts of water. Of carrots, potatoes, onions, tomatoes, cabbage, and turnips, take a teacup each chopped fine, salt and pepper to taste. Let the lamb be boiled in this water. Let it cool, skim off all the fat that rises to the top. The next day boil again, adding the chopped vegetables. Let it boil three hours the second day.

GREEN PEA SOUP.

One peck of green peas, four tablespoonfuls of lard, heated in the kettle; put in the peas and stir them until perfectly green; add pepper and salt, and pour in as much water as you want soup; boil three-quarters of an hour, then add one teacupful of milk, thickened with one tablespoonful of flour ; put in the soup two or three young onions, cut fine and fried a light brown in butter. Just as you take it up, add yolks of two eggs beaten in a little cream.

GUMBO SOUP.

Cut up a pair of good-sized chickens, as for a fricassee; flour them well, and put into a pan with a good-sized piece of butter, and fry a nice brown; then lay them in a soup-pot, pour on three quarts of hot water, and let them simmer slowly for two hours. Braid a little flour and butter together for a thickening, and stir in a little pepper and salt. Strain a quart or three pints of oysters, and add the juice to the soup. Next add four or five slices of cold boiled ham, and let all boil slowly together for ten minutes. Just before you take up the soup stir in two large teaspoonfuls of finely powdered sassafras leaves, and let it simmer five minutes, then add your oysters. If you have no ham, it is very nice without it. Serve in a deep dish, and garnish the dish with rice.

PLAIN GUMBO SOUP.

Take a piece of ham half the size of your hand, and a knuckle of veal; put them into a pot with two quarts of cold water; simmer slowly two or three hours, then add two quarts of boiling water. Twenty minutes before serving, put in one small can of okra and as many oysters as you please. Season to taste.

GIBLET SOUP.

Prepare first the vegetables, viz.: an onion, a small piece of turnip, and a carrot; cut in slices, and fry in hot butter; when hot and beginning to brown, dust in a tablespoonful or less of flour, and add the giblets, and let them all brown; then put all into a kettle with a gallon and a half of water, or half water and half broth, and some pieces of chicken if you have them; simmer for four or five hours; season to taste, and thicken with browned flour; serve with the yolks of hard-boiled eggs, one for each person, placed in the tureen before pouring the soup. It will require the giblets of five chickens for the above quantity.

GAME SOUP.

Roast, until about one-third done, two prairie hens, and put into a soup kettle with about one pound of lean beef, salt, and five pints of water; set on a slow fire; skim as needed, and add one-half a carrot, two stalks of parsley, one of celery, one onion, a bay-leaf, six pepper corns; simmer three hours, and take the birds out of the kettle; simmer then two hours, strain and serve.

GERMAN PEA SOUP.

Prepare a thickening by gradually mixing in a stew-pan three ounces of sifted flour, with one quart of chicken broth; in another stew-pan boil up two quarts of chicken broth, into which stir the thickening; add a little salt and sugar, and one quart of fresh shelled peas previously well washed; continue stirring with a spoon till the soup boils, then simmer till the peas are done; skim, pour the soup in a tureen, and stir in an ounce and a half of butter.

JULIENNE SOUP.

Scrape two carrots and two turnips, and cut in pieces an inch long; cut slices lengthwise about one-eighth of an inch thick; then cut again so as to make square strips; put them in a saucepan, with two ounces of butter, three tablespoonfuls of cabbage chopped fine, and half an onion chopped; set on the fire and stir until half fried; add broth as you wish to make thick or thin; boil until done; salt to taste; skim off the fat and serve; it takes about two hours; it can be served with rice or barley.

LOBSTER SOUP.

One large lobster; pick all the meat from the shell and chop fine; take one quart of milk and one pint of water, and, when boiling, add the lobster, nearly a pound of butter, salt and pepper to taste, and a tablespoon of flour. Boil ten minutes.

MACARONI SOUP.

Six pounds of beef put into four quarts of water, with one large onion, one carrot, one turnip, and a head of celery, and boiled three or four hours slowly. Next day take off the grease and pour into the soup kettle, season to taste with salt, and add a pint of macaroni broken into small pieces, and two tablespoonfuls of tomato ketchup. Half to three-quarters of an hour will be long enough to boil the second day.

MOCK TURTLE SOUP.

1. Boil a calf's head with a slice of ham till it all falls to pieces; strain, and set away to cool. The next day skim well, take a soup bunch of vegetables well boiled; strain and mix with the calf's head liquor, with a little of the meat from the head. Boil an hour before using. Take two tablespoonfuls of browned flour, moisten and stir into the soup before putting in the force-meat and egg balls. After putting in the force-meat balls, let it boil up, and dish right away, having in the tureen two hard-boiled eggs cut in thin slices, and two lemons, also cut in thin slices.

2. Take a calf's head and feet, boil them until the meat separates from the bones; pick the bones out and cut the meat in pieces, about an inch in size; put it back, and boil it about two hours more; chop the brains fine; add eight or nine onions and a little parsley; mix the spices with this (mace, cloves, pepper, and salt), and put it in the soup an hour or more before it is done; roll six or eight crackers with one half-pound of butter, and when nearly done, drop it in; brown a little flour and put it in; make force-meat balls of veal; fry them, and put them in the bottom of the tureen.

3. Put two ounces of butter in a saucepan and set it on the fire; when melted add a tablespoonful of flour, stir, and when turning brown add three pints of broth (either beef broth or broth made by boiling a calf's head); boil five minutes, and then add about four ounces of calf's head cut in dice; boil five minutes; cut two hard-boiled eggs and half a lemon in dice; mushrooms and truffles cut in dice; boil five minutes; cut two hard-boiled eggs and half a lemon in dice, and put into the tureen and turn the soup over.

MUTTON SOUP.

Boil a leg of mutton from two to three hours, and season with salt, pepper, and about a teaspoonful of summer savory rubbed fine; add rice or noodles as desired.

TO MAKE MUTTON BROTH QUICKLY.

One or two chops from a neck of mutton, one pint of cold water, a small bunch of sweet herbs, one-quarter of an onion, pepper and salt to taste. Cut the meat into small pieces; put it into a saucepan with bones in cold water, but no skin nor fat; add the other ingredients; cover the saucepan and bring the water quickly to boil; take the lid off and continue the rapid boiling for twenty minutes, skimming it well during the process; strain the broth into a basin; if there should be any fat left on the surface, remove it by laying a piece of thin paper on the top; the greasy particles will adhere to the paper and so free the preparation from them.

NOODLES FOR SOUP.

Beat one egg light; add a pinch of salt, and flour enough to make a stiff dough; roll out in a very thin sheet, dredge with flour to keep from sticking, then roll up tightly. Begin at one end and shave down fine like cabbage for slaw.

OKRA GUMBO.

Cut up one chicken, wash, dry, and flour it thoroughly; salt and pepper, fry very brown in a skillet with a lump of lard large as an egg. Put it into your soup-kettle with five quarts of water; add one onion cut up, and let it boil two hours; add two dozen okra pods, and let it boil another hour. Season to taste and serve with rice.

ONION SOUP.

Slice two medium-sized onions and fry brown in butter with a tablespoonful and a half of flour; put into a saucepan, and stir in slowly four or five pints of milk and water (about one-third water); season to taste, and add a teacup grated potato; set in a kettle of boiling water and cook ten minutes; add a cup of sweet cream and serve quickly.

OX-TAIL SOUP.

1. Take two tails, wash and put into a kettle with about one gallon of cold water and a little salt. Skim off the froth. When the meat is well cooked, take out the bones, and add a little onion, carrot, and tomatoes. It is better made the day before using, so that the fat can be taken from the top. Add vegetables next day, and boil an hour and a half longer.

2. Chop the ox-tail into small pieces; set on the fire with a tablespoonful of butter, and stir until brown, and then pour off the fat; add broth to taste, and boil gently until the pieces of tail are well cooked; season with pepper, salt, and three or four tomatoes; boil fifteen minutes and then serve. This soup can be made with water, in which case season with turnip, onions, carrot, and parsley.

POTATO SOUP.

Peel and slice one dozen potatoes to a quart of water; then boil thoroughly till the potatoes are done; then add two teacups of milk and a little butter; stir till butter is dissolved; take butter the size of an egg with two tablespoonfuls of flour; mix together well, and brown in a pan over the stove, after which stir it gradually into the soup; salt and pepper to suit one's taste.

POT-AU-FEU.

Take four pounds of beef without any bone, tie it into shape, and put into a pot with six quarts of water; when the water is boiling, put in half an ounce of salt; take two carrots, two turnips, one parsnip, one head of celery, and after washing, tie them together with a piece of string and put it into the pot after the meat has boiled an hour; then tie together one bay-leaf, sprig of parsley, thyme, and marjoram, and add, also, one onion, into which stick three cloves; when the vegetables have been in the pot two hours, add one cabbage cut in two; when the contents of the pot have simmered gently four hours, remove the meat on to a hot dish, and garnish with the carrots, turnip, and parsnip, and pour over it a little of the liquor; serve the cabbage in a hot vegetable dish; strain the liquor through a colander, and put aside to cool; do not remove the fat until required for use.

TOMATO SOUP.

1. One quart of tomatoes, one quart of milk, one pint of water; boil water and tomatoes together twenty minutes, then add the milk and one teaspoonful of soda. Season as you do oyster soup, with butter, salt, and pepper. Pour through a colander into a tureen.

2. One quart of tomatoes, one onion, two ounces of flour, four ounces of butter, two tablespoonfuls of sugar, two of salt, one-third of a teaspoonful of cayenne pepper, three pints of water, one-half pint of milk. Boil the tomatoes and onion in water for three-quarters of an hour. Add salt, pepper, sugar, butter, and flour, rub smoothly together like thin cream. Boil ten minutes. Boil separately. When both are boiling, pour the milk into the tomatoes, to prevent curdling. Serve with square of toasted bread.

3. Slice and fry a small onion in hot butter; then add a dozen large tomatoes, skinned and cut in pieces; after they have cooked ten or twelve minutes, take out the onion and press the tomatoes through a sieve; braid a teaspoon of flour with a small piece of butter, and put into a saucepan; when it has cooked a little, add the tomato, season, and add nearly a pint of broth; let it boil a minute or two, and then add a cup of boiled rice, hot, and a half teaspoonful of soda.

TURKEY SOUP.

Take the turkey bones and boil three-quarters of an hour in water enough to cover them; add a little summer savory and celery chopped fine. Just before serving, thicken with a little flour (browned), and seasoned with pepper, salt, and a small piece of butter.

VEAL BROTH.

Pick and wash a teacup of rice, and put into your dinner-pot; cut up three or four small onions and add to the rice; next, add your meat, which should be cut in pieces of about a quarter of a pound each; let the whole be covered with water from two to three inches above the meat. When it has boiled an hour, add a few small turnips and carrots sliced, with a tablespoonful of salt; a little before it is served add some parsley. This is a favorite broth with many people. It is very nice without the carrots. Some prefer it thickened with flour instead of rice.

VEGETABLE SOUP.

1. Scrape clean, and slice three carrots and three turnips; peel three onions; fry the whole with a little butter till it turns rather yellow; then add also two heads of celery cut in pieces, three or four leeks, also cut in pieces; stir and fry the whole for about six minutes; when fried, add also one clove of garlic, salt, pepper, two cloves, and two stalks of parsley; cover with three quarts of water; keep on rather a slow fire, skim off the scum carefully, and simmer for about three hours; then strain and use.

2. Seven ounces of carrot, ten ounces of parsnip, ten ounces of potatoes cut in thin slices, one and one-quarter ounces of butter, five teaspoonfuls of flour, a teaspoonful of made mustard, salt and pepper to taste, the yolks of two eggs, rather more than two quarts of water; boil the vegetables in the water two and one-half hours; stir them often, and, if the water boils away too quickly, add more, as there should be two quarts of soup when done. Mix up in a basin the butter and flour, mustard, salt and pepper, with a teacupful of cold water; stir in the soup and boil ten minutes. Have ready the yolks of the eggs in a tureen; pour on, stir well, and serve. Time, three hours is sufficient for eight persons.

3. Scrape clean and slice three carrots and three turnips, peel three onions; fry the whole with a little butter till it turns rather yellow, and then add two heads of celery cut in pieces; stir and fry for about six minutes; when fried add one clove of garlic, salt, pepper, two cloves, two stalks of parsley, and cover with about three quarts of water; keep on a rather slow fire, skim off the scum carefully, and simmer three hours; strain and serve.

SPRING VEGETABLE SOUP.

Take two pounds of shin of beef and two pounds of knuckle of veal; remove all the fat and break the bones and take out the marrow; put into a pot with five pints of water; add a teaspoonful of salt, and then cover and let it come to a boil quickly; remove the scum that rises, and set where it will simmer for five hours; one hour before serving, add two young carrots, scraped and cut in slices, half a head of celery, and a small onion cut into squares; in half an hour, add one turnip sliced, and in fifteen minutes one cauliflower broken in small pieces.

VERMICELLI SOUP.

Boil a shin of veal in three quarts of water. Put in a turnip, an onion, and one carrot, whole. Boil about three hours. Add salt and a small teacup of vermicelli, and boil for three-quarters of an hour. Before adding vermicelli, strain through a colander. Keep adding water if it boils away.

FISH.

Fish when fresh are hard when pressed by the finger—the gills red—the eyes full. If the flesh is flabby and the eyes sunken, the fish are stale. They should be thoroughly cleaned, washed, and sprinkled with salt.

Before broiling fish, rub the gridiron with a piece of fat, to prevent its sticking. Lay the skin side down first.

The earthy taste often found in fresh-water fish can be removed by soaking in salt and water.

Most kinds of salt fish should be soaked in cold water for twenty-four hours—the fleshy side turned down in the water.

Fish should be fresh, and always well cooked.

Never soak fresh fish in water, unless frozen. Clean, rinse, and wipe dry; in warm weather, lay on the ice until needed.

In boiling, put into cold water, to which add a little salt and vinegar, and allow eight minutes to the pound. If boiled whole do not remove the head and tail, and serve always with a sauce.

TO FRY.

Dredge with flour, dip lightly in beaten egg, roll in cracker crumbs, and fry in very hot lard. Serve with lemon slices.

TO BROIL.

Rub over with olive oil; cut in pieces or broil whole as preferred, over a clear, hot fire; when done, sprinkle with pepper and salt, a little lemon juice, a little chopped parsley, and some melted butter.

TO BAKE.

Stuff with a dressing as for poultry, and sew it up; lay strips of salt pork over it, sprinkle with pepper, salt, and crumbs, and bake in a hot oven; baste often.

BAKED FISH.

Stuff it with plain dressing; put in a pan with a little water, salt, pepper, and butter. Baste while baking. A fish weighing four pounds will bake in an hour. Garnish with hard-boiled eggs and parsley, and serve with drawn butter or egg sauce.

TO BOIL FISH.

Sew them in a cloth, and put in cold water, with plenty of salt. Most fish will boil in thirty minutes.

BOILED FISH.

Four or five pounds of fish, nearly cover with water and add two heaping tablespoonfuls of salt. Boil thirty minutes, and serve with drawn butter.

FISH.

PICKLING FISH.

Spice the vinegar as for cucumbers, put your fish in and let them boil slowly for a few minutes, until done, without breaking; then set them away for several weeks, and the bones will be entirely destroyed.

BREAD STUFFING FOR FISH.

Take about half a pound of stale bread and soak in water, and when soft press out the water; add a very little chopped suet, pepper, salt, a large tablespoonful of onion minced and fried, and, if preferred, a little minced parsley; cook a trifle, and after removing from the fire add a beaten egg.

BAKED BLACK FISH.

Rub a handful of salt over the surface, to remove the slime peculiar to the fish. For the stuffing, two ounces of beef drippings, two tablespoonfuls of chopped parsley and one ounce of salt pork; put in a saucepan and fry brown; then add a tablespoonful of chopped capers, half a saltspoonful of white pepper, one-half teaspoonful of salt, five ounces of bread, and one gill of broth; then stir until scalding hot; place inside the fish; cut a quarter of a pound of pork in thin slices and lay on either side of the fish, holding in place by twine wound around it—a generous sprinkle of salt and pepper completing it for the baking-pan. Bake in a hot oven one-half hour and serve on slices of fried bread with a sauce made of stock seasoned with one tablespoonful each of walnut and Worcestershire sauce, one tablespoonful of chopped capers and one tablespoonful of parsley.

BROOK TROUT.

1. If small, fry them with salt pork; if large, boil and serve with drawn butter.
2. Wash, drain and split; roll in flour, seasoned with salt; have some thin slices of salt pork in a pan, and when very hot put in the fish and fry a nice brown.

CREAM BAKED TROUT.

Clean the trout, put in pepper and salt, and close them. Place the fish in the pan, with just cream enough to cover the fins and bake fifteen minutes.

BAKED WHITE FISH.

Prepare a stuffing of fine bread crumbs, a little salt pork chopped very fine; season with sage, parsley, pepper, and salt. Fill the fish with the stuffing, sew it up, sprinkle the outside with salt, pepper, and bits of butter; dredge with flour and bake one hour. Baste often. Serve with egg sauce or parsley sauce.

BAKED CODFISH.

To a large teacup of codfish, picked fine, add two cups of mashed potatoes, two cups of milk, two well-beaten eggs, salt and pepper to taste, and half cup of butter, mix very thoroughly, and bake half an hour.

BAKED FISH.

Open the fish, wash, wipe perfectly dry, and rub over with salt; lay in a dripping-pan with a little butter and water, and bake thirty minutes in a hot oven.

BROILED SALMON.

Take slices of salmon, and half an hour before cooking sprinkle over them a little cayenne pepper, salt, lemon juice, and salad oil; grease the gridiron with a piece of pork; wrap the fish in buttered paper to prevent burning; serve with any sauce suitable for fish.

BOILED SALMON.

A piece of six pounds should be rubbed with salt, tied carefully in a cloth, and boil slowly for three-quarters of an hour. It should be eaten with egg or caper sauce. If any remains after dinner, it may be placed in a deep dish, a little salt sprinkled over, and a teacup of boiling vinegar poured upon it. Cover it closely, and it will make a nice breakfast dish.

TO BROIL SALMON.

The steaks from the center of the fish are the best; sprinkle with salt and pepper, spread on a little butter, and broil over a clear but slow fire.

CODFISH STEWED.

Soak the fish in cold water for several hours; pick fine, and put into a saucepan with cold water; boil a few minutes; pour off the water; add fresh and boil again, and then drain; next add sweet milk and butter, and thicken with flour or corn starch; stir well, and when taken from the fire add the yolks of two or three eggs well beaten; stir, pour into a hot dish, and serve.

CODFISH ON TOAST.

Take a bowl full of shredded codfish, put this in cold water in a skillet; let it come to a boil, then turn into a colander to drain; turn into the skillet again with a little cold milk; season with butter and pepper, stir smooth a tablespoonful of flour with a little cold milk; add, and let it boil for a moment; turn this on to buttered toast on a platter.

CODFISH BALLS.

Pick fine one quart bowl of codfish; let it simmer on the back of the stove a little while; then boil six good-sized potatoes, mash fine, and mix while hot with the fish thoroughly; season with pepper, salt and butter; add three eggs, well beaten, and drop in hot lard, serve in a napkin; lay the napkin on a platter, and the balls on the napkin to absorb the grease.

BAKED CODFISH.

Soak the fish over night; clean thoroughly, then put it into a stone crock, and cover with water; simmer until tender, then pick over, and mash fine. Take two-thirds mashed potatoes, seasoned, and one-third fish; mix well together, and bake until brown; then make a sauce of drawn butter, into which cut up two hard-boiled eggs.

CROQUETTES OF FISH.

Take cold fish of any kind, and separate it from the bones, and mince fine; add a little seasoning, an egg, a very little milk, and a teaspoonful of flour; brush with egg, roll in bread crumbs, and fry brown in hot lard.

FROGS FRIED.

Skin well, and cook for five minutes in salted water the hind legs only; then throw into cold water to cool, and drain; fry in hot fat, and serve, garnished with parsley.

FISH CHOWDER.

Cut a haddock into pieces about an inch thick and two inches square; place slices of salt pork in the bottom of a pot, and fry crisp; take out the pork, and chop fine, leaving the fat in the pot; next put in the pot a layer of fish, a layer of split crackers, some of the pork, and a little chopped onion seasoned with pepper, then another layer of fish, and so on; cover with water, and stew half an hour; put in the dish in which it is to be served, and thicken the gravy with flour; add a little ketchup; boil a moment, and pour over the chowder, and serve.

FRIED HALIBUT.

Place in your spider half a dozen slices of fat pork; fry to a brown, and place in a deep dish; add to the fat three tablespoonfuls of fresh lard; when boiling hot put in the halibut, which should be cut in pieces about three inches square, and dipped in sifted meal, sprinkle with salt, and fry a good brown. After the fish is all fried, put it into the dish with the pork, pour over it the boiling fat, add one tablespoonful of hot water, cover tightly, and stand in the oven twenty minutes.

FISH SCALLOP.

Remains of cold fish of any sort, half a pint of cream, half a tablespoonful of anchovy sauce, half a tablespoonful of made mustard, half a teaspoonful of walnut ketchup, pepper and salt to taste (the above quantities are for half a pound of fish when picked), bread crumbs; put all the ingredients into a stew-pan, carefully picking the fish from the bones; set it on the fire; let it remain till nearly hot; occasionally stir the contents, but do not allow it to boil; when done, put the fish into a deep dish or scallop shell, with a good quantity of bread crumbs; place small pieces of butter on the top; set in a Dutch oven before the fire to brown; it should take half an hour to cook it properly.

FRIED EELS.

Skin, remove head and tail, cut in desired length, and throw into boiling water for five minutes; then drain, season with pepper and salt, roll in flour or cornmeal and fry in boiling lard; serve with tomato sauce.

POTTED SHAD.

Cut into pieces, wash, and dry; mix two teaspoonfuls ground allspice, one of black pepper, one-half tablespoonful salt and sprinkle on each piece; put into a jar with good cider vinegar enough to cover; cover very closely and bake in a moderate oven twelve hours.

PICKLED SALMON.

Soak salt salmon twenty-four hours, changing the water frequently; afterwards pour boiling water *around* it, and let it stand fifteen minutes; drain, and then pour on boiling vinegar with cloves and mace added.

TO FRY SHAD.

Clean, wash, wipe dry, sprinkle with salt and pepper, dip in flour and fry in hot lard.

TO FRY SMELTS.

Wash, cut off the fins, and dry with a cloth; melt a spoonful of butter and into it stir the beaten yolks of two eggs; salt and flour the smelts a little, dip into the egg and butter, roll in grated bread crumbs, and plunge into boiling fat; fry until of a bright yellow-brown; serve upon a napkin, garnished with fried parsley.

SPICED SHAD.

Split and rub with salt and let it stand three or four hours; put into a pot with boiling water to cover, adding a teaspoonful of salt to every quart of water; boil twenty minutes, then drain; sprinkle with two tablespoonfuls allspice, one teaspoonful cayenne pepper; cover with cold vinegar.

SALT SALMON.

Soak well in cold water; when fresh enough, put in a kettle with cold water enough to cover and set over a slow fire; boil gently not more than two minutes and then remove and drain; fry a little parsley in butter and turn over the fish, adding lemon juice as preferred.

SALT MACKEREL BROILED.

Soak in warm water for an hour or two and then wipe dry; brush the fish over with dripping or melted butter; grease the bars of the gridiron and lay on the fish, setting it over a sharp fire; broil both sides, and serve spread with butter and chopped parsley.

TURBOT A LA CREME.

Boil a nice fresh fish, pick out the bones and season with pepper and salt; mix one-quarter pound of flour with one quart of milk, put in four small onions, small bunch of parsley and a sprig or two of thyme, salt, and one-half teaspoonful white pepper. Put over the fire and stir until it forms a paste; take off and add one-half pound butter and yolks of two eggs. Mix thoroughly and pass through a sieve; pour some of the sauce into a baking dish and add a layer of fish and sauce alternately until it is all used. Have sauce on the top, to which add bread crumbs and grated cheese. Bake half an hour.

SHELL FISH.

LOBSTER CROQUETTES.

Chop the lobster very fine; mix with pepper, salt, bread crumbs and a little parsley; moisten with cream and a small piece of butter; shape with your hands· dip in egg, roll in bread crumbs, and fry.

LOBSTER CUTLETS.

Mince the flesh of lobsters fine; season with salt, pepper, and spice; melt a piece of butter in a saucepan; mix with it one tablespoonful of flour; add lobster, finely chopped parsley; mix with some good stock; remove from the fire, and stir into it the yolks of two eggs; spread out the mixture, and, when cold, cut into cutlets, dip carefully into beaten egg, then into fine baked bread crumbs; let them stand an hour, and repeat, and fry a rich brown. Serve with fried parsley.

LOBSTER RISSOLES.

Boil the lobster, take out the meat, mince it fine, pound the coral smooth, and grate for one lobster the yolks of three hard-boiled eggs; season with cayenne and a little salt; make a batter of milk, flour, and well-beaten eggs—two tablespoonfuls of milk and one of flour to each egg; beat the batter well; mix the lobster with it gradually until stiff enough to roll into balls the size of a walnut; fry in fresh butter or best salad oil, and serve.

BROILED OYSTERS.

1. Dry large oysters with a napkin; season with pepper and salt, and broil on a fine wire broiler; turn frequently; or dip each oyster in butter, and roll in bread crumbs before broiling; serve on a hot dish with butter on them.

2. Drain select oysters in a colander. Dip them one by one in melted butter, to prevent sticking to the gridiron, and place them on a wire gridiron. Broil over a clear fire. When nicely browned on both sides, season with salt, pepper, and plenty of butter, and lay them on hot buttered toast, moistened with a little hot water. Serve very hot, or they will not be nice. Oysters cooked in this way and served on broiled beefsteak are nice.

OYSTER CHOWDER.

Fry out three rashers of pickled pork in the pot you make the chowder; add to it three potatoes and two onions, both sliced; boil until they are nearly cooked; soak two or three dozen crackers in cold water a few minutes, then put into the pot a half can of oysters, one quart of milk, and the soaked crackers. Boil all together a few minutes, season with salt, pepper, and butter. Fish chowder can be made the same way by using fresh fish instead of oysters.

OYSTER CROQUETTES

Take the hard end of the oyster, leaving the other end in nice shape for a soup or stew, scald them, then chop fine and add an equal weight of potatoes rubbed through a colander; to one pound of this add two ounces of butter, one teaspoonful of salt, half a teaspoonful of pepper, half a teaspoonful of mace, and one-half gill of cream; make in small rolls, dip in egg and grated bread, fry in deep lard.

FRIED OYSTERS.

1. Take large oysters, wash and drain. Dip them into flour; put in a hot frying pan with plenty of lard and butter; season with salt and pepper; fry brown on both sides. Fried in this way, are similar to broiled oysters.

2. Drain the oysters, and cover well with finest of cracker crumbs, seasoned with salt and pepper. Let them stand half an hour, then dip and roll again in the meal; fry brown in a good quantity of lard and butter.

3. Drain thoroughly in a colander; season with pepper and salt, and set in a cool place until needed; roll each oyster in bread crumbs, and fry in hot lard as you fry doughnuts; drain, and send to the table on a hot platter, garnished with chopped pickles or cold slaw.

OYSTER PIE.

1. Line a dish with a puff paste or a rich biscuit paste and dredge well with flour; drain one quart of oysters, season with pepper, salt, and butter, and pour into the dish; add some of the liquor; dredge with flour and cover with a top crust, leaving a small opening in the center.

2. Allow one can of oysters for two pies, roll out your paste and put in your pie-pan or dish, then put in oysters and cut up a piece of butter the size of an egg for each pie into small pieces; season with salt and pepper, sprinkle a tablespoonful in each, and roll out a top crust; bake from three-fourths of an hour to an hour.

OYSTER POT-PIE.

Have ready nice light-raised biuscuit dough, cut it into small squares season the oysters well with butter, pepper, and salt, and thicken them with a little flour; drop in the pieces of dough and boil till done. This may be baked in the oven in a pudding dish, allowing the dough to brown on the top.

PICKLED OYSTERS.

1. Take two quarts of oysters, put them in a saucepan, and, if they are fresh, salt them; let them simmer on the fire, but not boil; take out the oysters, and add to the liquor in the saucepan a pint of vinegar, a small handful of whole cloves, quarter of an ounce of mace, and two dozen pepper-corns; let it come to a boil, and when the oysters are cold in the jar, pour the liquor on them.

2. Choose the largest oysters and simmer over a slow fire, with a small bit of butter, for three minutes, and then skim out on to a dish to cool; take equal quantities of the liquor and cider vinegar, and heat; place a layer of oysters in a stone jar; throw over them some ground mace, a few cloves, whole allspice, and whole pepper then oysters and spice until all are used; pour over the hot liquor and set away in a cool place.

SHELL FISH.

SPICED OR PICKLED OYSTERS.

Put into a porcelain kettle one hundred and fifty large oysters with the liquor; add salt, and simmer till the edges roll or curl; skim them out; add to the liquor one pint of white wine vinegar, one dozen blades mace, three dozen cloves and three dozen pepper-corns; let it come to a boil and pour over the oysters. Prepared in this way, they will keep several weeks in cold weather.

ROASTED OYSTERS.

Take oysters in the shell, wash the shells clean and lay them on hot coals; when they are done they will begin to open. Remove the upper shell and serve the oysters in the lower shell, with a little melted butter poured over each.

OYSTERS, FANCY ROAST.

Toast a few slices of bread, and butter them; lay them in a shallow dish; put on the liquor of the oysters to heat, add salt, and pepper, and just before it boils, add the oysters; let them boil up once and pour over the bread.

OYSTER STEW.

Put two quarts of oysters in the saucepan with the liquor, and when they begin to boil skim them out and add a pint of cream or rich milk and seasoning; skim well; add to the oysters butter to taste, and pour the hot liquor over them, and serve.

STEWED OYSTERS.

Take one quart of liquor oysters; put the liquor (a teacupful for three) in a stewpan, and add half as much more water, salt, a good bit of pepper, a teaspoonful of rolled cracker for each. Put on the stove, and let it boil; have your oysters ready in a bowl; the moment the liquor boils pour in all your oysters, say ten for each person, or six will do. Now watch carefully, and as soon as it begins to boil take out your watch, count just thirty seconds, take your oysters from the stove. You will have your big dish ready, with one and a half tablespoonfuls of cream or milk for each person. Pour your stew on this, and serve immediately. Never boil an oyster in milk if you wish it to be good.

MARYLAND STEWED OYSTERS.

Put the juice into a saucepan, and let it simmer, skimming it carefully; then rub the yolks of three hard-boiled eggs and one large spoonful of flour well together, and stir into the juice. Cut in small pieces quarter of a pound of butter, half a teaspoonful of whole allspice, a little salt, a little cayenne, and the juice of a fresh lemon; let all simmer ten minutes, and just before dishing add the oysters. This is for two quarts of oysters.

OYSTERS WITH TOAST.

Broil or fry as many oysters as you wish, and lay them on buttered toast; salt and pepper; pour over them a cup of hot, rich cream; keep them perfectly hot until eaten.

OYSTER SOUP.

Drain one quart of oysters, and to the liquor add one quart of boiling water; let it boil; skim carefully; season with a little cayenne pepper and butter size of an egg; add the oysters, and let it boil up once; season with salt, and serve in a hot soup tureen.

OYSTER SHORT-CAKE.

Make a good short-cake, and bake on pie plates; put a quart of oysters on the stove with a little water, half a cup of milk, a good-sized piece of butter, salt, and pepper, and thicken with a tablespoonful of flour; when the cakes are baked, split and spread the oysters between, and some on top.

STEAMED OYSTERS.

Drain some select oysters; put into a pan, and place in a steamer over boiling water; steam until the oysters begin to curl, and then serve on a hot dish, with butter, salt, and pepper; garnish with chopped pickles.

OYSTER OMELET.

Beat six eggs separately very light; season with pepper and salt; add two tablespoonfuls of cream, and pour into a frying-pan, with a good tablespoonful of butter; drop in the omelet eight or ten large oysters, chopped fine, and fry; fold over, and send to table immediately.

SCOLLOPED OYSTERS.

Drain the oysters; place a layer of rolled cracker in the bottom of a buttered pudding-dish; then a layer of oysters; sprinkle with pepper, salt, and small bits of butter; moisten with a little of the liquor mixed with milk; then a layer of bread crumbs, then oysters, and so on until the dish is full, having crumbs on top; beat an egg into a little milk, and pour over the whole; sprinkle with small bits of butter; cover, and bake half an hour; remove the cover, and brown on top before sending to the table.

SOFT-SHELL CRABS.

Season with pepper and salt; roll in flour, then in egg, then in bread crumbs, and fry in hot lard.

DEVILED CLAMS

Chop fifty clams very fine; take two tomatoes, one onion, chopped equally fine, a little parsley, thyme, and sweet marjoram, a little salt, pepper, and bread crumbs, adding the juice of the clams until the mixture is of the consistency of sausage; put it in the shells, with a lump of butter on each; cover with bread crumbs, and bake one-half hour.

HOT CRAB.

Pick the crab; cut the solid part into small pieces, and mix the inside with a little rich gravy or cream, seasoning, and bread crumbs; put all into the shell of the crab, and put into the oven.

STEWED CLAMS.

Chop the clams, and season with pepper and salt, put in a saucepan butter the size of an egg, and when melted add a teaspoonful of flour; add slowly the clam liquor, and then the clams, and cook three minutes; then add half a pint of cream, and serve.

MEATS.

In selecting beef, choose that of a fine smooth grain, of a bright red color and white fat.

The sixth, seventh, and eighth ribs, are the choicest cuts for a roast. Have the bones removed and the meat rolled, but have the butcher send the bones for soup.

The flesh of good veal is firm and dry, and the joints stiff.

The flesh of good mutton or lamb is a bright red, with the fat firm and white.

If the meat of pork is young, the lean will break on being pinched; the fat will be white, soft, and pulpy.

Rules for Boiling Meat.—All fresh meat should be put to cook in boiling water, then the outer part contracts and the internal juices are preserved. For making soup, put on in cold water. All salt meat should be put on in cold water, that the salt may be extracted in cooking. In boiling meats. it is important to keep the water constantly boiling, otherwise the meat will absorb the water. Be careful to add boiling water, if more is needed. Remove the scum when it first begins to boil. Allow about twenty minutes for boiling for each pound of fresh meat. The more gently meat boils, the more tender it will be.

To Broil Meat well, have your gridiron hot before you put the meat on.

Broiling.—This is not only the most rapid manner of cooking meat, but is justly a favored one. It has nearly the same effect upon meat as roasting. The albumen of the outer portions is hardened, and, forming a skin, retains the juices. It should be turned rapidly, in order to produce an equal effect, but the meat should not be punctured with a fork.

Salt meat should be put into cold water and boil slowly.

A red pepper dropped into the water will prevent the rising of an unpleasant odor.

Fresh meat, unless for soup, should be put into boiling water, and be allowed to cook very gently; no salt to be added until nearly done.

In Roasting—Put into a hot oven, and baste frequently.

In Roasting Beef, it is necessary to have a brisk fire. Baste often. Twelve minutes is required for every pound of beef. Season when nearly done.

BEEFSTEAK.

"Farmer" Olcott, in the Hartford *Courant*, writes: "It is sometimes more convenient for the cook to get the beefsteak done tender without watching. I remember catching a Sacramento cook broiling his beef in the oven. No cook ought to be hung for treating a steak to a hot oven when the other conveniences are limited, but a friend tells me of a better way that I think is original with him. He smothers the steak in corn meal and so bakes it, declaring that if there is any way of making a tough steak tender, that is it."

BOILED TONGUE.

In choosing a tongue, ascertain how long it has been dried or pickled, and select one with a smooth skin, which denotes its being young and tender; if a dried one, and rather hard, soak it at least for twelve hours previous to cooking it; if, however, it is fresh from the pickle, two or three hours will be sufficient for it to remain in soak; put the tongue into a stew-pan with plenty of cold water and a bunch of savory herbs; let it gradually come to a boil, skim well, and simmer very gently until tender; peel off the skin, garnish with tufts of cauliflower or Brussels sprouts, and serve; boiled tongue is frequently sent to table with boiled poultry instead of ham, and is by many persons, preferred; if to serve cold, peel it, fasten it down to a piece of board by sticking a fork through the root and another through the top to straighten it; when cold glaze it, and put a paper ruche round the root, and garnish with tufts of parsley; cook a large smoked tongue four to four and a half hours, a small one two and a half to three hours, a large unsoaked tongue three to three and a half hours, a small one, two to two and a half hours.

BROILED HAM AND EGGS.

Cut the ham in thin slices, take off the rind, wash the slices in cold water, and lay them on the gridiron over quick coals; turn frequently, and they will soon be broiled; take them up on a platter, previously warmed, butter and pepper the ham; have ready on the fire a pan of boiling water from the teakettle; break into it as many eggs as you require for the meal, and when the "white" is done, dip out each egg carefully with a spoon, so as to keep it whole, and set it on one of the slices of ham; after all are arranged, sprinkle pepper over each egg and serve.

BEEF HASH.

Chop fine cold steak or roast beef, and cook in a little water; add cream or milk, and thicken with flour; season to taste, and pour over thin slices of toast.

BEEF STEW.

Cut cold beef into small pieces, and put into cold water; add one tomato, a little onion, chopped fine, pepper, and salt, and cook slowly; thicken with butter and flour, and pour over toast.

BEEF A-LA-MODE.

Take a round of beef, remove the bone from the middle, also all the gristle and tough parts about the edges. Have ready half a pound of fat salt pork. Cut into strips as thick and long as your finger. Prepare a nice dressing the same as for stuffing a turkey. With a thin sharp knife make perpendicular incisions in the meat about half an inch apart. Thrust into them the pork and work in with them some of the dressing. Proceed thus until the meat is thoroughly plugged. Put it into a baking pan with a little water at the bottom, cover tightly and bake slowly four hours; then uncover and spread the rest of the dressing over the top, and bake until a nice brown. After taking up, thicken the gravy and pour over the beef. It should be sliced horizontally. Is good either hot or cold.

BOILEAU.

Take a piece of beef weighing six or eight pounds, have the bone taken out; then rub it well with a mixture composed of ground cloves, allspice, black pepper, sweet marjoram, and salt, one teaspoonful of each rubbed fine. After the mixture is well rubbed in, roll it up tightly and tie it; put it into a pot half full of water, with three or four potatoes, a carrot, two turnips, if small, and two onions, and let it stew six houss.

BREAKFAST DISH.

Chop fine as much cold beef or mutton as is required; add a pint, more or less of good soup stock; season with pepper, salt, and ground cloves; thicken with browned flour and pour boiling hot over little bits of nicely-toasted bread. Garnish with slices of lemon and serve at once.

CROQUETTES.

Raw pork chopped fine, two cups; one medium-sized onion, chopped fine; teaspoonful powdered sage; one cup bread, soaked until soft; salt and pepper to taste; two eggs beaten light; mix thoroughly into small flat cakes; roll in flour or crumbs, and fry in hot lard.

CORNED BEEF.

1. Put into cold water enough to cover well, and place where it will cook very slowly for three or four hours; if to be used cold, simmer until the bones can be easily removed, and then press in a square mold.

2. Select a nice piece of fresh beef; rub over sufficient salt to "corn" it, but not to make it very salt; let it stand two or three days, judging of the time by the size of the meat; then wash thoroughly in cold water, and putting in the pot, cover with cold water and boil gently till quite tender; add such vegetables as are desired, like the old time-honored "boil dish;" judge of the quantity of vegetables by the strength of flavor desired in the soup to be made from the water in which the whole is boiled; when done, dish beef and vegetables, and serve hot.

DEVILED BEEF.

Take slices of cold roast beef, lay them on hot coals and broil; season with pepper and salt, and serve while hot, with a small lump of butter on each piece.

DRIED BEEF IN CREAM.

Shave your beef very fine; pour over it boiling water; let it stand for a few minutes; pour this off and pour on good rich cream; let it come to a boil. If you have not cream, use milk and butter, and thicken with a very little flour; season with pepper, and serve on toast or not, as you like.

FRIZZLED BEEF.

Shave beef very fine; put into a frying pan when good and hot; put in the beef and shake and stir until heated through; season with pepper; serve in this way, or just before serving beat one egg light and stir in.

PRESSED BEEF.

Cure a piece of brisket with salt and pulverized saltpetre for five days; boil gently until tender; press until perfectly cold.

BEEF TONGUE.

If it is corned it should be soaked for twenty-four hours before boiling. It will require from three to four hours, according to size. The skin should always be removed as soon as it is taken from the pot. An economical method is to lay the tongue, as soon as the skin is removed, in a jar, coiled up, with the tip outside the root, and a weight upon it. When it is cold, loosen the sides with a knife and turn it out. The slices being cut horizontally all round, the fat and lean will go together.

SAVORY BEEF.

Take a shin of beef from the hind quarter, saw it into four pieces, put it into a pot and boil it until the meat and gristle drop from the bones; chop the meat very fine, put it in a dish and season it with a little salt, pepper, clove, and sage to your taste; pour in the liquor in which the meat was boiled and place it away to harden. Cut in slices and eat cold.

SCRAMBLED EGGS WITH BEEF.

Dried beef chipped very fine; put butter and lard into a skillet, and when hot put in the beef; heat for a few minutes, stirring to prevent burning; break up some eggs into a bowl; season and stir in and cook a few minutes.

YORKSHIRE PUDDING TO SERVE WITH ROAST BEEF.

Three eggs well beaten, to which add nine tablespoonfuls of flour, a small teaspoonful of salt, and beat up with milk until about the consistency of thick cream. This batter pour into a pan in which the beef has been roasted, having enough grease (which must be hot) to bake it. Bake in a quick oven.

BEEFSTEAK SMOTHERED WITH ONIONS.

Put in the skillet a little lard and the steak; peel and slice the onions and lay them over the meat till the skillet is full; season with pepper and salt, cover tightly and place over the fire. After the juice of the onions has boiled away and the meat begins to fry, remove the onions, turn the meat to brown on the other side, then replace the onions as before, being careful that they do not burn.

CHOPPED STEAK,

Take a sirloin steak raw, remove the bone and all gristle or stringy pieces, and chop until a perfect mince; season with salt and pepper; make into a large flat cake about one-half of an inch thick; put into a skillet a good-sized piece of butter and when quite hot put in the steak, and fry brown on both sides. Make a little gravy in the skillet and pour over the meat. This is a nice way to use the ends from tenderloin steaks. The meat can not be chopped too fine.

STUFFED BEEFSTEAK.

Take a rump steak about an inch thick; make a stuffing of bread, herbs, etc., and spread it over the steak. Roll it up, and with a needle and coarse thread sew it together. Lay it in an iron pot on one or two wooden skewers, and put in water just sufficient to cover it. Let it stew slowly for two hours; longer if the beef is tough; serve it in a dish with the gravy turned over it. To be carved crosswise, in slices, through beef and stuffing.

BEEFSTEAK WITH OYSTERS.

Broil a sirloin or tenderloin steak; season; take one quart of oysters, drain off all the liquor, put them into the stew-pan with half of a small cupful of butter, or less butter and a little sweet cream; let them boil, and turn them over the steak on the platter. Oysters broiled and laid on the steak are very nice.

STEAK AND OYSTERS.

Take one pound best rump steak without any fat; put in an oval dish a dozen and a half oysters (taking care to remove the hard part and beard), with the liquor from the oysters to cover them; put the steak on them, cover the top of the steak with two onions cut in the thinnest possible manner; put another dish inverted over the steak, then put a paste round the edge of both dishes and put this into a gentle oven for an hour. Reverse the dishes for five minutes, then take off the dish which was originally at the top, and serve.

BROILED BEEFSTEAK.

Have the choice steaks cut three-quarters of an inch thick; grease the gridiron and have it quite hot. Put the steak over a hot, clear fire and cover. When the steak is colored turn it over, which must be done without sticking a fork into it and thus letting out the juice. It should be quite rare or pink in the center, but not raw. When cooked sufficiently, lay on a hot platter and season with pepper and salt, and spread over the top some small bits of butter, and serve immediately.

MOCK DUCK.

Take a round steak; make stuffing as for turkey; spread the stuffing on the steak, roll it up and tie it; roast from half to three-quarters of an hour.

ROAST VEAL.

Take a loin of veal, make a stuffing the same as for roast turkey, fill the flat with the stuffing and secure it firmly on to the loin; rub the veal with salt, pepper, and a little butter; put it into a pan with a little water. While roasting baste frequently, letting it cook until thoroughly done, allowing two hours for a roast weighing from six to eight pounds. When done remove the threads before sending to the table; thicken the gravy with a little flour.

FILLET OF VEAL (ROASTED IN THE POT).

Remove the bone and fill the cavity with a force-meat made of bread crumbs, a very little salt pork chopped fine, sage, pepper, salt, and ground cloves. Lay in the pot a layer of slices of salt pork, put in the fillet, fastened with skewers, cover in the same manner, pour over a pint of good stock, cover down close and let it cook slowly two or three hours, then take off the cover, let it brown, and serve.

VEAL CUTLETS.

1. Take one egg and beat it a little, roll the cutlet in it, then cover with rolled crackers. Have a lump of butter and lard mixed, hot in the skillet, put in the meat and cook slowly. When nicely browned on both sides stir in one tablespoonful of flour for gravy; add half pint of sweet milk and let it come to a boil. Season to taste and pour over the meat or serve in a separate dish as preferred.

2. Cut in nice pieces, season, dip in egg, then in bread crumbs, with a little lemon and parsley chopped fine. Have plenty of grease in your pan, hot; fry brown on one side, then turn over. Make a rich brown gravy in another vessel and serve. Garnish with parsley and lemon.

VEAL CUTLETS BROILED.

1. Broil them on a moderate fire, basting them occasionally with butter and turning them often. Serve with tomato sauce.

2. Trim evenly; sprinkle salt and pepper on both sides, dip in melted butter, and place upon the gridiron over a clear fire; baste while broiling with melted butter, turning over three or four times; serve with melted butter sauce or tomato sauce.

VEAL.

Cut two pounds of veal into thin pieces; roll with flour, and fry with hot lard; when nearly done, add one and a half pints of oysters; season, thicken with a little flour; serve hot.

VEAL CUTLETS BAKED.

Take cutlets and trim nicely; mix half a pound of sausage meat with two eggs; lay a buttered paper on the bottom of the dripping-pan, and cover with half the sausage meat, and then lay on it the cutlet, and cover with the remainder of the sausage meat; baste with melted butter and veal stock, and serve with the gravy when done.

VEAL CUTLETS.

Pound and season, cut the outer edges, and beat into good shape;

take one egg, beat it a little, roll the cutlet in it, then cover thoroughly with rolled crackers. Have a lump of butter and lard mixed hot in your skillet; put in the meat, and cook slowly; when nicely browned on both sides, stir in one teaspoonful of flour for the gravy, add half a pint of sweet milk, and let it come to a boil; salt and pepper.

PATE DE VEAU.

Of veal three and one-half pounds of fat and lean, a slice of salt pork about one-half pound, six small crackers powdered very fine, two eggs, a bit of butter the size of an egg, one tablespoonful of salt, one of cayenne pepper, one of black or white pepper, one grated nutmeg. Chop the meat all very fine, and mix the ingredients thoroughly, put it in a dripping-pan with a little water, make it into a loaf pyramidical or round from a bowl. Bake about two hours, basting it constantly. Leave it to get cold, and slice as head-cheese. A very palatable and convenient lunch or tea relish.

VEAL SCALLOP.

Chop some cold roast or stewed veal very fine; put a layer on the bottom of a pudding-dish, well buttered. Season with pepper and salt. Next have a layer of fine powdered crackers; wet with a little milk or some of the gravy from the meat. Proceed until the dish is full. Spread over all a thick layer of cracker crumbs, seasoned with salt, and wet into a paste with milk and two beaten eggs. Stick bits of butter all over it, cover closely, and bake half an hour; then remove the cover, and bake long enough to brown nicely. Do not get it too dry.

VEAL STEAKS.

Beat them until tender, then broil over clear hot coals until a nice brown on both sides; season with salt, pepper, and butter; send to the table while hot. A gravy made by stewing in a little hot water some bits of veal, with a few oysters or mushrooms, seasoned, and poured over the steak, is very nice.

STEWED VEAL.

Break the shank bone, wash it clean, and put into two quarts of water an onion, peeled, a few blades of mace, and a little salt; set it over a quick fire, and remove the scum as it rises; wash carefully a quarter of a pound of rice, and when the veal has cooked for about an hour skim it well, and throw in the rice. Simmer for three-quarters of an hour slowly. When done put the meat into a deep dish, and the rice around it. Mix a little drawn butter, stir in some chopped parsley, and pour over the veal.

MARBLED VEAL.

Take some cold roasted veal, season with spice, beat in a mortar; skin a cold boiled tongue, cut up and pound it to a paste, adding to it nearly its weight of butter; put some of the veal into a pot, then strew in lumps of the pounded tongue; put in another layer of veal, and again more tongue; press it down, and pour clarified butter on top. This cuts very prettily like veined marble. White meat of fowls may be used instead of veal.

A GOOD PREPARATION OF VEAL.

1. The following is an excellent mode of preparing veal to be eaten cold, and for keeping it on hand for several days, ready for immediate use: Take say three and a half pounds—the thick part of the leg is preferable, with the tough, tendenous parts removed—chop it fine without cooking; mix well with it four soda crackers rolled fine, three well-beaten eggs, one tablespoonful of salt, one tablespoonful of pepper, half a nutmeg, two tablespoonfuls of cream, or a small piece of butter; make it into a loaf, and bake in a dripping-pan without water, with quick heat at first, to close the outside and retain the juices, and continue the baking about one and a quarter to one and a half hours; serve cut in thin slices; an excellent lunch in traveling.

2. Butter a good-sized bowl, and line it with thin slices of hard-boiled eggs; have veal and ham both in very thin slices; place in the bowl a layer of veal, with pepper and salt, then a layer of ham, omitting the salt, then a layer of veal, and so on, alternating with veal and ham, until the bowl is filled; make a paste of flour and water, as stiff as it can be rolled out; cover the contents of the bowl with the paste, and over this tie a double cotton cloth; put the bowl into a saucepan, or other vessel, with water just up to the rim of the bowl, and boil three hours; then take it from the fire, remove the cloth and paste, and let it stand until the next day, when it may be turned out and served in very thin slices.

PRESSED VEAL OR CHICKEN.

Put four pounds of veal, or two chickens in a pot; cover with water, stew slowly until the meat drops from the bone, then take out and chop it; let the liquor boil down until there is a cupful; put in a small cup of butter, a tablespoonful of pepper, a little allspice, and a beaten egg; stir this through the meat; slice a hard-boiled egg; lay in your mold, and press in the meat; when put upon the table garnish with celery tops or parsley.

SANDWICHES.

Chop cold boiled ham very fine, and mix it with the yolks of eggs (beaten), a little mustard and pepper, and spread on very thin slices of bread, buttered on the loaf; trim off the crust, and cut into neat squares.

MINCED LIVER.

Cut liver into small pieces and fry with salt pork; cut both into square bits, nearly cover with water, add pepper and a little lemon juice; thicken the gravy with fine bread crumbs, and serve.

VEAL CROQUETTES.

Mince veal fine, mix one-half cup of milk with one teaspoonful of flour, a piece of butter the size of an egg; cook until it thickens; stir into the meat; roll into balls; dip in egg, with a little milk stirred in, roll in brown bread crumbs; fry in hot lard.

MEATS. 39

VEAL CHEESE.

Take equal quantities of sliced boiled veal and sliced boiled tongue. Pound each separately in a mortar, adding butter as you do so. Mix them in a stone jar, press it hard, and pour on melted butter. Keep it covered in a dry place. When cold cut in thin slices for tea or lunch.

VEAL HASH.

Take a teacupful of boiling water in a saucepan, stir into it an even teaspoonful of flour wet in a tablespoonful of cold water, and let it boil five minutes, add one-half teaspoon of black pepper, as much salt, and two tablespoonfuls of butter, and let it keep hot, but not boil. Chop the veal fine and mix with half as much stale bread crumbs. Put into a pan and pour the gravy over it, then let simmer ten minutes. Serve this on buttered toast.

CALF'S LIVER STEWED.

Cut the liver into small slices, about three inches square. Into your saucepan place two onions, sliced fine, a tablespoonful of sage, one of summer savory, a little pepper, and salt; then add your liver, and cover with water, and let it stew for two hours. Just before you serve it, dredge on a little flour, and add a tablespoonful of butter.

TO DRESS CALF'S HEAD LIKE TURTLE.

Let them boil an hour and a half, with salt in the water; tie the brains in a cloth bag, and boil half an hour; when all is done, take out the bones and cut in pieces. Add to your liquor a little sweet marjoram, a nutmeg grated, clove, mace, and pepper, to taste, half a pint of ketchup, half a pound of butter; then put in the meat, and boil a few minutes, and it is done.

MOCK TERRAPIN.

Half a calf's liver, season and fry brown, hash it, but not very fine, flour it thickly, then add a teaspoonful of mixed mustard, a little cayenne pepper, two hard-boiled eggs chopped fine, a lump of butter the size of an egg, a teacup of water. Let it boil a minute or two. Cold veal will do as well as liver.

BROILED CALF'S LIVER WITH BACON.

Procure a nice calf's liver, wash and cut in thin slices, broil over a clean fire, with thin slices of breakfast bacon. Season with butter, salt, and pepper.

SWEETBREADS WITH MUSHROOMS.

Parboil sweetbreads, allowing eight medium-sized ones to a can of mushrooms; cut the sweetbreads about half an inch square, stew until tender; slice mushrooms and stew in the liquor for one hour, then add to the sweetbreads a coffee cup of cream, pepper and salt, and a tablespoonful of butter. Sweetbreads boiled and served with green peas make a very nice dish.

SWEETBREADS WITH TOMATOES.

Take sweetbreads and parboil them, put them into a stew-pan and season with salt and cayenne pepper to taste; place over a slow fire; mix one large tablespoonful of browned flour with a small piece of butter, add a leaf of mace; stir butter and gravy well together, and let all stew for half an hour; then set the stew-pan in the oven, and when the sweetbreads are nicely browned place them on a dish; pour the gravy into a half pint of stewed tomatoes thickened with a teaspoonful of flour and a small piece of butter and seasoned. Strain it through a wire sieve into the stew-pan, let it come to a boil, and stir until done; then pour over the sweetbreads, and send to the table very hot.

FRIED TRIPE.

Scrape the tripe well; cut into squares the size of your hand; boil in salt and water (a tablespoonful of salt to one quart of water) till very tender. The next day cut into smaller pieces, season with salt and pepper, dredge with flour, fry brown on both sides in a pan of hot lard. When done, take it out, pour nearly all the lard out, add a good gill of boiling water, thicken with flour mixed smooth with a tablespoon of vinegar; season to taste, and pour hot over the tripe. A nice breakfast dish.

SPICED TRIPE.

Take fresh tripe, cut it into pieces four or five inches square, put a layer of the tripe in an earthen jar, then sprinkle a few cloves, allspice, and whole pepper over it; then another layer of tripe, then spice, and so on, until the jar is full; cover it up and let it stand away in a cold place for a few days, until it tastes of the spice. Serve up cold.

BALTIMORE MEAT PIE.

Pare two pounds of potatoes, cover them with hot water, and let them simmer till done; mash them and add a little cream and salt; lay them in the style of paste in a dish; place on thin slices of underdone meat, either mutton, beef, or veal; lay them in thickly; pour over them some gravy, a wineglass of ketchup, then cover thick with mashed potatoes, and bake moderately for about forty minutes.

CROQUETTE.

Take cold veal, chicken, or sweetbreads, a little of each, or separately, cut very fine a little fat and lean of ham, half the quantity of the whole of bread crumbs, two eggs, butter the size of an egg, pepper, salt, and a little mustard. Knead like sausage meat, adding a little cream; form in any shape, dip in egg, and then roll in cracker crumbs; fry in lard until a light brown. Dry them in the oven. Celery or mushrooms are an improvement.

MEAT RISSOLES.

Chop fine the cold meat, carefully excluding every particle of fat, skin, and outside; pound in a mortar with a small piece of butter, adding pepper, salt, and powdered fine herbs; moisten with stock; put this into a pan on the fire and take off as soon as hot; stir in the yolk of an egg beaten up with a little lemon juice, and put the mixture by to cool; make a paste of six ounces of flour, two ounces of butter, a pinch of salt, the yolks of two eggs, and a little water; roll it out, and cut it into small squares; put the meat in the center, and paste the corners over, pressing them well down; fry in hot lard, and serve with parsley.

BREADED LAMB CHOPS.

Grate plenty of stale bread, season with salt and pepper, have ready some well-beaten egg, have a spider with hot lard ready, take the chops one by one, dip into the egg, then into the bread crumbs, repeat it, as it will be found an improvement, then lay separately into the boiling lard, fry brown, and then turn. To be eaten with currant jelly or grape ketchup.

CUTLETS A-LA-DUCHESSE.

Cut the neck of lamb, about two pounds, into cutlets, trim them and scrape the top of the bone clean, fry in butter and set away to cool. Put a piece of butter into a stew pan with three mushrooms and a sprig of parsley, chop fine, stir over the fire until very hot; then pour over a cupful of white sauce—the yolks of three or four eggs well beaten. Stir constantly until as thick as cream, but do not let it boil. Dip each cutlet into it, covering thickly with the sauce, again set away to cool. Then egg and bread-crumb them. Fry lightly.

TO FRY LAMB STEAKS.

Dip each piece into well-beaten egg, cover with bread crumbs or corn meal, and fry in butter or new lard. Mashed potatoes and boiled rice are a necessary accompaniment. It is very nice to thicken the gravy with flour and butter, adding a little lemon juice, and pour it hot upon the steaks, and place the rice in spoonfuls around the dish to garnish it.

SPICED LAMB (COLD).

Boil a leg of lamb, adding to the water a handful of cloves and two or three sticks of cinnamon broken up. Boil four hours.

STEWED LAMB CHOPS.

Cut a loin of lamb into chops, cover with water and stew them until tender, keeping well covered except when skimming. When done season with salt and pepper, and thicken the gravy with a little flour, stirred until smooth, with a piece of butter the size of a walnut. Have pieces of bread previously toasted, and pour the stew over them.

MUTTON CHOPS.

1. Trim neatly, season, and dip each chop into a beaten egg, and then in cracker-crumbs; put into the oven in a dripping-pan, with two spoonfuls of butter and a little water; baste frequently, and bake until well browned.

2. Have them trimmed from fat and skin; dip each one into beaten

egg, then in pounded cracker, and fry in hot lard or dripping. It is still better to bake them very slowly in the oven

HARICOT MUTTON.

Loin chop fried until brown, dredge with flour, put into boiling water, or, if you have it, weak soup; cut carrots into small pieces, then simmer for two hours. Season with pepper and salt. Steak cooked in the same way is very nice.

CAPTAIN CHIRAZ RAGOUT.

Brown four tablespoonfuls of flour in a pot, then add a piece of butter the size of a walnut, with as much water as will make it the consistency of cream, and stir well. Cut up the meat—two pounds of lamb or mutton—not fine, but into pieces an inch or more in thickness and length, one-half teaspoonful of black pepper, a pinch of cayenne, with salt to taste, then add one and a half pints of boiling water, and stir well. Then one dozen and a half of large tomatoes peeled and chopped up, four carrots sliced lengthwise, three onions, and one dozen potatoes. Boil slowly for three hours.

IRISH STEW.

Take mutton chops, cover well with water, and let them come to a boil; pour this off and add more water; then a lump of butter the size of an egg, two tablespoonfuls of flour, one teacupful of milk, season; potatoes, and two small onions. Boil until the potatoes are done.

RAGOUT.

1. Take three pounds of veal from the neck or breast, and cut into small pieces, and fry in butter or dripping a light brown; remove from the pan, and to the butter add a tablespoonful of flour; cook a few minutes; then add two cups of warm water, one onion, a sprig each of thyme and parsley, a carrot, sliced, salt and pepper, then the meat, and cover; when done, place the meat on the dish; strain with gravy around it, and garnish with small onions fried.

2. Take pieces of mutton, veal, beef, or rabbit, cut into any size and and shape desired; heat a tablespoonful of drippings or lard in a saucepan, and when hot, fry the meat until almost done. Take out the meat and add a tablespoonful of flour, brown it, add a little lukewarm water, mix it well and then add a quart of boiling water, season with salt and cayenne pepper, add the meat, three or four onions, and six or seven potatoes—partially boiled before being put into the ragout; cover closely and stew until the vegetables are done. Take out the meat and vegetables and skim off all the fat from the gravy, season more, if necessary, and pour over the ragout and serve.

A RAGOUT OF COLD VEAL.

Cut the veal into slices, put a large piece of butter into a frying-pan, and as soon as it is hot, dredge the meat well with flour, and fry a nice brown. Remove the meat, and put into the pan as much of your cold gravy as you think proper, season with pepper and salt, and a wine glass of tomato ketchup; then cut a few slices of cold ham, lay into the gravy, and add your slices of veal. It must be sent to the table hot.

BAKED HAM.

A ham of sixteen pounds to be boiled three hours, then skin and rub in half a pound of brown sugar, cover with bread crumbs and bake two hours.

PORK STEAKS, BROILED.

Trim, season, and roll them in melted butter and bread crumbs; broil them over a moderate fire until thoroughly done. Make a sauce of five tablespoonfuls of vinegar and half a teacupful of stock; let it boil, and thicken with a little flour. Strain, and then add pepper and some pickles chopped fine.

ROAST PORK.

Select either the leg, loin, fillet, or shoulder for roasting. Make a stuffing as for turkey, or a stuffing seasoned with onion and sage. If the skin is left on it should be cut into small squares; otherwise sprinkle it with powdered sage. Baste frequently; and allow twenty minutes for each pound.

HAM AND EGGS.

Cut the ham into thin slices and broil, and spread over it a little butter. Poach the eggs in salted water, and lay neatly upon the ham.

BOILED HAM.

Soak twenty-four hours; put into a pot with cold water and boil gently for five or six hours; take it off the fire and let it remain in the water until cold. Peel off the skin and sprinkle with bread or cracker crumbs, and brown in the oven. Slice very thin for the table.

HAM BALLS.

Take one-half cupful of bread crumbs and mix with two eggs well beaten; chop fine some bits of cold boiled ham and mix with them. Make into balls and fry.

HAM TOAST.

Boil one-fourth of a pound of lean ham, mix with the yolks of three eggs, well beaten, one ounce of butter, two tablespoons of cream, a little cayenne pepper, stir over the fire until it thickens. Spread on hot toast.

PIGS' FEET HASH.

Singe and scrape the feet, then wash clean and put them into salt and water to soak over night, or for several hours, then scrape again until they are perfectly clean, and boil them till the meat falls from the bones, chop with a knife, season with salt and pepper; pack in a crock, and if the weather be cool it will keep some time. It can be sliced and eaten cold, or put into a skillet and fried until brown.

PIG'S HEAD.

Have the head nicely cleaned, and boil it till very tender. Chop it very fine, and season with salt, pepper, sage, and a little clove, while hot. Put in a deep dish, and cover with a plate that is smaller than the dish, that it may rest on the meat. Place on the plate a very heavy weight, and let it stand for twenty-four hours. This makes the famous "Pig's Head Cheese."

PORK AND BEANS.

Take two pounds of side pork, not too fat nor too lean, to two quarts of marrowfat beans; put the beans to soak the night before you boil them in a gallon of milk-warm water. After breakfast scald and scrape the rind of the pork, and put on to boil an hour before putting in the beans; as soon as the beans boil up pour off the water, and put on one gallon of fresh water; boil until quite tender, adding more water if necessary; great care must be taken that they do not scorch. When nearly as stiff as mashed potatoes put into a baking dish, score the pork, and put in the center; brown in the oven one hour. If preferred, use corned beef instead of pork.

BOSTON BAKED BEANS.

Put a quart of beans to soak over night; in the morning pour off the water, and add fresh water enough to cover, to which add about one tablespoonful of molasses. Put a small piece of salt pork in the center, almost covering it with the beans, and bake slowly from six to eight hours, adding hot water as needed until nearly done, when they can be allowed to cook nearly dry, or according to taste.

TO FRY APPLES AND PORK CHOPS.

Season the chops with salt and pepper, and a little powdered sage and sweet marjoram; dip them into beaten egg, and then into beaten bread crumbs. Fry about twenty minutes, or until they are done. Put them on a hot dish; pour off part of the gravy into another pan, to make a gravy to serve with them, if you choose. Then fry apples, which you have sliced about two-thirds of an inch thick, cutting them around the apple, so that the core is in the center of each piece. When they are browned on one side and partly cooked, turn them carefully with a pancake turner, and let them finish cooking; dish around the chops, or on a separate dish.

SPARE RIBS BROILED.

Crack the bones, and broil over a clear fire, taking care that the fire is not hot enough to scorch them.

ROAST LAMB.

Choose a hind quarter of lamb, stuff it with fine bread crumbs, pepper, salt, butter, and a little sage. Sew the flap firmly to keep it in place, rub the outside with salt, pepper, butter, a little of the stuffing, and roast two hours. Eat with mint sauce.

MUTTON A-LA-VENISON.

Take a fat loin, remove the kidney, and let it hang a week, if the weather permits. Two days before dressing it for cooking take ground allspice, clove, and pepper, mix them, and rub into the meat a tablespoonful of each twice a day for two days. Before cooking wash it off, and roast as a leg. To preserve the fat and keep it in, make a paste of flour and water, and spread thickly over the meat. Over this tie a double sheet of coarse paper, well buttered. About a quarter of an hour before it is done remove the paper and paste, return to the oven, and baste and dredge with flour. It is equal to venison.

BOILED LEG OF MUTTON.

Put on in boiling water, with a little salt; boil two hours and a half; make a sauce of melted butter; a piece of butter the size of an egg, stir with a tablespoonful of flour well, then stir into a pint of boiling water, with a tablespoonful of capers. Put into a sauce-tureen on the table, and garnish the dish with boiled cauliflower and parsley.

BREAST OF MUTTON AND GREEN PEAS.

Select a breast of mutton, not too fat, cut it into small, square pieces, dredge it with flour, and fry it a fine brown in butter; add pepper and salt, cover it with water, and set it over a slow fire to stew, until the meat is perfectly tender. Take out the meat, skim off all the fat from the gravy, and just before serving add a quart of young peas, previously boiled with the strained gravy, and let the whole boil gently until the peas are done.

SWEET-BREADS.

Take two large parboiled sweet-breads, put into a stewpan with one and one-half gills of water, season with salt, black and cayenne pepper, put over a slow fire. Mix one large tablespoonful of browned flour with a piece of butter, stir butter and gravy well together. After stewing slowly for half an hour set the pan in a quick oven, and when nicely browned place in a dish, pour the gravy into one-half pint stewed tomatoes, thicken with one dessertspoonful of flour, butter, salt, and pepper, strain through a sieve into stewpan, let it come to a boil, stir till done, pour over the sweet-bread, and send to the table hot.

SWEET-BREADS BROILED.

Parboil, after soaking in salt and water, then rub well with butter, and broil. Turn often, and dip into melted butter, to prevent them from becoming hard and dry.

SWEET-BREADS FRIED.

Wash in salt and water, parboil, cut into pieces the size of a large oyster, season, dip in rolled cracker crumbs, and fry a light brown in lard and butter.

SWEET-BREADS STEWED.

Wash, remove all the bits of skin, soak in salt and water one hour, then parboil; when half cooked take from the fire, cut into small pieces, stew in a little water till tender, add a piece of butter, a teaspoonful of salt, a teaspoonful of flour, and boil up once. Serve on toast very hot. Another way is to prepare as above and serve with tomato sauce.

TRAVELING LUNCH.

Sardines chopped fine, also a little ham, a small quantity of chopped pickles, mix with mustard, pepper, ketchup, salt, and vinegar; spread between bread nicely buttered. To be like jelly cake, cut in slices crossways.

SWEET-BREAD FRITTERS.

Parboil the sweet-breads; cut into small pieces, and season with salt, pepper, and parsley; dip into batter, and fry in hot lard.

TO BROIL SWEET-BREADS.

Soak an hour in salt and water; drain; parboil, then rub well in butter, and broil; turn often, and each time they are turned roll them in a plate of hot melted butter, so they need not become hard and dried.

STEWED TRIPE.

Five pounds of tripe cut in small slices and fried in a half-pound of lard; put in the tripe and let it cook a little, then add a cup of vinegar, a bowl of beef broth, salt, pepper, and three tablespoonfuls of flour; mix the whole, and let it stew about fifteen minutes; this is the English method, but I have a simpler and more delicate way of cooking tripe, which I prefer: Take three pounds of fresh tripe, cut it in pieces about three inches square; cut up about three good-sized onions in thin slices; place tripe and onions (after washing the former) in warm water, and let it stew gently until the tripe is tender; then simmer away all the water; add unskimmed milk thickened with flour, butter size of an egg, a trifle of pepper and a little salt; when the thickened milk is well boiled, dish up for the table.

BEEF HEART.

Wash it carefully and stuff it nicely, with dressing as for turkey; roast it about one and a half hours, and serve with the gravy, which should be thickened with some of the stuffing. It is very nice hashed.

MEAT CROQUETTES.

Use cold roast beef, chop it fine, season with pepper and salt, and one-third the quantity of bread crumbs, and moisten with a little milk; have your hands floured, rub the meat into balls, dip it into beaten egg, then into fine pulverized cracker, and fry in butter; garnish with parsley.

BEEF OMELET.

Three pounds of beefsteak, three-fourths of a pound of suet, chopped fine; salt, pepper, and a little sage, three eggs, six Boston crackers rolled; make into a roll and bake.

POUNDED BEEF.

Boil a shin of twelve pounds of meat until it falls readily from the bone; pick it to pieces; mash gristle and all very fine, pick out all the hard bits. Set the liquor away; when cool take off all the fat; boil the liquor down to a pint and a half. Then return the meat to it while hot; add pepper and salt and any spice you choose. Let it boil a few times, stirring all the while. Put into a mold or deep dish to cool. Use cold and cut in thin slices for tea or warm it for breakfast.

MUTTON PIE.

Cover the bottom of a dish with bread crumbs; then a layer of cold mutton, cut in very thin slices; then a layer of tomatoes, sliced thin; season with pepper, salt, and small bits of butter, and so on, until the dish is full, or you have sufficient, having tomatoes and bread crumbs on top; cover and bake about forty minutes, and serve hot.

POT PIE.

Cut veal, beef, or chicken into pieces and put into boiling water enough to cover, with two slices of bacon; cover closely and boil an hour, and season to taste; make a batter of two well beaten eggs, two cups of milk, a teaspoonful baking powder, and flour to make a batter; drop in separate spoonfuls while boiling, and cook five minutes; serve immediately.

TOMATO STEW.

Two pounds of any kind of meat used for stewing; put into a saucepan with a can of tomatoes, or a quart of fresh ones; season with pepper and salt; cover closely, and when the tomatoes are cooked, add two tablespoonfuls of butter, rubbed into a tablespoonful of flour; stew until the meat is tender, and then pour over dry toast.

GAME.

Broiling is the favorite way for cooking game, for which allow about forty minutes; butter well and serve hot on hot dishes,
For roasting allow thirty minutes.
Serve with jelly.
Garnish with lemon slices, Saratoga potatoes, or water-cresses.

BROILED QUAIL.

Dress carefully, and soak a short time in salt and water; split down the back; dry with a cloth, and rub them over with butter, and place on the gridiron over a clear fire; turn frequently, and dip in melted butter; season with salt; prepare a slice of thin toast, nicely buttered and laid on a hot dish, for each bird, and lay a bird breast upward, on on each slice; garnish with currant jelly.

BROILED PRAIRIE CHICKEN.

Wash thoroughly and remove the skin; put in hot water and boil fifteen or twenty minutes; take out and sprinkle with salt, pepper, and rub over with butter, and broil over a clear fire; place each on a piece of toast; garnish with currant jelly.

BROILED PIGEONS.

Split down the back; roll them in butter and cracker-crumbs, and broil; serve them on toast like quail, laying a piece of butter on each.

PARTRIDGE PIE.

Line a deep baking-dish with veal cutlets, and over them place thin slices of ham and a seasoning of pepper and salt; pluck, draw, wipe, and quarter four partridges, rub each part with a seasoning of pepper, salt, minced parsley, and butter; put in a baking-dish, pour over them a pint of strong soup-stock, line the edges of the dish with a light puff-paste, cover with the same, brush over with the yolk of an egg, and bake one hour. If the paste is in danger of becoming too brown, cover with a thick paper.

ROAST QUAIL OR PRAIRIE CHICKEN.

Dress carefully and wipe dry; tie a piece of salt pork over the breast of each bird, and put into a steamer over boiling water, covering closely, and steam twenty minutes; take out, remove the pork, and put into the oven, basting them often with butter, and brown.

WILD DUCK.

To BAKE.—Use a stuffing or not, as preferred; place an onion in the pan in which they are baking, and baste at first with water, afterward with butter; sprinkle with salt and flour, and brown; half an hour will cook them; make a gravy of the giblets, and serve with currant or cranberry jelly.

To BROIL.—Split down the back, dip in melted butter, and broil over a clear fire; garnish with lemon slices.

VENISON STEWED.

Cut into small steaks; make a dressing as for duck, with bread-crumbs, onion, butter, pepper, and salt, thyme (or pork instead of butter, if preferred), and spread upon each steak; then roll and tie; then put into boiling water and stew; thicken the gravy with flour.

BROILED VENISON STEAK.

Broil quickly over a clear fire, and, when sufficiently done, pour over two tablespoonsfuls of currant jelly melted with a piece of butter. Pepper and salt to season. Eat while hot, on hot plates.

TO COOK VENISON.

Broil as you would a beefsteak, rare. Have ready a gravy of butter, pepper, and salt, and a very little water. Heat the gravy without boiling it. Score the steak all over, put it in the gravy and cover tight; keep hot enough to steam the meat, and send in a covered dish to table.

PIGEON COMPOTE.

Truss six pigeons as for boiling. Grate the crumbs of a small loaf of bread, scrape one pound of fat bacon, chop thyme, parsley, an onion, and lemon peel fine, and season with salt and pepper, mix it up with two eggs, put this force-meat into the craws of the pigeons, lard the breasts and fry brown; place them in a stew-pan with some beef stock, and stew them three-quarters of an hour, thicken with a piece of butter rolled in flour. Serve with force-meat balls around the dish and strain the gravy onto the pigeons.

TO ROAST WILD FOWL.

The flavor is best preserved without stuffing. Put pepper, salt, and a piece of butter into each. Wild fowl require much less dressing than tame. They should be served of a fine color, and a rich, brown gravy. To take off the fishy taste which wild fowl sometimes have, put an onion, salt, and hot-water into the dripping-pan, and baste them for the first ten minutes with this, then take away the pan and baste constantly with butter:

TO ROAST PARTRIDGES, PHEASANTS OR QUAILS.

Pluck, singe, draw, and truss them, season with salt and pepper, roast for about a half an hour in a brisk oven, basting often with butter. When done, place on a dish together with bread crumbs fried brown and arranged in small heaps. Gravy should be served in a tureen apart.

TO BROIL QUAIL OR WOODCOCK.

After dressing, split down the back, sprinkle with salt and pepper, and lay them on a gridiron, the inside down. Broil slowly at first. Serve with cream gravy.

TO ROAST WILD DUCK OR TEAL.

After dressing, soak them over night in salt and water, to draw out the fishy taste. Then in the morning put them into fresh water, changing several times before roasting. Stuff or not, as desired. Serve with currant jelly.

PIGEON PIE.

Dress and wash clean, split down the back, and then proceed as for chicken pie.

ROAST PIGEONS.

When cleaned and ready for roasting, fill the bird with a stuffing of bread crumbs, a spoonful of butter, a little salt and nutmeg, and three oysters to each bird (some prefer chopped apple). They must be well basted with melted butter, and require thirty minutes' careful cooking. In the autumn they are best, and should be full grown.

TO ROAST PIGEONS.

They should be dressed while fresh. If young they will be ready for roasting in twelve hours. Dress carefully, and after making clean, wipe dry and put into each bird a small piece of butter dipped in cayenne. Truss the wings over the back and roast in a quick oven, keeping them constantly basted with butter. Serve with brown gravy. Dish them with young water-cresses.

FRIED RABBIT.

After the rabbit has been thoroughly cleaned and washed, put it into boiling water for about ten minutes; drain, and, when cold, cut it into joints, dip into beaten egg, and then into fine bread-crumbs, seasoned with salt and pepper. When all are ready fry them in butter over a moderate fire fifteen minutes, thicken the gravy with an ounce of butter and a small teaspoonful of flour, give it a minute's boil, stir in two tablespoonfuls of cream, dish the rabbit, pour the sauce under it, and serve quickly.

STEWED RABBIT.

Skin and clean the rabbit, cut into pieces, put one-fourth of a pound of butter into a stew-pan and turn the pieces of rabbit about in it until nicely browned; take out the meat, add one pint of boiling water to the butter, one tablespoonful of flour stirred to a paste in cold water, one tablespoonful of salt, and a little grated onion if liked, let this boil up, add the meat, stew slowly till the rabbit is tender. Serve hot.

ROAST RABBIT.

1. Clean and put into a dripping-pan with a small onion and carrot sliced; sprinkle with salt, pepper, and spread with butter; put into a quick oven with water enough to cover the bottom of the pan, and baste frequently; add more water if needed; when done, strain the gravy over the rabbit, and serve with cranberry sauce.

2. Dress nicely and fill with a dressing made of bread crumbs, a little onion, sage, pepper and salt, and a small piece of butter; tie a piece of salt pork over it; put into a dripping-pan with a little water, in a quick oven; baste often; serve with currant jelly.

RABBIT PIE.

Line a deep dish with a puff paste or rich biscuit crust; stew the rabbit, season well, and pour into the dish; cover with an upper crust, and bake.

SNIPE.

Clean nicely and singe; put a piece of butter into each one, and tie a small piece of bacon over the breast, and bake, basting frequently; serve with water-cress.

POULTRY.

HOW TO CHOOSE POULTRY.

Young, plump, and well fed, but not too fat poultry are the best. The skin should be fine-grained, clear, and white; the breast full, fleshed, and broad; the legs smooth. The birds must be heavy in proportion to their size. As regards ducks and geese, their breasts must also be plump; the feet flexible and yellow. For boiling, white-legged poultry must be chosen, because when dressed their appearance is by far the more delicate. But darker-legged ones are juicy and of a better flavor when roasted. The greatest precaution ought to be taken to prevent poultry from getting at all tainted before it is cooked. It should be killed and dressed from eight to ten hours before cooking. Pigeons are far better for being cooked the day they are killed, as they lose their flavor by hanging. Care must be taken to cook poultry thoroughly, for nothing is more revolting to the palate than underdone poultry.

PLAIN STUFFING.

Take stale bread, cut off all the crust, rub very fine and pour over it as much melted butter as will make it crumble in your hands; salt and pepper to taste.

POTATO STUFFING.

Take two-thirds bread and one-third boiled potatoes grated, butter size of an egg, pepper, salt, one egg, and a little ground sage; mix thoroughly.

APPLE STUFFING.

Take half a pound of the pulp of tart apples which have been baked or scalded; add two ounces of bread-crumbs, some powdered sage, a finely shred onion; season well with cayenne pepper. For roast goose, duck, etc.

CHESTNUT STUFFING.

Boil the chestnuts and shell them, then blanch them and boil until soft; mash them fine and mix with a little sweet cream, some bread-crumbs, pepper, and salt. For turkey.

ROAST TURKEY.

A turkey weighing not more than eight or nine pounds (young) is the best. Wash and clean thoroughly, wiping dry, as moisture will spoil the stuffing. Take one small loaf of bread grated fine, rub into it a piece of butter the size of an egg, one small teaspoonful of pepper, and one of salt; sage, if liked. Rub all together, and fill only the breast of the turkey, sewing up so that the stuffing cannot cook out. Always put the giblets under the side of the fowl, so they will not dry up. Rub salt and pepper on the outside, put into the dripping-pan, with one teacupful of water, basting often, turning it till brown all over. Bake about three hours. Have left in the chopping-bowl a little stuffing, take out the giblets, and chop fine. After taking out the turkey put in a large tablespoonful of flour; stir until brown. Put the giblets into a gravy-boat, and pour over them the gravy.

BOILED TURKEY.

Soak it in salt and water for an hour and a half, to make it white. Make the stuffing of bread crumbs and about half the quantity of suet, a little parsley, and a little lemon-peel, chopped fine. Scald the parsley, in order to have it green. Put all these in the breast. Tie lightly in cloth, and boil. A young turkey will boil in two hours; an older one will of course require a longer time. Garnish with parsley and lemon cut in slices.

BOILED TURKEY.

Stuff the turkey as for roasting. A very nice dressing is made by chopping half a pint of oysters, and mixing them with bread crumbs, butter, pepper, salt, thyme, and wet with milk or water. Baste about the turkey a thin cloth, the inside of which has been dredged with flour, and put it to boil in cold water with a teaspoonful of salt in it. Let a large turkey simmer for three hours; skim while boiling. Serve with oyster sauce, made by adding to a cupful of the liquor in which the turkey was boiled the same quantity of milk, and eight oysters chopped fine; season with minced parsley, stir in a spoonful of rice or wheat flour wet with cold milk; a tablespoonful of butter. Boil up once, and pour into a tureen.

TURKEY DRESSED WITH OYSTERS.

For a ten-pound turkey take two pints of bread crumbs, half a teacupful of butter cut in bits (not melted), one teaspoonful of powdered thyme or summer savory, pepper, salt, and mix thoroughly. Rub the turkey well inside and out with salt and pepper, then fill with first a spoonful of crumbs, then a few well-drained oysters, using half a can for a turkey. Strain the oyster liquor, and use to baste the turkey. Cook the giblets in the pan, and chop fine for the gravy. A fowl of this size will require three hours in a moderate oven.

TURKEY SCALLOP.

Pick the meat from the bones of cold turkey, and chop it fine. Put a layer of bread crumbs on the bottom of a buttered dish, moisten them with a little milk, then put in a layer of turkey with some of the filling, and cut small pieces of butter over the top; sprinkle with pepper and salt; then another layer of bread crumbs, and so on until the dish is nearly full; add a little hot water to the gravy left from the turkey, and pour over it; then take two eggs, two tablespoonfuls of milk, one of melted butter, a little salt, and cracker crumbs as much as will make it thick enough to spread on with a knife; put bits of butter over it, and cover with a plate. Bake three-quarters of an hour. About ten minutes before serving remove the plate, and let it brown.

CURRIED CHICKEN.

Fry out in the pot you make the curry three large rashers of pickled pork and three onions sliced; fry until the onions are brown; cut the chicken into small pieces, and slice three potatoes thin; add them to the pork and onions, cover well with water, cook until the chicken is done and the potatoes have thickened the water; salt to taste. Put two tablespoonfuls of curry powder in a tumbler, and mix with water; slice two or three more potatoes very thin; add the potatoes and mixed powder to the stew, and boil until the potatoes are cooked but not broken; serve with rice; the above is for one extra large chicken or two small ones. Green peas and corn are a valuable addition.

STEWED CHICKEN WITH OYSTERS.

Season and stew a chicken in a quart of water until very tender; take it out on a hot dish, and keep it warm; then put into the liquor a lump of butter the size of an egg; mix a little flour and water smooth, and make thick gravy; season well with pepper and salt, and let it come to a boil. Have ready a quart of oysters, picked over, and put them in without any liquor; stir them round, and as soon as they are cooked pour all over the chicken.

CHICKEN PIE.

Stew chicken till tender, season with one-quarter of a pound of butter, salt, and pepper; line the sides of a pie-dish with a rich crust, pour in the stewed chicken, and cover loosely with a crust, first cutting a hole in the center. Have ready a can of oysters, heat the liquor, thicken with a little flour and water, and season with salt, pepper, and butter the size of an egg; when it comes to a boil pour it over the oysters, and about twenty minutes before the pie is done lift the top crust and put them in.

FRIED CHICKEN.

Joint young, tender chickens; if old, put in a stew-pan with a little water and simmer gently till tender; season with salt and pepper, dip into flour, and fry in hot lard and butter until nicely browned. Lay on a hot platter and take the liquor in which the chicken was stewed, turn into the frying-pan with the browned gravy, stir in a little flour; when it has boiled stir in a teacup of rich, sweet cream, and pour over the chicken.

PRESSED CHICKEN OR VEAL.

Boil three chickens until the meat comes off the bones, then removing all bones, etc., chop, not very fine; add a piece of butter as large as an egg, salt and pepper to season well. Have about a pint of the broth, into which put one-half box gelatine until dissolved; then put back the chopped chicken and cook until the broth is evenly absorbed. Press under a weight in a pan until cold.

JELLIED CHICKEN OR VEAL.

Boil a chicken in as little water as possible, until the meat falls from the bones; chop rather fine, and season with pepper and salt; put in a mold a layer of the chopped meat and then a layer of hard-boiled eggs cut in slices; then layers of meat and egg alternately until the mold is nearly full; boil down the liquor left in the pot one-half; while warm, add one-quarter of an ounce of gelatine, and when dissolved pour into the mould over the meat. Set in a cool place over night to jelly.

CHICKEN POT-PIE.

Cut and joint a large chicken. Cover with water, and let it boil gently until tender. Season with salt and pepper, and thicken the gravy with two tablespoonfuls of flour mixed smooth in a piece of butter the size of an egg. Have ready nice light bread dough; cut with a biscuit-cutter about an inch thick; drop this into the boiling gravy, having previously removed the chicken to a hot platter, cover, and let it boil from one-half to three-quarters of an hour. To ascertain whether they are done or not, stick into one of them a fork, and if it comes out clean they are done. Lay on the platter with the chicken, pour over the gravy, and serve.

BROILED CHICKEN.

Only young, tender chickens are nice broiled. After cleaning and washing them, split down the back, wipe dry, season with salt and pepper, and lay them inside down on a hot gridiron over a bed of bright coals. Broil until nicely browned and well cooked through, watching and turning to prevent burning. Broil with them a little salt pork, cut in thin slices. After taking them from the gridiron, work into them plenty of butter, and serve garnished with the pork, slices of lemon, and parsley.

CHICKEN CROQUETTES.

One cold boiled chicken chopped fine; then take a pint of sweet milk, and when the milk is boiled, stir into it two large tablespoonfuls of flour, made thin in a little cold milk; after the flour is well cooked with the milk, put in a piece of butter the size of an egg, and salt and cayenne pepper; stir all well into the chicken: roll up with your hand, and dip first into an egg beaten up, then into crackers rolled fine, and fry in hot tallow (fresh tallow, half and half lard, is very nice.)

BAKED CHICKEN.

Split open in the back, season with salt and pepper and plenty of butter. Pour a little water into a pan, and, while baking, baste often, turning the chicken so as to nicely brown all over. When done, take up the chicken; thicken the gravy with a little flour, and serve in a gravy boat. Chickens are nice stuffed and baked in the same manner as turkey

A NICE WAY TO COOK CHICKEN.

Cut the chicken up, put into a pan, and cover with water. Let it stew as usual. When done, make a thickening of cream and flour. Add butter, pepper, and salt. Have ready a nice shortcake, baked and cut in squares, rolled thin as for crust. Lay the cakes on the dish, and pour the chicken and gravy over them while hot.

CHICKEN PUDDING.

Cut up the chickens and stew until tender. Then take them from the gravy, and spread on a flat dish to cool, having first well seasoned them with butter, pepper, and salt. Make a batter of one quart of milk, three cups of flour, three tablespoonfuls of melted butter, one-half teaspoon of soda, one teaspoon of cream tartar, a little salt. Butter a pudding dish and put a layer of chicken at the bottom, and then a cupful of the batter over it. Proceed till the dish is full. The batter must form the crust. Bake an hour, and serve the thickened gravy in a gravy boat.

SCALLOPED CHICKEN.

Mince cold chicken and a little lean ham quite fine, season with pepper and a little salt; stir all together, add some sweet cream, enough to make it quite moist, cover with crumbs, put it into scallop shells or a flat dish, put a little butter on top, and brown before the fire or front of a range.

BOILED CHICKEN.

The same as boiled turkey. They can be stuffed or not as desired.

CROQUETTES.

Chop fine any cold pieces of cooked meat or chicken, or whatever you may wish to use, first removing all fat, bone, etc.; add half the quantity of bread crumbs, one egg, pepper, and salt; make into balls and cook in a buttered spider; serve hot.

FRICASSEED CHICKEN.

Stuff two chickens as if to boil, put in a pot, do not quite cover over with water, put them on two hours before dinner; chop an onion, some parsley, and a little mace, rub a piece of butter twice as large as an egg with flour and stir it all in. Before dishing, beat the yolks of six eggs, and stir in carefully; cook five minutes.

POULTRY CROQUETTE.

Melt a bit of butter in a stew-pan; put into it chopped parsley, mushrooms, two spoonfuls of flour, salt, and pepper to taste. Fry it and pour in stock and a little cream. This sauce ought to have the consistency of thick cream. Cut up any poultry which has been cooked the day before into dice. Put into the saucepan, and let get cold. Form into balls, and cover them with bread-crumbs. Wash in eggs which have been beaten up, and roll in bread-crumbs a second time. Drop in boiling lard, and fry to a good color. Garnish with parsley. Croquette made of veal may be prepared in the same way.

MINCED FOWLS.

Remove from the bones all the flesh of either cold, roast, or boiled fowls. Clean it from the skin, and keep covered from the air until ready for use. Boil the bones and skin with three-fourths of a pint of water until reduced quite half. Strain the gravy and let it cool. Next, having first skimmed off the fat, put it into a clean saucepan with a half cup of cream, three ounces of butter, well mixed with one tablespoon of flour. Keep these stirred until they boil. Then put in the fowl, finely minced, with three hard-boiled eggs, chopped, and sufficient salt and pepper to season. Shake the mince over the fire until just ready to boil. Dish it on hot toast and serve.

ROAST DUCK.

Prepare the same as for turkey, adding to the dressing two or three finely-chopped onions. Serve with apple sauce or cranberries.

ROAST GOOSE.

Two ounces of onions, and half as much green sage, chopped fine, and one coffee cup of bread crumbs, a little pepper and salt, the yolks of two eggs. Do not quite fill the goose, but leave room to swell. Roast from one hour and a half to two hours, and serve with gravy and apple sauce.

BONED TURKEY.

Boil a large turkey in as little water as possible until the meat falls from the bones; remove all the bones and skin; pick the meat into small pieces, and mix dark and light together; season with pepper and salt; put into a mold and pour over it the liquor, which must be kept warm, and press with a heavy weight.

CHICKENS FRIED WITH RICE.

Take two or three chickens, cut them up, and half fry them; then boil half a pint of rice in a quart of water, leaving the grains distinct, but not too dry; one large tablespoonful of butter stirred in the rice while hot; let five eggs be well beaten into the rice, with a little salt, pepper, and nutmeg, if the last is liked; put the chickens into a deep dish, and cover with the rice; brown in an oven not too hot.

CHICKEN SANDWICHES.

Stew a chicken until very tender; season with a little salt; take out the bones and pack the meat firmly into a deep dish, mixing the white and dark nicely together; pour the broth in which the chicken is stewed over it—there should be just enough to cover the meat; when it is cold, cut in smooth slices and place between slices of good bread or biscuit.

GIBLET PIE.

Take the gizzards, heads, legs, livers, ends of wings, and necks, and stew in sufficient water; season with pepper, salt, and a little butter; line the sides of a deep dish with a rich crust; pour in the giblets, cover with an upper crust, and bake.

PICKLED CHICKEN.

Boil until the meat falls from the bones; pick the meat and put into a jar, and pour over it a liquor made with vinegar, to which has been added one-half the quantity of the water in which the chickens were cooked; season to taste.

SMOTHERED CHICKEN.

Dress your chickens; wash and let them stand in water half an hour to make them white; put into a baking-pan (first cutting them open at the back); sprinkle salt and pepper over them, and put a lump of butter here and there; then cover tightly with another pan the same size and bake one hour; baste often with butter. A delicious dish. . It is a Southern method.

SPRING CHICKEN.

Cut into pieces, season, roll in flour, and fry in hot lard, covering closely; when done, remove from the pan, pour out nearly all the fat, and add a cup of cream; thicken with a little flour; season with pepper and salt, and, when done, pour over the chicken.

STEWED PIGEONS.

Dress, tie down the wings and legs, and put a small piece of bacon onto the breast of each bird; place in the bottom of a kettle a slice or two of bacon, and lay the pigeons carefully on them; cover with stock; cover the kettle very closely, and simmer slowly until tender; serve on toast.

JUGGED PIGEON.

Truss and season the pigeons with pepper and salt; stuff them with a mixture of their own livers, shred with beef suet, bread crumbs, parsley, marjoram, and two eggs; sew them up and put into the jar with half a pound of butter; stop up the jug, so that no steam can get out, then set them in a pot of water to stew; they will take two hours, and must boil all the time; when stewed enough take them out of the gravy, skim off the fat. put in a spoonful of cream, a little lemon peel, an anchovy shred, a few mushrooms, and thicken it with butter and flour; dish up the pigeons, pour the sauce over them, and garnish with sliced lemon.

STEWED GIBLETS.

Put the giblets in a pan with butter, and fry a light brown; add parsley, an onion, a little thyme, and thicken with a little flour, and cover with stock; boil nearly two hours, and then take up the giblets; let the gravy boil a little longer, and then strain over the meat.

SALADS.

MAYONNAISE SALAD DRESSING.

The yolk of one egg, raw; stir into this all the olive oil it will hold, in as fine a stream as possible. Season with cayenne pepper, salt, and mustard.

SIMPLE DRESSING FOR SALADS.

Mix three tablespoonfuls of olive oil and one tablespoonful of scraped onion with one saltspoonful of salt and one saltspoonful of pepper (mixed), and then add one tablespoonful of vinegar. When thoroughly mixed, pour over the salad.

CHICKEN SALAD DRESSING.

Take two hard-boiled eggs, lay them into water till quite cold, put the yolks into a small bowl and mash them very fine, adding the yolks of two raw eggs, one teaspoonful of salt, one large tablespoonful of dry mustard, a very little cayenne pepper; stir this well, always one way; when well mixed, add a very little sweet oil, stirring all the time. After this is mixed, put in more, a very little at a time, until you have used a third of a bottle, then add a large spoonful of vinegar or lemon juice, then more oil as before, using in all two-thirds of a bottle, then another spoonful of vinegar; when well mixed it must be very light, and a nice color. Set on the ice for two or three hours; not more than twenty minutes before using the salad, mix it and prepare for the table by putting with the meat about half the dressing, stir it up well, and then pour on to the meat one wine glass of best vinegar; stir this up well, it will turn the chicken very white; if it requires a little more salt, add it now. Place the chicken in the centre of a flat dish, large enough to lay lettuce or celery around the meat, wipe the lettuce as dry as you can, and lay around the meat, then with a spoon put the rest of the dressing on the lettuce.

CHICKEN SALAD.

1. To two large boiled fowls (cold) take two large heads of celery or four small ones; having removed all the skin and the fat, cut the meat from the bones into very small pieces; it is best not to mix the dressing with the salad until just before it is to be eaten. Put into a porcelain kettle the gravy from the chicken, one-half pint of vinegar, one-half pint of sweet oil or melted butter, one large tablespoonful of Colman's mustard, one small teaspoonful of cayenne pepper, one teaspoonful of salt, the yolks of eight eggs beaten and stirred in just before taken off, one teacup of cream stirred into the dressing when cold; mix together with a silver fork, and garnish with celery tops.

2. Three chickens boiled until tender; when cold chop, but not too fine, add twice the quantity of celery cut fine, and three hard-boiled eggs sliced; make a dressing with two cups of vinegar, half cup of butter (or two tablespoonfuls of oil) two eggs beaten with a large tablespoonful of mustard, saltspoonful of salt, two tablespoonfuls of sugar, and tablespoonful of pepper, or a little cayenne pepper, put the vinegar into a tin pail and set in a kettle of boiling water; beat the other ingredients together thoroughly, and stir slowly into the vinegar until it thickens. Pour over the salad just before serving.

LOBSTER SALAD.

1. The above receipt makes excellent lobster salad by adding lobster cut into small pieces, and mixed lightly with a fork.

2. Boil the lobster, break in two and drain; remove all the flesh from the shell and chop into dice; add lettuce, chopped fine; season with salt, pepper, vinegar, mustard, and a little oil, and spread over it a Mayonnaise sauce.

3. To a three-pound lobster take the yolk of one raw egg, beat very lightly, then take the yolks of three hard-boiled eggs (cold), and add to the raw yolk, beating all the time; add, gradually, a few drops at a time, one-half bottle of the finest olive oil, still stirring all the time, then add one and a half tablespoonfuls of the best English mustard, salt and pepper to taste; beat the mixture until light, add a tablespoonful of strong vinegar. Cut the lobster into small pieces and mix with it salt and pepper; pour over it the dressing just before sending to the table; garnish with the white of egg (boiled), celery tops, and the small claws.

4. Pick the meat from the shell, chop and season the same as for chicken salad; garnish with the claws and parsley.

LETTUCE SALAD.

1. Two heads of lettuce, two hard-boiled eggs, two teaspoonfuls of butter, one-half teaspoonful of salt, one teaspoonful white sugar, one-half teaspoonful made mustard, one teaspoonful pepper, four tablespoonfuls of vinegar; rub the yolks of the eggs to a powder, add sugar, butter, pepper, salt, and mustard, let it stand five minutes, then beat

in the vinegar. Cut the lettuce with a knife and fork, put into a bowl, and mix in the dressing by tossing with a fork.

2. Serve with simple dressing, and garnish with hard-boiled eggs.

Lettuce, cold boiled potatoes, and cold boiled beets; potatoes in the center, beets next, and lettuce around the edge of the dish. Simple dressing.

POTATO SALAD.

1. Potatoes boiled in the "jacket," and peeled while warm, cut evenly into fine slices, and when cold mixed with fine olive oil. After having drawn with this for a little while, add salt, pepper, chopped onion, and mix all this by shaking it up, as using a spoon would break the potatoes, and make them unsightly. Add good vinegar.

2. Small onions sliced and cold boiled potatoes, over which pour the simple dressing.

3. Cut a dozen cold boiled potatoes into fancy shapes, one-quarter of an inch thick; mix with some flakes of cold boiled fish (halibut, cod, or salmon), and pour over them a salad dressing, made with six tablespoonfuls of melted butter, or salad oil, six tablespoonfuls of cream or milk, one tablespoonful of salt, half that quantity of pepper, and one teaspoonful of ground mustard. Into this mix one cupful of vinegar. Boil well, then add three raw eggs, beaten to a foam; remove directly from the fire, and stir for five minutes; when thoroughly cold turn over the salad. Garnish with slices of pickled cucumber, cold beet, hard-boiled egg, and fresh parsley.

4. Steam and slice the potatoes; add a very little raw onion chopped very fine, and a little parsley, and pour over the whole a nice salad dressing; serve either warm or cold.

5. One pound mashed potato, one-quarter pound mashed beet; mix smooth and add two tablespoonfuls salad oil, same of vinegar, pepper, salt, and parsley chopped fine.

CUCUMBER SALAD.

Peel and slice and put into a dish, with salt over every layer, and leave an hour; drain dry, and then dress with oil, vinegar, and pepper; add onions if the flavor is liked.

SWEET-BREAD SALAD.

Boil the sweet-breads twenty minutes, then drop them into cold milk, split them and fry brown in butter, break in small pieces with lettuce and mix with the dressing. Make a dressing with the yolks of two eggs, two tablespoonfuls of vinegar, two teaspoonfuls of mixed mustard, the least bit of sugar, one bottle of olive oil poured into this with a thread-sized stream, stirring all the time. The dressing for salmon salad is also nice for this.

SALMON SALAD.

For a pound can of California salmon, garnished with lettuce, make a dressing of one teacup of vinegar, butter half the size of an egg, one teaspoon of Colman's mustard, one-half teaspoonful of cayenne pepper; one-half teaspoonful of salt, one teaspoonful of sugar, two eggs; when cold, add one-half teacup of cream and pour over the salmon.

COLD SLAW.

Two-thirds of a cup of vinegar, one egg, two tablespoonfuls sugar, one teaspoon of salt, half teaspoon of mixed mustard, and butter size of an egg; stir until it boils. When cold, pour over the shaved cabbage.

KOHL SLAU.

Cut very fine and pack in a small jar; sprinkle a little salt and pepper over it; take vinegar—a pint will answer for a small head; butter the size of a walnut; one spoonful of sugar or more if liked; heat this to the boiling point; mix a well beaten egg in a cup of cream and pour into the vinegar, stirring briskly until it again boils; then instantly pour it over the cabbage and cover tightly, pressing down with a little weight or plate; the slau is better when two days old, although it can be eaten at once, or after a week if kept in a cool place.

HOT SLAW.

With a sharp knife—there are knives made for the express purpose—cut up nicely a firm head of cabbage; sprinkle it with as much pepper and salt as you think necessary; beat up the yolk of one egg, add a lump of butter the size of a walnut, a gill of cream, the same quantity of vinegar, a tablespoonful of sugar, an even teaspoonful of mustard, and a pinch of bruised celery seed; heat these condiments, mix together, in a tin cup; put the slaw in an oven, and pour the mixture over it boiling hot; stir it till well mixed, and the cabbage slightly coddled, then send to the table hot.

BEEF SALAD.

Cut in very thin small slices and put on a dish with chopped parsley; mix in a bowl some vinegar and sweet oil—one part vinegar to two of oil—pepper, salt, and mustard; beat together and pour over the meat.

CABBAGE SALAD.

One quart of cabbage chopped fine; make a dressing with the yolks of two or three hard-boiled eggs rubbed smooth, butter the size of an egg, melted, one tablespoonful of sugar, half tablespoonful of pepper, teaspoonful of salt, and half teacup of cider vinegar; heat together, and when cool mix thoroughly with the cabbage. Use the whites of the eggs for garnishing.

CELERY SALAD.

1. Cut in pieces one-quarter of an inch long; make a dressing of the yolks of three hard-boiled eggs, one-half cup of vinegar, three tablespoonfuls of salad oil, one teaspoonful French mustard, a little salt and cayenne pepper; mix well, and pour over the celery.

2. One head of cabbage, three bunches of celery, chopped very fine. Take one teacupful vinegar, lump of butter size of an egg, yolks of two eggs, one teaspoonful mustard, one of salt, pinch of cayenne pepper, two teaspoonfuls of sugar. Mix these well; put the mixture on the stove, and heat until it thickens, stirring all the time; when cold add two tablespoonfuls of rich sweet cream; pour over the salad; if not moist enough add cold vinegar.

SALADS.

CHICKEN CELERY.

Chop the remains of chicken or turkey, and mix with an equal proportion of celery; a little salt and vinegar only, although some like a dressing as for slaw, but this takes away too much of celery taste. It may be prepared with lettuce instead of celery.

CABBAGE SALAD.

Cut the cabbage very fine, and put into the dish in layers, with salt and pepper between; then take two teaspoonfuls of butter, two of sugar, two of flour, two of mustard, one cup of vinegar, and one egg. Stir all together, and let it come to a boil on the stove. Pour it hot over, and mix well with the cabbage; cover up.

FISH SALAD.

Cut cold salmon, or fish of any kind, into slices, and place them in a dish with hard-boiled eggs and lettuce, crisped and broken into small pieces, and pour over it a salad dressing made either with or without mustard.

SALAD DRESSING.

Beat the yolks of eight eggs, and add one cup of sugar, one tablespoonful of mustard, salt and pepper; mix; boil three cups of vinegar, to which add a cup of butter, and while boiling pour over the mixture, and mix thoroughly; bottle and set in a cool place, and use when needed.

SALAD DRESSING FOR LETTUCE.

Take the yolks of two hard-boiled eggs; add one-half teaspoonful mixed mustard, and mix to a paste with a silver fork; then add slowly, mixing carefully, about one-half cup of vinegar, one teaspoonful of sugar, and salt to taste; cut the lettuce with a sharp knife, and pour the dressing over it; garnish with hard-boiled eggs.

SALMON SALAD.

Put a can of salmon into boiling water, and boil a quarter of an hour; remove from the can; drain off the oil; sprinkle with pepper and salt, and a few whole cloves; cover with vinegar, and let it stand twenty-four hours, and then take from the vinegar into a salad dish, and add a head of lettuce, cut fine; over the whole pour a nice salad dressing; garnish with lettuce leaves, and serve.

TOMATO SALAD.

1. Peel and cut into six pieces six large tomatoes; make a dressing of one tablespoonful of oil, one of vinegar, one-half teaspoonful of mustard, a little cayenne pepper, and salt; pour over the tomatoes; mix well, and serve.

2. One dozen medium-sized tomatoes peeled and sliced, yolks of four hard-boiled eggs, one raw egg well beaten, teaspoon sugar, salt to taste, and one-half saltspoon of cayenne pepper, one tablespoonful of butter, and one teacup of vinegar. Or, slice and serve with mayonnaise dressing.

SAUCES.

ANCHOVY.

Make as for caper sauce, adding a tablespoonful of anchovy extract or paste.

BUTTER SAUCE.

Mix well together two tablespoonfuls of butter, some chopped parsley, juice of half a lemon, salt, and pepper; use for broiled meat or fish.

BROWN BUTTER SAUCE.

Put butter into a frying-pan, and let it stand on the fire until very brown, and then add a little parsley, and fry a moment longer.

DRAWN BUTTER SAUCE.

One-quarter pound of butter, rub with it two teaspoonfuls of flour. When well mixed, put into a saucepan with one-half pint of water or stock; cover it, and set the saucepan into a larger one of boiling water; shake it constantly till completely melted and beginning to boil; season with salt and pepper.

CAPER SAUCE.

1. Mix together two large tablespoonfuls of butter and a tablespoonful of flour; put into a saucepan, and add two cups of broth or water; set on the fire, and when thick add capers to taste; salt; take from the fire, add the yolk of an egg beaten and serve. This sauce can be greatly varied; by using chopped cucumbers or hard-boiled eggs, or herbs, or mushrooms, you have cucumber, egg, herb, or mushroom sauce.

2. Make a drawn-butter sauce, and then add two or three tablespoonfuls of French capers; remove from the fire and add a little lemon juice.

SUBSTITUTE FOR CAPER SAUCE.

Half a pint of melted butter, two tablespoonfuls of cut parsley, half a teaspoonful of salt, one tablespoonful of vinegar. Boil the parsley slowly to let it become a good color; cut, but do not chop it fine; add to it a half-pint of smoothly-made melted butter, with salt and vinegar in the above proportions; let it simmer two minutes and then serve.

BOILED EGG SAUCE.

Add to half a pint of drawn-butter sauce two of three hard-boiled eggs, chopped.

PICKLE SAUCE.

Add to half a pint of drawn-butter sauce three tablespoonfuls of pickled cucumbers, minced fine.

TOMATO SAUCE.

1. Stew one can of tomatoes, one small onion for twenty minutes, and then strain through a sieve. Put an ounce and a half of butter into a saucepan, and when it boils dredge in an ounce and a half of flour. When thoroughly cooked, pour in the tomatoes.

2. One can of **tomatoes** boiled down and strained; rub together one heaping teaspoonful of flour, **one** tablespoonful of butter, and a little salt, with a very little cayenne **pepper**, and stir into the tomatoes; then let all come to a boil.

MUSHROOM SAUCE.

Prepare the mushrooms by **cutting off the stalks, and** throw them **into boiling** water; season **with salt pepper, and butter.** Boil until **tender, and** then thicken **the gravy with a little butter and flour:** add **a little lemon juice and pour over the meat.**

CELERY SAUCE.

1. Six heads of celery, one pint of white stock, two blades of mace, one small bunch of savory herbs; thickening of butter and flour, or arrowroot, half a pint of cream, lemon juice; boil the celery in salt and water until tender, and cut into pieces two inches long; put the stock into a stew-pan with the mace and herbs, and let it simmer for one-half hour to extract their flavor; then strain the liquor, add the celery and a thickening of butter kneaded with flour, or, what is still better, with arrowroot; just before serving, put in the cream, boil it up and squeeze in it a little lemon juice; if necessary, add a seasoning of salt and white pepper. This sauce is for boiled turkey, poultry, etc.

2. Pick and wash two heads of celery; cut them into pieces one inch long, and stew them in a pint of water with one teaspoonful of salt, until the celery is tender. Rub a large spoonful of butter and a teaspoonful of flour well together; stir this into a pint of cream; put in the celery, and let it boil up once. Serve hot with boiled poultry.

3. Mix two tablespoonfuls of butter with a tablespoonful of flour, add two cups of stock, or water, and boil; when thick, add celery chopped fine; season; boil ten minutes; strain and serve.

CREAM DRESSING.

Take a large tablespoonful of sweet cream and whip to a stiff froth; add two tablespoonfuls of fine sugar, and nearly a half cup of vinegar, beat, and use for cabbage dressing.

HORSE RADISH.

Mix together thoroughly one small tablespoonful of melted butter, or, if preferred, olive oil, and one of mixed mustard, two of horse radish, one of vinegar, and a dessertspoonful of vinegar and a little salt.

MAYONNAISE SAUCE.

Put the yolk of an egg into a bowl with a saltspoonful of salt, and beat until light with a wooden spoon; then add half a teaspoonful of dry mustard, and beat again for a minute; then add olive oil, drop by drop until it is thickening, then a few drops of vinegar, and the same of lemon juice; continue the process until the egg has absorbed a little more than a gill of oil; finish by adding a little cayenne pepper.

MUSTARD FOR TABLE.

One-half teacup of vinegar put on to boil, butter size of a walnut, one teaspoonful of salt, one tablespoonful of sugar, one-half teacup of Colman's mustard, mixed with a little cold vinegar.

ONION SAUCE.

Boil one cup of milk; season to taste; add a small piece of butter and a tablespoonful of flour moistened with some of the milk; when thick, add three onions that have been boiled and chopped fine.

TOMATO SAUCE.

Stew one-half dozen tomatoes with a little chopped parsley; salt and pepper to taste; strain; and, when it commences to boil, add a spoonful of flour, stirred smooth with a tablespoonful of butter. When it boils, take up.

PARSLEY SAUCE.

Wash a bunch of parsley in cold water, then boil it about six or seven minutes in salt and water. Drain it; cut the leaves from the stalks and chop them fine. Have ready some melted butter, and stir in the parsley; allow two small tablespoonfuls of leaves to one-half pint of butter. Serve with boiled fowls and fish.

MELTED OR DRAWN BUTTER.

Cut two large spoonfuls of butter into small pieces, and put it into a saucepan with a large spoonful of flour, and ten of new milk. When thoroughly mixed, add six large spoonfuls of water. Shake it over the fire until it begins to simmer, shaking it always the same way; then let it stand quietly and boil up. It should be of the consistency of rich cream, and not thicken.

APPLE SAUCE.

Pare, core and slice some apples; stew them with sufficient water, to prevent burning; when done, mash them through a colander, sweeten to taste, add a small piece of butter, a little nutmeg or lemon.

CRANBERRY SAUCE.

One quart of cranberries, one quart of water and one pound of white sugar; make a syrup of the water and sugar. After washing the berries clean and picking out all poor ones, drop them into the boiling syrup; let them cook from fifteen to twenty minutes. They are very nice strained.

EGG SAUCE.

Three ounces of butter, beaten with one ounce of flour; stir into it one pint of boiling water; salt and pepper. Cook fifteen minutes; pour into sauce-boat, having hard-boiled eggs, sliced or chopped, in it.

WHITE SAUCE.

Take one cup of butter and melt it, and while in the saucepan, shake in three tablespoonfuls of flour until well mixed. Then add one quart of milk, stirring all the time till it boils.

OYSTER SAUCE.

One pint of oysters cut small, boiled for five minutes in their own liquor; a cup of milk, a tablespoonful of butter rubbed smooth into a tablespoon of flour; salt and pepper; let it boil. Serve with turkey.

MINT SAUCE.

Wash the mint very clean; pick the leaves from the stalk, and chop them fine; pour on to them vinegar enough to moisten the mint well; add fine sugar to sweeten.

CREAM SAUCE.

Mix two tablespoonfuls of butter with one of flour; then add two small cups of cream, and set on the fire; stir until thick, and then remove from the fire; then add the yolk of an egg, well beaten with a teaspoonful of water, and season with salt and pepper.

GRAVY FOR ROAST BEEF.

Melt a little butter in a gill of water; pour it over a roast when put in the oven; place under it an earthen dish to catch the drippings; baste often for half an hour, then set it to cool; when cool, remove all fat, heat the gravy, and pour it over the roast.

PIQUANTE SAUCE.

One small onion chopped fine and fried with two tablespoonfuls of butter; when nearly done add a tablespoonful of flour and cook a minute; then add one cup of stock, seasoning, chopped cucumber, parsley and a little mustard; boil ten minutes, and when done add a teaspoonful of vinegar.

SAUCE FOR BOILED TURKEY OR CHICKEN.

Make as for caper sauce, using milk instead of broth or water, and add cauliflower cut into small pieces; or, add lemon, and the livers boiled and mashed.

VEGETABLE SAUCE.

Equal quantities of ripe tomatoes and young okras; chop the okras fine, skin the tomatoes and slice one onion. Stew all together very slowly until tender, and season with half tablespoonful of butter and a little cayenne pepper and salt. For cold meat.

VEGETABLES.

Have your vegetables fresh as possible. Wash them thoroughly. Lay them in cold water until ready to use them.

Vegetables should be put to cook in boiling water and salt. Never let them stand after coming off the fire; put them instantly into a colander over a pot of boiling water, if you have to keep them back from dinner.

Peas, beans, and asparagus, if young, will cook in twenty-five or thirty minutes. They should be boiled in a good deal of salt water. Cauliflower should be wrapped in a cloth when boiled, and served with drawn butter. Potato water is thought to be unhealthy; therefore do not boil potatoes in soup, but in another vessel, and add them to it when cooked.

LIMA BEANS.

Shell, wash and put into boiling water with a little salt; when boiled tender, drain and season them, and either dress with cream or large lump of butter, and let simmer for a few moments.

CABBAGE A-LA-CAULIFLOWER.

Cut the cabbage fine as for slaw; put it into a stewpan, cover with water and keep closely covered; when tender drain off the water; put in a small piece of butter with a little salt, one-half a cup of cream, or one cup of milk. Leave on the stove a few minutes before serving.

CREAM CABBAGE.

Beat together the yolks of two eggs, one-half cup of sugar, one-half cup of vinegar; butter size of an egg, salt, and a little cayenne pepper. Put the mixture into a saucepan and stir until it boils; then stir in one cup of cream. Let it boil. Pour over the cabbage while hot.

STEWED CELERY.

Clean the heads thoroughly. Take off the coarse, green, outer leaves. Cut in small pieces, and stew in a little broth. When tender, add some rich cream, a little flour and butter, enough to thicken the cream. Season with pepper, salt, and a little nutmeg if that is agreeable.

GREEN CORN ON THE COB.

Take off the outside leaves and the silk, letting the innermost leaves remain on until after the corn is boiled, which renders the corn much sweeter. Boil for half an hour in plenty of water, drain, and after removing the leaves, serve.

CORN FRITTERS.

1. To a can of corn add two eggs well beaten, two tablespoonfuls of flour, one teaspoonful of salt, one-half teaspoon of pepper; mix thoroughly; have the pan hot; put in two tablespoonfuls of lard, and drop in the corn in large spoonfuls. Cook brown.

2. One pint of corn meal, one-half cup of milk, one tablespoonful of salt, one egg, one pint of wheat flour, one teaspoon of soda.

GREEN CORN PUDDING.

One quart of milk, five eggs, two tablespoonfuls of melted butter one tablespoonful of white sugar, one dozen large ears of corn; grate the corn from the cob; beat the whites and yolks of the eggs separately; put the corn and yolks together, stir hard, and add the melted butter, then the milk gradually, stirring hard all the time; next, the sugar, and then the whites and a little salt. Bake slowly, covering the dish at first. It will bake in about an hour.

FRENCH MUSHROOMS CANNED.

Pour off the liquid, pour over them a little cream, season and let them simmer for a short time. To be served on broiled beefsteak.

MUSHROOMS BROILED.

Gather them fresh, pare, and cut off the stems, dip them in melted butter, season with salt and pepper, broil them on both sides over a clear fire; serve on toast.

BAKED ONIONS.

Wash, but do not peel the onions; boil one hour in boiling water, slightly salt, changing the water twice in the time; when tender, drain on a cloth, and roll each in buttered tissue paper, twisted at the top, and bake an hour in a slow oven. Peel and brown them; serve with melted butter.

SUCCOTASH.

1. Use double the quantity of corn that you do beans. Cook the beans for three or four hours. Put in the corn one hour before dinner. Have just water enough to cook them in. Care must be taken not to let it stick. Season with salt, pepper, and lump of butter.

2. Boil Lima beans and sweet corn in separate pots; when done, cut the corn from the cob, allowing twice as much corn as beans; put them together and let them boil. Just before serving, add a little butter, pepper, and salt.

TOMATOES A-LA-CREME.

Pare and slice ripe tomatoes, one quart of fresh ones or a pound can, stew until perfectly smooth, season with salt and pepper, and add a piece of butter the size of an egg; just before taking from the fire, stir in one cup of cream, with a tablespoonful of flour stirred smooth in a part of it; do not let it boil after the flour is put in. Have ready in a dish pieces of toast, pour the tomatoes over this and serve.

BROWNED TOMATOES.

Take large round tomatoes and halve them, place them the skin side down in a frying-pan in which a very small quantity of butter and lard have been previously melted, sprinkle them with salt and pepper, and dredge well with flour. Place the pan on a hot part of the fire, and let them brown thoroughly; then stir and brown again, and so on until they are quite done. They lose their acidity, and their flavor is superior to stewed tomatoes.

TO BROIL TOMATOES.

Take large round tomatoes, wash and wipe, and put them in a gridiron over lively coals, the stem side down. When brown, turn them and let them cook till quite hot through. Place them on a hot dish, and send quickly to the table, when each one may season for himself with pepper, salt, and butter.

BAKED TOMATOES.

1. Fill a deep pan (as many as will cover the bottom) with ripe tomatoes, round out a hole in the center of each, fill up with bread crumbs, butter, pepper, and salt; put a teacup of water in the pan; bake till brown; send to the table hot.

2. Cut in slices good fresh tomatoes (not too ripe); put a layer of them in a dish suitable for baking; then a layer of bread crumbs over them, salt, pepper, and plenty of butter; another layer of tomatoes, and so on until the dish is full. Bake one hour.

SCALLOPED TOMATOES.

Butter an earthen dish, then put in a layer of fresh tomatoes, sliced and peeled, and a few rinds of onion (one large onion for the whole dish); then cover with a layer of bread crumbs, with a little butter, salt, and pepper. Repeat this process until the dish is full. Bake for an hour in a pretty hot oven.

SWEET POTATOES.

Sweet potatoes require more time to cook than common potatoes. To Boil—Take large, fine potatoes, wash clean, boil with the skins on in plenty of water, but without salt. They will take at least one hour. Drain off the water, and set them for a few minutes in a tin pan before the fire or in the stove, that they may be well dried. Peel them before sent to the table. To Fry—Choose large potatoes; half boil them, and then, having taken off the skins, cut the potatoes into slices, and fry in butter or in nice drippings. To Bake—Bake as the common potato, except give them a longer time.

MASH POTATOES.

Steam or boil potatoes until soft in salted water; pour off the water, and let them drain perfectly dry; sprinkle with salt, and mash; have ready some hot milk or cream in which has been melted a piece of butter; pour this onto the potatoes, and stir until white and very light.

BROWNED POTATOES.

Boil, and three-quarters of an hour before a round of beef is taken from the oven put them in the dripping-pan, after skimming off the fat from the gravy; baste them frequently, and when quite brown drain on a sieve.

QUIRLED POTATOES.

Peel, boil, mash, and season a few potatoes; then put them into a colander, pressing them through into the dish you wish to serve them in; set in the oven, and brown.

POTATO PUFF.

Take two large cups of cold mashed potatoes, and stir into it two tablespoonfuls of melted butter, beating to a white cream before adding anything else; then put with this two eggs beaten very light, and a teacupful of cream or milk, salting to taste. Beat all well, pour into a deep dish, and bake in quick oven until nicely browned.

SARATOGA POTATOES.

Peel, and slice on a slaw-cutter into cold water, wash thoroughly, and drain; spread between the folds of a clean cloth, rub and pat until dry. Fry a few at a time in boiling lard· salt as you take them out. Saratoga potatoes are often eaten cold. They can be prepared three or four hours before needed, and if kept in a warm place they will be crisp and nice. They are used for garnishing game and steaks.

POTATO CAKES.

Two pounds of mashed potatoes, two tablespoonfuls of butter, and a little salt, two pounds of flour, and milk enough to make a batter, one-half cupful of yeast; set it to rise, and when light bake in cakes size of a muffin.

MASHED POTATOES.

Wash and cut in halves or quarters, put into boiling water, boil one-half hour; when done pour off all the water, adding salt; mash perfectly smooth; then add cream if you have it; if not, milk, and beat well with fork and spoon. The beating makes them light.

BROILED POTATOES.

Take cold boiled potatoes, peel and slice them in slices one-third of an inch thick, dip them into dissolved butter, place on a gridiron over a very clear fire, grill them until nicely browned underneath; then turn them and when a nice color put them into a heated dish; sprinkle with salt and pepper and serve hot.

POTATOES A-LA-DELMONICO.

Cut the potatoes with a vegetable cutter into small balls about the size of a marble; put them into a stew-pan with plenty of butter, and a good sprinkling of salt; keep the saucepan covered, and shake occasionally until they are quite done, which will be in about an hour.

FRIED POTATOES WITH EGGS.

Slice cold boiled potatoes, and fry in good butter until brown; beat up one or two eggs, and stir into them just as you dish them for the table; do not leave them a moment on the fire after the eggs are in, for if they harden they are not half so nice; one egg is enough for three or four persons, unless they are very fond of potatoes; if they are, have plenty, and put in two.

POTATO BALLS OR CROQUETTES.

Four large, mealy potatoes, cold, mash them in a pan with two tablespoonfuls of fresh melted butter, a pinch of salt, a little pepper, one tablespoonful of cream, and the beaten yolk of one egg; rub it together for about five minutes, or until very smooth; shape the mixture into balls about the size of a walnut, or small rolls, dip them into an egg well beaten, and then into the finest sifted bread crumbs; fry them in boiling lard.

STEWED POTATOES.

Put into a frying-pan a small piece of butter, a little parsley chopped fine, salt, and pepper, and half a cup of cream, set on the fire and let come to a boil. Cut cold boiled potatoes into small pieces and turn into the cream, let the cream boil up well around the potatoes, add another small piece of butter, and serve.

LYONNAISE POTATOES.

Into a saucepan put a large lump of butter and a small onion, finely chopped, and when the onion is fried to an amber color, throw in slices of cold boiled potatoes, which must be thoroughly stirred until they are turning brown; at this moment put in a spoonful of finely-chopped parsley, and as soon as it is cooked drain through a colander, so the potatoes retain the moisture of the butter and many particles of the parsley. Thus you may have Lyonnaise potatoes.

FRIED OYSTER PLANT.

Parboil oyster plant; scrape off the outside; cut in slices; dip in beaten egg, roll in bread crumbs, and fry in hot lard.

SALSIFY, OR VEGETABLE OYSTERS.

Wash and scrape them thoroughly, and as you wash throw them into a bowl of cold water. Cut into pieces about half an inch long, boil three-fourths of an hour, when tender pour off all the water, season with pepper and salt, a small lump of butter, and enough cream to almost cover them; if no cream, use milk, with more butter, and thicken like gravy with a little flour. They are nice served on toast.

BAKED EGG PLANT.

Cut in halves a nice smooth egg plant scoop out the center, leaving with the skin about one-third of an inch, chop the inside of the egg plant very fine, two ripe tomatoes, one onion, some bread-crumbs, a little parsley, and green pepper—onion and pepper to be chopped separately very fine, salt, butter, and very little pepper, mix very smooth, put in the shell, butter on top, and bake about one-half hour.

FRIED EGG PLANT.

Pare and slice them, then sprinkle each slice with salt, and let them stand for about one hour with a weight on them, then dip into egg well beaten, then flour, and fry light brown in lard and butter.

EGG PLANT—BAKED.

Boil until soft, and scoop out all the inside; mash fine, and to every cupful add a teaspoonful of cracker crumbs, a teaspoonful of butter, and pepper and salt to taste; put into a dish for the table; beat an egg very light, and spread a part over the top of the dish, then sprinkle with rolled cracker, and lastly spread with the remainder of the egg, and set into the oven to brown.

EGG PLANT.

Put into water and boil until soft, then cut in two and scoop out all the inside; season; take a tablespoonful at a time, dip in egg and bread-crumbs, and fry in hot lard.

STUFFED CABBAGE,

Cut the heart out of a large cabbage; take cold chicken or any cold meat, and chop very fine, and season highly, and mix with the yolk of an egg; fill the cabbage with this stuffing, and then tie it firmly in a cloth, and boil an hour and a half or two hours.

TO BOIL ASPARAGUS.

Scrape the stems lightly to within two inches of the points; throw them into cold water for a few minutes; tie in bunches of equal size, cut the ends that they may be all of the same length, then throw into boiling water a little salted, and boil fast for twenty or twenty-five minutes, or until quite tender; have prepared a round of bread nicely toasted, which dip quickly into the boiling asparagus water, then dish the asparagus upon it, with the points meeting in the center; send rich melted butter to the table with it.

BAKED BEETS.

Wash and put into a pan; set into a moderate oven, and bake slowly; when soft, remove the skin, and dress to taste.

BEANS.

We must not forget beans, which abound so much in nourishment, but they must be thoroughly cooked; for bean soup they should be boiled about five hours seasoned then with cream or butter, and with salt, they ought to be relished by everybody. However I may have seasoned this soup, my children always wish to add milk upon their plates. Baked beans must be either boiled until very soft before baking, or must be baked a long time—from three to six hours, if not previously very tender—with a good deal of liquor in the jar or pan. Those who use pork at all, usually put a piece of fat pork in the dish of beans prepared for baking, but some of us very much prefer a seasoning of cream or butter. Split pea-soup or common unsplit dried peas, boiled five to six hours without meat, is very nutritious, and much liked by many; I season it with salt, and cream or milk, if I have it—the more the better—otherwise with butter.

BAKED BEANS.

Soak a pint and a half of dried beans over night; in the morning pour off the water, cover with fresh water, and boil until they crack open, or are very tender; then put them with the water in which they were boiled, into a deep earthen dish, adding a little salt, and, if agreeable, a tablespoonful of molasses; put on top of the dish one half pound of fat and lean pork or corned beef, which should be gashed or scored across the rind; bake four hours, and longer, if convenient; it will be better for it, only bake slowly; keep nearly covered with water till two-thirds done, then allow it to dry away.

GREENS.

This is the simplest of dishes, yet it is not always a well-served one. Greens should be properly boiled; the water should be soft, and a tablespoonful of salt added to a large-sized pot of it, which should be boiling hot when the greens are thrown in; it should be kept boiling until they are done, which can be told by their sinking to the bottom of the pot, and then they should be skimmed out as quickly as possible into a colander so that all the water will run out; press them with a small plate, and then turn upon a platter, add a large piece of butter, and cut up fine. Serve smoking hot.

LIMA BEANS.

They should be gathered young; shell them, lay them in a pan of cold water, and then boil them about two hours, till they are quite soft; drain well, and add to them some butter.

MACARONI.

Boil macaroni until tender; butter the bottom of a pudding-dish, and put in a layer of the macaroni, then a layer of grated cheese; season with butter, pepper, and salt; then another layer of macaroni, and so on, finishing with a layer of cheese; cover with milk and bake forty minutes.

MACARONI AS A VEGETABLE.

Simmer one-half pound of macaroni in plenty of water till tender, but not broken; strain off the water. Take the yolks of five and the whites of two eggs, one-half pint of cream; white meat and ham chopped very fine, three spoonsfuls of grated cheese. Season with salt and pepper, heat all together, stirring constantly. Mix with the macaroni, put into a buttered mold, and steam one hour.

MACARONI WITH CHEESE.

Throw into boiling water some macaroni, with salt according to quantity used; let it boil one-fourth of an hour, when it will be a little more than half-cooked, drain off the water; place the macaroni in a saucepan with milk to cover, boil till done. Butter a pudding-dish, sprinkle the bottom with plenty of grated cheese, put in the macaroni a little white pepper, plenty of butter, sprinkle on more cheese, cover that with bread-crumbs, set in a quick oven to brown; serve hot.

MACARONI WITH OYSTERS.

Boil macaroni in salt water, after wich draw through a colander; take a deep earthen dish or tin; put in alternate layers of macaroni and oysters; sprinkle the layers of macaroni with grated cheese; bake until brown.

STEWED MACARONI.

Boil two ounces of macaroni in water, drain well, put into a saucepan one ounce of butter, mix with one tablespoonful of flour, moisten with four tablespoonfuls of veal or beef stock, one gill of cream; salt and white pepper to taste; put in the macaroni, let it boil up, and serve while hot.

MACARONI WITH TOMATOES.

Boil one-half pound of macaroni till tender, pour off all the water, then add one-half cup of sweet cream, one-third of a cup of butter, pepper, and salt; let simmer for a short time, but be careful that it does not become much broken; turn into vegetable dish; have ready one pint of stewed tomatoes; season with butter, salt, and pepper; pour over the macaroni.

BOILED ONIONS.

Skin them thoroughly. Put them to boil; when they have boiled a few minutes, pour off the water and add clean cold water, and then set them to boil again. Pour this away and add more cold water, when they may boil till done. This will make them white and clear, and very mild in flavor. After they are done, pour off all the water, and dress with a little cream, salt and pepper to taste.

ESCALLOPED ONIONS.

Boil till tender six large onions; afterward separate them with a large spoon; then place a layer of onions and a layer of grated bread-crumbs alternately in a pudding-dish; season with pepper and salt to taste; moisten with milk; put into the oven to brown.

SCOTCH ESCALLOPS.

Peel potatoes and slice, not quite as thin as for Saratoga chips, and cover the bottom of a dripping-pan with them; sprinkle with salt and pepper and small pieces of butter, or butter and lard mixed; continue this until the pan is full; lay a slice of salt pork or two on the top; cover closely and bake in a good hot oven. Very nice sweet potatoes can be prepared in the same way. They are very nice without the pork.

TURNIPS.

Pare and cut into pieces; put them into boiling water well salted, and boil until tender; drain thoroughly and then mash and add a piece of butter, pepper, and salt to taste, and a small teaspoonful of sugar. Stir until they are thoroughly mixed, and serve hot.

FRIED PARSNIPS.

Scrape, cut into strips, and boil until tender in salted water; drain and dip into batter, made with one egg beaten light, one-half cup of milk, and flour enough to make a batter, and fry in hot butter or lard.

ASPARAGUS.

Cook only the tender green stalks; cut them of equal lengths, and boil in water with a little salt till tender. While the asparagus is cooking prepare some nicely toasted bread, lay the asparagus on the toast and season with butter, salt, and pepper, or pour over it a little cream previously scalded.

SPINACH.

Spinach requires good washing and close picking. Boil twenty minutes in boiling water, drain, season with butter, pepper, and salt; garnish the dish with slices of hard-boiled eggs.

FRESH CORN MUSH.

Take several ears of green corn, grate it down; take some milk, stir into the corn briskly with a little salt; strain through a coarse sieve, and put in a hot cooking-pot with a spoonful of lard. Keep it well stirred for at least twenty minutes without stopping, while cooking. When thickened put into a deep dish, slice, and fry.

PARSNIP FRITTERS.

Four parsnips, boiled and mashed fine; add three well-beaten eggs, two tablespoonfuls of sifted flour, butter the size of an egg, one teacup of milk, and salt to taste. Upon a hot buttered griddle drop the mixture, and bake after the style of flannel-cakes. Serve quite hot.

PARSNIP STEW.

Three slices of salt pork, boil one hour and a half; scrape five large parsnips, cut in quarters lengthwise, add to the pork, and let boil one-half hour, then add a few potatoes, and let all boil together until the potatoes are soft; the fluid in the kettle should be about a cupful when ready to take off.

GREEN PEAS.

Put the pods into a pot, cover and boil thoroughly, then strain and put the peas into the same water and boil tender. Season with butter, pepper, a little salt, and the least bit of sugar.

BOILED HOMINY.

Soak one cup of fine hominy in three cups of water and salt to taste; in the morning turn it into a quart pail; then put the pail into a kettle of boiling water, cover tightly and steam one hour; then add one teacupful of sweet milk, and boil fifteen minutes.

CAULIFLOWER.

Trim off all the outside leaves, and put into boiling water well salted; boil until tender, and then serve with a white sauce or with cream.

TO FRY PARSLEY.

This, when done as it should be, is one of the nicest as well as cheapest of garnishings. The parsley should be washed and dried in a cloth; then if one is the happy possessor of a wire basket, put in the parsley and hold from two to three minutes in boiling drippings; take from the basket and dry until crisp before the kitchen fire. It may be fried without a basket, but requires more care in so doing.

STEWED MUSHROOMS.

Wash them, cut off the ends of the stalks and peel them; put them in a stew-pan without any water, and season with salt and pepper; add two ounces of butter rolled in two teaspoonfuls of flour to every pint of mushrooms; cover them closely and let them simmer slowly until they are soft.

TOMATO TOAST.

Rub tomatoes through the colander, and cook to taste; toast three slices of bread, butter and lay upon a hot dish; just before serving add a cup of cream or milk to the tomatoes and pour over the toast.

STUFFED TOMATOES.

Select large tomatoes of even size, and scoop out a small place in the top and fill with stuffing made as follows: Fry a small onion chopped fine in a tablespoonful of butter; when nearly done add some bread crumbs, moistened with a little milk or water, and seasoned with pepper and salt; put a little bit of butter on each and then bake. Another dressing is made as follows: Chop very fine cold meat or fowl of any kind with a very small piece of bacon added; fry an onion chopped fine in a tablespoonful of butter, and when nearly done add the meat, some bread-crumbs, pepper and salt; cook a minute; mix well; add the yolk of an egg, and fill the tomatoes; place in a baking dish; sprinkle bread-crumbs over them with some small bits of butter, and bake. Use either as a garnish or as a dish by itself.

AN EXCELLENT DISH.

Place alternate layers of tomatoes, sliced onions, and **bread and butter** in a pudding dish and bake.

PARSNIP FRITTERS.

Boil in salted water until very tender; then mash, seasoning with a little butter, pepper, and salt, add a little flour and one or two eggs, well beaten; make into small balls or cakes and fry in hot lard.

POTATO CAKES.

Grate raw **potatoes**; season; **add flour** and well-beaten **eggs; make** into cakes and fry.

BAKED POTATOES.

Slice them and put into cold water for a time before using; then put into a baking-dish, with seasoning and half-pint of milk; bake slowly, and when done, lay a piece of butter on the top.

POTATO-CHEESE PUFFS.

Take some grated cheese, some cold mashed potato, and a beaten egg, with a little butter; mix well, adding salt and pepper; put into patty-pans, and bake in a quick oven. Serve hot.

POTATO PUFF.

Beat a pint of mashed potatoes; butter the size of an egg, melted, until very light; then add half a cup of cream and two eggs beaten separarely; beat well and pile irregularly in a dish, and bake quickly.

CARROTS STEWED.

Cut the carrots lengthways, and boil until soft; then slice very thin and put into a saucepan with two tablespoonfuls of butter and a cup of cream or milk; season, and stew a quarter of an hour.

CAULIFLOWER, WITH CHEESE.

Boil in salted water until tender; put them into a baking-dish and pour over them a drawn-butter sauce in which has been mixed a little grated cheese; sprinkle with bread-crumbs, and place in a quick oven for ten minutes.

CABBAGE A-LA-CREME.

Boil and drain the cabbage; put into a saucepan one cup of cream, two tablespoonfuls of butter, and thicken with a little flour, and season with salt and pepper, and then add the cabbage, and boil slowly five or ten minutes.

EGGS AND OMELETS.

PROPER WAY TO COOK EGGS.

Butter a tin plate and break in your eggs; set in a steamer; place over a kettle of boiling water, and steam until the whites are cooked; they are more ornamental when broken into patty-tins, as they keep their form better; the whites of the eggs, when cooked in this manner, are tender and light, and not tough and leathery, as if cooked by any other process; they can be eaten by invalids, and they certainly are very much richer than by any other method; if cooked in the shell, they taste of the lime contained in them, and, if broken into boiling water, it destroys their flavor.

TO PRESERVE EGGS.

Pack them when perfectly fresh, in wheat bran, the small ends down, and so loosely as to prevent their coming in contact with each other, or the sides or bottom of the vessel which contains them. Cover carefully with bran, well pressed down.

A NICE CHEESE RELISH.

Four ounces of flour, four ounces of cheese, and three of butter, salt, pepper, and a dash of cayenne pepper, knead it all together, roll thin, cut in strips like ladies' fingers, and bake a delicate brown.

SCRAMBLED EGGS WITH HAM.

Put into a pan, butter, a little pepper and salt and a little milk; when hot drop in the eggs, and with a knife cut the eggs and scrape them from the bottom; add some cold ham chopped fine, and when done serve in a hot dish.

EGGS AND OMELETS.

TO POACH EGGS.

Have the water well salted, and not let it boil hard. Break the eggs separately into a saucer, and slip gently into the water; when nicely done, remove with a skimmer, trim neatly, and lay each egg upon a small, thin square of buttered toast, then sprinkle with salt and pepper. Some persons prefer them poached, rather than fried, with ham, in which case, substitute the ham for toast.

STUFFED EGGS.

Boil the eggs hard, remove the shells, and then cut in two, either way, as preferred. Remove the yolks, and mix with them pepper, salt, and a little dry mustard—some like cold chicken, ham, or tongue, chopped very fine—and then stuff the cavities, smooth them, and put the halves together again. For picnics, they can simply be wrapped in tissue paper to keep them together. If for home use, they can be egged and bread-crumbed, and browned in boiling lard; drain, and garnish with parsley.

EGG TOAST.

Beat four eggs, yolks and whites together, thoroughly; put two tablespoonfuls of butter into a saucepan, and melt slowly; then pour in the eggs, and heat without boiling over a slow fire, stirring constantly; add a little salt, and when hot, spread on slices of nicely-browned toast, and serve at once.

CHEESE OMELET.

Butter the sides of a deep dish and cover with thin slices of rich cheese; lay over the cheese thin slices of well-buttered bread, first covering the cheese with a little red pepper and mustard; then another layer of cheese; beat the yolk of an egg in a cup of cream—milk will do—and pour over the dish, and put at once into the oven; bake till nicely brown. Serve hot, or it will be tough, hard, and worthless.

OMELET WITH OYSTERS.

Allow one egg for each person, and beat separately very light; season; just before cooking add the oysters, which have been previously scalded in their own liquor.

TOMATO OMELET.

One quart of tomatoes, chopped finely (after the skin is removed), and put into a saucepan with two finely-chopped onions, a little butter, salt, and pepper, one cracker pounded finely; cover tight and let it simmer about an hour; beat five eggs to a froth; have your griddle hot; grease it well; stir your eggs into the tomato, beat together, and pour into the griddle; brown on one side, fold and brown on the other. To be served hot.

BREAD OMELET.

One cup of bread crumbs wet with a little milk, salt and pepper, let stand until soft, beat eight eggs light, heat the skillet, adding a large lump of butter, mix the bread and eggs, pour into the skillet, and after eggs harden divide in the middle.

BAKED OMELET.

1. Beat the yolks of six eggs, and add the whites of three eggs beaten very light; salt and pepper to taste; a tablespoonful of flour mixed in a cup of milk; pour into a well-buttered pan, and put into a hot oven; when thick pour over it the whites of three eggs beaten light, and brown. Serve immediately.

2. Set one-half pint of milk on the fire and stir in one-half cup of flour mixed with a little cold milk and salt; when scalding-hot, beat the yolks of six eggs and add them, stir in whites and set immediately in the oven; bake twenty minutes, and serve as soon as done.

OMELET.

Beat the yolks and whites of eight eggs separately until light, then beat together; add a little salt and one tablespoonful of cream. Have in the omelet pan a piece of butter; when the butter is boiling-hot, pour in the omelet, and shake it until it begins to stiffen, and then let it brown. Fold double, and serve hot.

APPLE OMELET.

Eight large apples, four eggs, one cup of sugar, one tablespoonful of butter, nutmeg or cinnamon to taste. Stew the apples and mash fine, add butter and sugar; when cold, add the eggs, well beaten. Bake until brown, and eat while warm.

OYSTER OMELET.

Allow for every six large oysters or twelve small ones, one egg, remove the hard part, and mince the rest very fine; take the yolks of eight eggs and whites of four, beat till very light, then mix in the oysters, season, and beat all up thoroughly; put into a skillet a gill of butter, let it melt; when the butter boils, skim it, and turn in the omelet, stir until it stiffens, fry light brown; when the under side is brown, turn on to a hot platter. If wanted the upper side brown, hold a red-hot shovel over it.

OMELET SOUFFLEE.

Stir five tablespoonfuls of sifted flour into three pints of milk, strain through a sieve; add the yolks of eight eggs; beaten very light, and, just as it goes into the oven, the whites beaten stiff. Bake quickly.

FRENCH OMELET.

One quart of milk, one pint of bread-crumbs, five eggs, one tablespoonful of flour, one onion chopped fine, chopped parsley, season with pepper and salt. Have butter melted in a spider; when the omelet is brown, turn it over. Double when served.

OMELET WITH HAM.

Make a plain omelet, and just before turning one half over the other, sprinkle over it some finely-chopped ham. Garnish with small slices of ham. Jelly or marmalade may be added in the same manner.

EGGS AND OMELETS.

BOILED EGGS, WITH SAUCE.

Boil hard, remove the shell, set in a hot dish, and serve with **piquante sauce.**

BAKED EGGS.

1. Mix some finely chopped ham and bread crumbs in about equal proportions, and season with salt and pepper, and moisten with milk and a little melted butter; half fill some patty pans with the mixture, break over the top of each an egg, sprinkle with fine bread-crumbs, and bake; serve hot.

2. Break the eggs into a buttered dish and season; add small bits of butter and a little cream; bake fifteen minutes.

3. Butter a clean, smooth saucepan, break as many eggs as will be needed into a saucer, one by one. If found good, slip it into the dish. No broken yolk allowed, nor must they crowd so as to risk breaking the yolk after put in. Put a small piece of butter on each, and sprinkle with pepper and salt. Set into a well-heated oven, and bake till the whites are set. If the oven is rightly heated, it will take but a few minutes, and is far more delicate than fried eggs.

HOMINY FRITTERS.

Two teacupfuls of cold boiled hominy; stir in one teacupful of sweet milk and a little salt; four tablespoonfuls of sifted flour and one egg; beat the white separately and add last; drop the batter by spoonfuls into hot lard, and fry a nice brown.

BAKED CABBAGE.

Cook as for boiled cabbage, after which drain and set aside until cold. Chop fine, add two beaten eggs, a tablespoonful of butter, pepper, salt, three tablespoonfuls rich cream; stir well and bake in a buttered dish until brown. Eat hot.

BEETS.

Wash thoroughly, being careful not to prick the skin, as that will destroy the color; put into boiling water and boil five or six hours; if served hot season with butter; pepper, and salt; if cold, cover with vinegar.

EGG A-LA-MODE.

Remove the skin from a dozen tomatoes, medium size, cut them up in a saucepan, add a little butter, pepper, and salt; when sufficiently boiled, beat up five or six eggs, and just before you serve, turn them into the saucepan with the tomato, and stir one way for two minutes, allowing them time to be well done.

EGG BASKETS.

Boil quite hard as many eggs as will be needed. Put into cold water till cold, then cut neatly into halves with a thin, sharp knife; remove the yolk and rub to a paste with some melted butter, adding pepper and salt. Cover up this paste and set aside till the filling is ready. Take cold roast duck, chicken, or turkey, which may be on hand, chop fine and pound smooth, and while pounding mix in the paste prepared from the yolks. As you pound moisten with melted butter and some gravy which may have been left over from the fowls; set this paste when done over hot water till well heated. Cut off a small slice from the end of the empty halves of the whites, so they will stand firm, then fill them with this paste; place them close together on a flat round dish, and pour over the rest of the gravy, if any remains, or make a little fresh. A few spoonfuls of cream or rich milk improves this dressing.

FRENCH EGG CAKE.

Beat up thoroughly six eggs, a teaspoonful of sweet cream or milk, and a little salt. Fry in a pan in which there is one-half ounce of melted butter, over a quick fire. In order that the omelet may remain soft and juicy, it is necessary that the pan should be hot before the eggs are poured in. During the frying move the pan continually to and fro; continue this until a cake is formed, then let it remain still a moment to brown. Turn out and serve immediately.

BREAD, BISCUIT, ETC.

In selecting flour first look to the color. If it is white, with a yellowish straw-color tint, buy it. If it is white, with a bluish cast, or with black specks in it, refuse it. Next examine its adhesiveness—wet and knead a little of it between your fingers; if it works soft and sticky, it is poor. Then throw a little lump of dried flour against a smooth surface; if it falls like powder, it is bad. Lastly, squeeze some of the flour tightly in your hand; if it retains the shape given by the pressure that, too, is a good sign. It is safe to buy flour that will stand all these tests.

Three things are indispensable to success in bread making; good flour, good yeast, and watchful care; a fourth might be added: experience.

In winter, always warm the flour for bread, and keep the sponge near the stove, where it will not get chilled.

Bread should be put into a rather hot oven. An hour is the time usually allowed for baking.

Rolls and biscuits should bake quickly. To make them a nice color, rub them over with warm water just before putting them into the oven, to glaze them, brush lightly with milk and sugar.

Baking powder and soda biscuit should be made as rapidly as possible, laid into hot pans and put in a quick oven.

Gem pans should be heated and well greased.

Fritters should be made quickly and beaten very thoroughly.

Pancakes should be well beaten, the eggs separately, the whites to a stiff froth and added the last thing.

HOP YEAST.

Six potatoes boiled in a gallon of water with a handful of hops tied in a bag; put in a jar one-half cup of flour, and when the potatoes are done, pour the water over it, adding the potatoes when mashed; when lukewarm, add a cup of yeast, and when cold a half cup of sugar, **one-fourth cup of salt**, and a tablespoonful of ginger.

POTATO YEAST.

Take half a dozen medium-sized potatoes, **boil and** mash fine, and two cups of flour, a good tablespoonful ginger, one of salt, one-half cup white sugar; add two cups of boiling water, **and beat** until smooth; **when lukewarm**, add a cup of yeast or two **yeast cakes.**

YEAST.

1. **Take** two good-sized **potatoes, grate them raw.** Add one-half teacup **of white** sugar, **one** teaspoon **of salt, a little ginger.** Pour over the mixture one-half pint of boiling water, **in which one** tablespoonful of **hops has been** boiled. Save half a cup each time to start anew.

2. To one cup of grated raw potato add half cup salt and half cup sugar, pour over all one quart boiling water, stirring well; it will thicken like starch; when nearly cold add one cup of good yeast. In about twelve hours it should be light. Put in jug or bottle, and cork tightly.

3. A double handful of hops, one-half-dozen large potatoes; boil together in one-half gallon of water till done; strain and mash on to one-half cupful of ginger, small cup of flour, and one cup of brown sugar, and half cup of salt. Let stand until cool, then add **one** cupful of good yeast. Next day cork **up tight in a jug.**

YEAST AND BREAD.

Take ten large potatoes, **pare, and put** them **in a** kettle with three **quarts of water; put a pint** of **hops in a thin muslin bag** in the same **kettle with** potatoes; boil until potatoes are **soft, then** pour **the** water from this kettle boiling hot over a pint of flour in a crock. Squeeze all the strength from the hops; mash the potatoes, add a quart of cold water to them, and put through a colander into the crock, and add one-half teacup of salt, a cup of sugar, one tablespoonful of ginger. Let **this stand for two days** until it stops fermenting and settles; then put **into a jug, cork tight,** and keep in a cool place.

FOR THE BREAD.

Pare and boil six good-sized potatoes, **drain** off the water, mash fine, and pour over them about three pints of **cold** water, and run through a colander; add flour until this is a thin **batter,** then put in a cupful of yeast from the jug. Let stand until it **rises, and** then stir into flour as much **as you can** with a spoon, and let **rise again.** Work in enough more flour to make as stiff as bread, **and let rise** the third time. When light this time work out into loaves, **and let rise.** All the flour must be sifted.

VIENNA BREAD.

The following is the recipe by which the Vienna bread was made **that became** so famous on the Centennial grounds: Sift in a tin pan **four pounds of** flour; bank up against the sides; pour in one quart of milk and water, and mix into it enough flour to form a thin batter; then quickly and lightly add one pint of milk, in which is dissolved one ounce of salt and one and three-quarter ounces of yeast; leave the remainder of the flour against the sides of the pan; cover the pan with a cloth, and set in a place free from draught for three-quarters of an hour; then mix in the rest of the flour until the dough will leave the bottom and sides of the pan, and let it stand two and a half hours; finally, divide the mass into one-pound pieces, to be cut in turn into twelve parts each; this gives square pieces about three and a half inches thick, each corner of which is taken up and folded over to the center, and then the cases are turned over on a dough-board to rise for half an hour, when they are put in a hot oven that bakes them in ten minutes.

BREAD.

The first thing is the yeast, which is made with hops, a small handful boiled and stirred into flour with a little salt, and sometimes a little ginger and brown sugar. To "set" the sponge, the flour is sifted carefully, and into the center is poured the yeast, thoroughly mixed with water and salt, and about a peck of finely-mashed potatoes is needed for a baking of a dozen loaves of medium size. This mixture is made thoroughly fine, and the ingredients when mixed (about new milk-warm in summer, and a little warmer in colder weather) poured slowly upon the flour, and made into a fine batter. It is at night, which is our plan; the first thing in the morning it is again worked and set to rise before breakfast, so that by dinner time our large baking is finished. The potatoes, without a doubt, keep the bread moist, are a healthful addition, and where cheap effect a saving in flour of some importance.

STEAMED BROWN BREAD.

One cup of molasses, two and a half cupfuls of sour milk, one teaspoonful of soda dissolved in a teaspoonful of warm water, two cups of graham flour, one cup corn meal, teaspoonful of salt; steam three hours, and then set a few minutes in the oven.

BUCKWHEAT CAKES.

Take warm water, and thicken it with flour, to which add a tablespoonful of molasses to make them brown well. Brewers' yeast is best, but it cannot generally be obtained except in large towns. In the morning add a little soda. If the batter is of the right consistency, and the cakes baked quickly and eaten direct from the griddle, they will be quite different from the tough, heavy things too often stacked up before the fire.

BREAD PANCAKES.

Soak the bread and drain; to two cups of bread add one of flour, milk enough to make a thin batter, two teaspoonfuls baking powder, and one egg, beaten light.

CORN MEAL PANCAKES.

Take two cups of Indian meal and a teaspoonful of salt; pour over it boiling water to make a batter; stand until cool, and then add the yolks of three eggs beaten, flour to make the proper consistency, one and a half teaspoonfuls baking powder; just before baking add the whites, beaten stiff.

RICE PANCAKES.

One-half cup of cold boiled rice, mixed with one pint of milk and the yolks of three eggs, and flour (in which has been mixed a good teaspoonful of baking powder and a little salt) to make a batter; bake on the griddle, and while hot spread with jelly or jam; roll up, trim and sprinkle over with sugar; must be eaten hot.

TOMATO PANCAKES.

Make a batter with one cup of flour, two teaspoonfuls sugar, salt, teaspoonful baking powder and two cups of milk, adding last three eggs, beaten light; slice large tomatoes, season, cover with the batter, and bake on a griddle.

YEAST WAFFLES.

One quart of flour mixed with a pint of warm milk; add one-half cup of yeast, salt, two eggs (well beaten), and piece of butter size of an egg, melted; when light, bake.

WAFFLES.

Rub a large teaspoonful of baking powder and the same quantity of butter into a pint of flour; one-half teaspoonful of salt; beat the yolks of two eggs very light, and mix with a coffee-cupful of milk, and add to the flour; lastly, the whites of the eggs, beaten to a stiff froth.

BROWN BREAD.

1. Take two cups of rye meal, two cups of Indian meal, and one-half cup of flour; salt, and a teaspoonful of saleratus should be added to this; it can be mixed with water, but is nicer when sour milk is used; it must be made soft enough to run; bake slow and long.

2. Four cups sour milk, four cups corn meal, two cups rye meal, one-half cup New Orleans molasses, soda to sweeten milk; bake it in a deep dish two hours.

BISCUITS.

Into a quart of sifted flour put two heaping teaspoonfuls of baking powder and a pinch of salt; mix together while dry; then rub into it a piece of lard a little larger than an egg; mix with cold sweet milk; roll thin; cut with a tin cutter, and bake a light brown in a hot oven; send to the table immediately.

CORN BREAD.

Two cups of Indian, one cup wheat,
One cup sour milk, one cup sweet,
One good egg that well you beat,
Half a cup molasses, too,
Half cup sugar add thereto,
With one spoon of butter new

Salt and soda each a spoon;
Mix up quickly and bake it soon;
Then you'll have corn bread complete,
Best of all corn bread you meet.
It will make your boy's eyes shine
If he's like that boy of mine.
If you have a dozen boys
To increase your household joys,
Double then this rule I should,
And you'll have two corn cakes good.
When you've nothing nice for tea,
This the very thing will be;
All the men that I have seen
Say it is of all cakes queen—
Good enough for any king
That a husband home can bring;
Warming up the human stove,
Cheering up the hearts you love;
And only Tyndall can explain
The links between corn bread and brain.
Get a husband what he likes,
And save a hundred household strikes.

CORN MEAL GEMS.

To two cups of boiling milk add two cups of corn meal, salt, two tablespoonfuls of sugar, and butter size of a hickory nut; mix well, and leave until cool; then add three eggs, beaten very light; bake in gem-pan

GRAHAM PUFFS.

One egg, one pint sweet milk, one pint graham flour, and a pinch of salt; beat the egg thoroughly, add the milk, then the flour gradually; beat the whole mixture briskly with an egg-beater; pour into cast-iron gem-pans, well greased and piping hot; bake in very hot oven; this mixture is just sufficient for twelve gems.

GRAHAM MUFFINS.

Two cups of graham flour, one cup of milk, one-third of a cup of sugar, one egg, butter the size of an egg, two teaspoonfuls of baking-powder; bake in rings twenty or thirty minutes in a hot oven.

GRAHAM CRACKERS.

Seven cups graham, one cup thick sweet cream or butter, one pint sweet milk, two teaspoonfuls baking-powder; rub the baking-powder into the flour, add the cream, with a little salt, then the milk; mix well, and roll as thin as soda crackers; cut in any shape; bake quickly, then leave about the stove for a few hours to dry thoroughly.

GRAHAM BISCUITS.

Take one quart water or milk, butter the size of an egg, three tablespoonfuls of sugar, two of baker's yeast, and a pinch of salt; take enough white flour to use up the water, making it the consistency of batter cakes; add the rest of the ingredients, and as much graham flour as can be stirred in with a spoon; set it away till morning; in the morning grease pan, flour hands; take a lump of dough the size of a large egg, roll lightly between the palms; let them rise twenty minutes, and bake in a tolerably hot oven.

GERMAN PUFFS.

Two cups of sweet milk, two cups of flour, three eggs, and a little salt.

GRAHAM GEMS.

One quart of graham flour, three teaspoonfuls of baking-powder, two eggs beaten light, butter the size of an egg (melted), one tablespoonful brown sugar, a little salt, and milk enough to make a batter.

BROWN BREAD.

One cup of corn meal, one cup of graham flour, one cup of sour milk, one cup of warm water, one-half cup of molasses, one teaspoonful of soda, a little salt; steam two hours; serve at table hot.

BOSTON BROWN BREAD.

Take three teacups of corn meal, stir into it two cups of boiling sweet milk; when cold, add one teacup of molasses, one cup of wheat flour, and one cup of sour milk; into the sour milk stir well one teaspoonful of soda; add one-half teaspoonful of salt; steam three hours.

CORN BREAD.

1. Three cups of corn meal, one and one-half cups of flour, one and one-half cups of sweet milk, five eggs, four teaspoonfuls of baking-powder, a little sugar.

2. One cup of corn meal, two cups of flour, one-half cup of sugar, three-fourths of a cup of melted butter, one cup of milk, three eggs, three teaspoonfuls of baking-powder.

BOILED INDIAN BREAD.

Two cups meal, one quart sour milk, one cup flour, two-thirds of a cup syrup, one teaspoonful soda, one egg; put in pudding-bag, set in boiling water, and boil three hours.

CORN CAKE (DELICIOUS).

One quart of corn meal, one quart of milk, two eggs, half cup of sugar, or three tablespoonfuls of molasses, teaspoon of salt, three tablespoonfuls baking-powder.

CORN BREAD WITHOUT EGGS.

Two cups of corn meal, one cup of flour, two cups of milk, two tablespoonfuls of melted butter, two tablespoonfuls of sugar, two tablespoonfuls of baking powder.

CORN MEAL MUFFINS.

1. Three pints of corn meal, one pint of flour, two eggs, five tablespoonfuls of baking-powder.

2. One and one-half cups of corn meal, the same of flour, two tablespoons of baking-powder, one-half cup of sugar, one-half teaspoon of salt, small tablespoon of melted butter, two eggs, milk enough to make a stiff **batter**.

CORN BREAD.

Two cups **sour milk,** three-quarters of a cup **molasses, two cups of** corn meal, one and one-half **cups** of white flour, small tablespoon **of** soda, dissolved in sour milk; **salt; steam** three hours; to be eaten hot. Slice and steam when you wish to warm it up.

CORN GRIDDLE CAKES.

One dozen ears of corn grated, two eggs, one cup sweet milk, salt, pepper, flour enough to make batter; then bake on buttered griddle.

STEAMED CORN BREAD.

Scald two cups of **corn meal with boiling** water, then add one cup of cold meal and one cup **of flour, two cups** of milk, one cup of molasses, and three teaspoonfuls **of baking-powder.** Steam three hours.

MISS PLATER'S CORN MUSH.

Put a quart of water on to boil. Stir a pint of cold milk with one pint of corn meal and one tablespoonful of salt. When the water boils, pour in the mixture gradually, stirring well; boil half an hour, stirring often.

DROP BISCUITS,

One quart of flour, three teaspoonfuls of baking-powder, teaspoonful of salt, butter the size of an egg rubbed into the flour, one pint of milk, drop from a spoon in buttered pan; bake in **a** quick oven.

SODA BISCUITS.

One quart of flour, two teaspoonfuls of cream tartar, one of soda, a piece of butter the size **of** an egg, one and a half cups of sweet milk; mix very thoroughly the flour, cream tartar, butter, salt; then add the **milk and soda.** Roll out and bake in a quick oven ten minutes.

NEWPORT BREAKFAST CAKES.

Six eggs, **six spoonfuls of sugar,** three pints of milk, one-half cup of butter, six teaspoonfuls of cream tartar, three teaspoonfuls soda; **stir stiff**; makes six loaves.

CRUMPETS.

Take **one quart of** dough **from the bread at** an early hour in the morning; break three eggs, separating yolks and whites, both to be whipped to **a light** froth, mix them in the dough, **and** gradually add milk-warm water, until it is a batter the consistency of buckwheat cakes; beat it well **and let** it rise till breakfast time. Have the griddle **hot and nicely greased; pour on the batter in** small round cakes, and bake a light brown.

ENGLISH ROLLS.

Two pounds of flour, **two** ounces of butter, three tablespoonfuls of yeast, one pint of warm milk; mix well together, and set in a warm place to rise; knead, and make into rolls. Bake twenty minutes.

HOW TO MAKE ROLLS.

When mashing potatoes for dinner, put a tablespoonful of it into one pint of the water they were boiled in, and set aside till bed-time; then strain it through a colander, add one pint of milk, one large spoonful nice lard, one large spoonful white sugar, one teaspoonful salt, one penny-worth of yeast, and flour to make a stiff batter. Leave it in a moderately warm place. In the morning add flour enough to make a soft dough, working it well. Let it rise again, roll out half an inch thick, cut into round cakes, fold together, drawing a buttered knife through as you fold them. Let them rise again for half an hour, or till light, bake in a quick oven from fifteen to twenty minutes. In cold weather the milk should be lukewarm; in hot weather the milk should be scalded and cooled. The potatoes must be pared before boiling, and the kettle in which they are boiled must be perfectly clean.

RUSKS.

In one large coffee cup of warm milk, dissolve one cake of compressed yeast, then add three eggs and one cup of sugar, and beat all together; use only flour enough to roll out, to which add two ounces of butter; let it raise. When very light, knead, mold into shape, and set in a warm place. When light, bake in a hot oven; when done, cover the top with sugar dissolved in milk.

SWEET RUSK.

One pint of warm milk—new is best—one-half cup of butter, one cup of sugar, two eggs, one teaspoonful of salt, two tablespoonfuls of yeast; make a sponge with the milk, yeast, and enough flour to make a thin batter, and let rise over night. In the morning add the sugar, butter, eggs, and salt, well beaten up together, with enough flour to make a soft dough. Let it rise again; then make out into round balls, and rise a third time. Bake in a moderate oven.

FRENCH ROLLS.

Into one pound of flour, rub two ounces of butter, and the whites of three eggs, well beaten; add a tablespoonful of good yeast, a little salt, and milk enough to make a stiff dough, cover and set in a warm place till light, which will be in an hour or more, according to the strength of the yeast; cut into rolls, dip the edges into melted butter to keep them from sticking together, and bake in a quick oven.

CINNAMON ROLLS.

Take a piece of pie-crust; roll it out; cut it in narrow strips; sprinkle cinnamon over it; roll it up tight; put it in a clean tin pan, which has been well oiled with butter; brown nicely and bake; then serve on the table.

BREAKFAST ROLLS.

Two quarts flour, one tablespoonful sugar, one tablespoonful butter, one-half cup yeast, one pint scalded milk, or water, if milk is scarce, and a little salt, set to rise until light; then knead until hard and set to rise, and when wanted make into rolls; place a piece of butter between the folds, and bake in a slow oven.

POTATO ROLLS.

Boil four good sized potatoes, with their skins on; squeeze them in a towel, to make them dry and mealy, then remove the skin and mash them perfectly smooth, with a spoonful of butter and a little salt; add the yolks of three eggs, well beaten, and stir into the potatoes, then add one pint and a half of milk, and a large spoonful of yeast; beat in flour enough to make a stiff dough; set it to rise, and when risen, make it into cakes the size of an egg; let them rise again, and bake a light brown.

VIENNA ROLLS.

One quart of milk, one-half teaspoonful salt, three teaspoonfuls baking-powder, one teaspoon lard, one pint of milk. Mix into a dough easily to be handled without sticking to the hands; turn on the board, and roll out to the thickness of half an inch, cut it out with a large cake-cutter, spread very lightly with butter, fold one-half over the other, and lay them in a greased pan without touching; wash them over with a little milk, and bake in a hot oven.

ENGLISH TEA CAKE.

Take a light bread dough, enough for a small loaf, mix with it one tablespoonful of lard, one of sugar, one large spoonful of currants; let rise again until very light, then bake; cut into round slices and toast them; butter while hot.

BROWN LOAF.

One coffeecup of molasses, one teaspoonful of soda dissolved in one-half teacupful of boiling water; stir into the molasses until it foams, then mix into it graham flour and corn meal (in the proportion of three to one) enough to make a thick batter, and then add one tablespoonful of lard; pour into a mold, and steam four hours; to be eaten hot; very nice as a pudding with sauce.

STEAMED GRAHAM BREAD.

Two cups of graham flour, one egg, one tablespoonful melted butter, three-quarters of a cup of milk, one-half cup of molasses, two teaspoonfuls of baking powder; steam one and a half hours.

MRS. M.'S BROWN BREAD.

Scald one pint of brown flour, make it thick as thick mush, then put in half a cup of yeast, and let this sponge stand over night; in the morning mix it up with white flour, and sweeten to taste. This quantity makes into two small loaves. It requires longer to bake than white bread.

GRAHAM MUFFINS.

One quart of graham flour, two teaspoonfuls of baking powder, a piece of butter the size of a walnut, one egg, one tablespoonful of sugar, one-half teaspoonful of salt, milk enough to make a batter as thick as for griddle cakes.

GRAHAM BREAKFAST ROLLS.

Two pounds of potatoes boiled and pressed through a colander, one pint of water, one-half cup of sugar, one-half teaspoonful of salt, one-half cup of yeast; mix into a stiff dough with graham flour, and let rise over night; in the morning mold into small cakes, and when light bake.

GRAHAM BISCUIT.

One pint of sweet milk, one-half cup of butter, one-half cup of sugar, two eggs, flour enough to make stiff, and a spoonful baking powder; drop on buttered tins.

BOSTON BROWN BREAD.

One quart rye meal (not flour), two quarts of corn meal, two-thirds of a cup of molasses, into which beat a teaspoonful of soda; add a teaspoonful of salt, and mix quite soft with boiling water, and bake.

TO FRESHEN STALE BREAD.

Pump on or pour water over the loaf until moistened through, put in a pan, set in the oven, and bake until the moisture is all absorbed.

MILK SPONGE BREAD.

Put a pint of boiling water in a pitcher, with a teaspoonful of sugar, one-quarter teaspoonful salt, and the same of soda; let it stand till you can bear your finger in it; then add flour to make a thick batter; beat it hard for two minutes; now place the pitcher in a kettle of hot water—not hot enough to scald the mixture; keep the water at the same temperature till the emptyings are light. If set early in the morning they will be ready, if watched carefully, at eleven o'clock to make a sponge, the same as for other bread, with a quart of very warm milk. Let this sponge get very light; then make into loaves, and set to rise again, taking care they do not get too light this time before putting in the oven, or the bread will be dry and tasteless,

SALT-RISING BREAD.

1. Take newly-ground middlings; put six heaping teaspoonfuls of it in a coffeecup; add one teaspoon of sugar one saltspoon of salt, one-half saltspoon of soda; mix thoroughly; pour boiling water in the mixture, stirring it well together until it will nearly fill the cup; remove the spoon; cover the cup of dough; set it where it will keep warm, not scald; set it Friday morning, and it will be light for Saturday's baking; if in a hurry, set in a dish of warm water. Now put in bread-pan flour enough for bread; add salt; take one quart of boiling water for three loaves, and turn into the middle of your flour, stirring in slowly; put enough cold water or milk to cool sufficiently to bear your finger in it; then add middlings; stir in well; cover with some of the flour, and set in a warm place. When light enough mix

soft into loaves, grease bread-pans, also top of the loaves, which makes a tender upper crust; cut gashes quite deep across, and they will rise evenly; set near the stove, and when light enough bake three-quarters of an hour.

2. In the morning take a quart dish and scald it out; then put in a pint of warm water; put in a teaspoonful of salt; stir flour enough in to make a thick batter; set the dish in a kettle of warm water, and where it will keep of the same temperature, just warm enough to bear your hand in. If the flour is good it will be at the top of the dish in two hours; then take flour enough in a pan to make three loaves of bread; make a hole in the middle; put in the yeast, and the same dish full of warm water; stir it up thick with a spoon, and cover it up with some flour, and set it to rise. When light mold into loaves, and set it in a warm place to rise again. When light enough, bake three-quarters of an hour.

BAKING POWDER BISCUIT.

One important point is in having a hot oven; another is, have flour sifted, and roll dough as soft as you can handle; then more baking powder is needed. For each teacup of flour take a teaspoon of powder; butter the size of a small hen's egg is sufficient for a quart of flour. After rubbing butter and powder into the amount of flour needed, turn in cold water (milk will do), stirring all of the time, till the right consistency is reached; salt; then roll lightly, and bake at once. They will prove flakey, feathery, delicious and more nutritious than biscuit raised with yeast.

SODA BISCUITS.

Three pints of flour, a tablespoon of butter, and a tablespoon of lard, a teaspoon of salt, and a teaspoon even full of cream of tartar, with the flour dry, rub the butter and lard very thoroughly through it; dissolve the soda in a pint of milk, and mix all together. Roll out, adding as little flour as possible; cut with a biscuit cutter, and bake twenty minutes in a quick oven.

TREMONT HOUSE ROLLS.

Take two quarts of flour, add one teaspoonful of salt; make a hole in the middle and put into it one tablespoonful of sugar, butter about the size of an egg, one pint of boiled milk, and one teacupful of yeast. Do not stir, but put them together at night, and set in a cool place until morning. Then mix all together and knead fifteen minutes. Set in a cool place again for six hours, and roll out about one-half an inch thick and cut with a biscuit cutter. Moisten one edge with butter, and fold together like rolls. Lay in the pan so that they will not touch, set for half an hour in a warm place to rise, and bake in a quick oven.

LIGHT BISCUIT.

1. Take about as much dough, after it is light, as would make a good sized loaf of bread; put in a pie-pan; mix in that a small cup of lard and butter, more lard than butter, one tablespoon of fine sugar; do not put in any more flour; never mind if sticky; then let rise very light,

keeping in warm place; roll out about one-half inch thick without molding. Bake in rather quick oven. Will bake in fifteen or twenty minutes.

2. In kneading bread, set aside a small loaf for biscuits. Into this work a heaping tablespoonful of lard and butter mixed, and a teaspoon of sugar. The more it is worked the whiter it will be. As it rises, mold it down twice before making into biscuits. Roll out and cut with a biscuit cutter. The dough should be quite soft.

FRENCH ROLLS.

One pint of milk come to a boil, one-half cup of butter, one cup of sugar, one cup of yeast, stirred into a sponge; when light knead up stiff, add one cup of milk, put in just when light, roll out, cut with a round cutter, butter one-half side, and lay the other over. Bake fifteen minutes.

ROLLS.

Take one quart of flour and mix quite soft with warm milk and one-half cup of yeast; mix in the morning and set to rise until noon; then break into it two eggs, three tablespoonfuls of sugar, one tablespoonful of butter, and teaspoonful of salt; mix up well together with hands, and set to rise again until about an hour before tea. Then knead a little, and cutting off a piece about the size of a common biscuit, roll out to about the size of a saucer, spread thinly with butter and turn over. After they are molded let them stand until light enough, and bake in a very quick oven.

WHEAT MUFFINS.

One quart of flour, five teaspoonfuls of baking powder, two tablespoonfuls of butter, five eggs, milk enough to make a thick batter.

WHITE MUFFINS.

One teacup of milk, three cups of flour, two eggs, one-half cup of sugar, piece of butter the size of an egg, baking powder.

POPOVERS.

1. One cup rich milk, one egg, one cup flour, a little salt; beat together thoroughly, first the milk and flour, then egg and salt; fill buttered cups half full; bake in a hot oven.

2. One pint sifted flour, one and one-half teaspoonfuls of baking powder, one tablespoonful sugar, one-half teaspoonful of salt, large teaspoonful melted butter, and, lastly, two eggs beaten very light; bake in gem-pans.

CREAM PUFFS.

Boil one pint water, rub together one-half pound of butter with three-fourths of a pound of sifted flour; stir into the water while boiling. When it thickens like starch remove from the fire. When cool stir into it ten well-beaten eggs and one small teaspoon of soda. Drop the mixture on to the buttered tins with a large spoon. Bake until a light brown, in a quick oven. When done open on one side and fill with mock cream, made as follows : One cup of fine sugar, four eggs, one cup of flour, one quart of milk; beat eggs to a froth; stir in the sugar, then flour; stir them in the milk while boiling; stir till it thickens; then remove from the fire and flavor with lemon or vanilla. It should not be put into the puffs until cold.

PUFFETS.

One quart flour, one pint milk, two eggs, beaten light, butter size of an egg, three tablespoonfuls sugar, three teaspoonfuls baking powder; bake quick.

ROSETTES.

To three eggs, the yolks beaten very light, add one quart of milk, a piece of butter the size of an egg cut in little pieces into the milk and eggs, three coffeecups of flour, a little salt, three teaspoonfuls of baking powder, and lastly the whites of the eggs beaten very light and stirred quickly into the mixture. Bake in a quick oven.

SALLY LUNN.

1. One quart of flour, a piece of butter the size of an egg, three tablespoonfuls of sugar, two eggs, two teacups of milk, two teaspoonfuls of cream tartar, one of soda and a little salt. Scatter the cream of tartar, sugar, and the salt into the flour; add the eggs, the butter melted, and one cup of milk; dissolve the soda in the remaining cup, and stir all together steadily a few moments. Bake in two round pans.

2. Rub into a quart of flour two teaspoonfuls of baking-powder; beat together nearly half a cup of butter and two tablespoonfuls of sugar; put into the flour and mix with a pint of milk; then add two eggs beaten light.

STRAWBERRY SHORTCAKE.

Make a good biscuit crust, and roll out about one-quarter of an inch thick, and cut into two cakes the same size and shape; spread one over lightly with melted butter, and lay the other over it, and bake in a hot oven. When done they will fall apart. Butter them well, as usual. Mix the berries with plenty of sugar, and set in a warm place until needed. Spread the berries in alternate layers, having berries on the top, and over all spread whipped cream or charlotte russe. The juice that has run from the fruit can be sent to the table in a tureen, and served as cut.

LEMON SHORTCAKE.

Make a nice rich shortcake, split and butter; then take the rind, juice and pulp of two lemons, one cup of sugar and one cup of cream. Mix thoroughly, and spread.

YEAST WAFFLES.

Take three pints of milk, one tablespoonful of butter, put them into a pan on the stove until the butter melts, add five eggs, well beaten, one tablespoonful of salt, one and one-half tablespoonfuls of yeast, and about three pints of flour. Make up, and let them rise three or four hours before baking.

WAFFLES.

1. Four eggs beaten separately, one quart of milk, a piece of butter the size of an egg, melted; three teaspoonfuls of baking-powder, a little salt, enough flour to make a rather thick batter.

2. Sift together one quart of flour, one-half teaspoonful of salt, one teaspoonful of sugar, and three teaspoonfuls of baking-powder; then add two eggs, well-beaten, and one and a half pints of milk. When done, sift sugar over them, and serve hot.

CREAM WAFFLES.

One pint of rich sour cream; stir into it one teaspoonful of saleratus, then add flour to make rather a stiff batter. To be split and buttered.

LEMON TURNOVERS.

Four dessert spoonfuls of flour, one of powdered sugar, the rind of one lemon, two ounces of melted butter, two eggs and a little milk. Mix flour, sugar, and lemon with the milk to the consistency of batter; add the butter and eggs well beaten. Fry, and turn over.

VARIETIES.

Two eggs beat light, teaspoon of salt, the egg thickened with flour to roll out thin as a wafer; cut in strips one inch wide and four inches long, wind it round your finger, and fry them as you do doughnuts.

DROP BISCUIT.

Rub into one quart of flour one-half teacup of butter, one small teaspoonful of salt, two tablespoonfuls of baking-powder, enough sweet milk to mix with a spoon. Drop on buttered pans.

MILK TOAST.

Place the milk to heat, mix a teaspoonful of flour smoothly with a little milk, stir it in, and let it come just to a boil, with a piece of butter the size of an egg to a quart of milk, and some salt. Place your toast on a deep dish, and pour your gravy over it.

MOCK CREAM TOAST.

Melt in one quart of morning's milk about two ounces of butter, a large teaspoonful of flour, freed from lumps, and the yolks of three eggs, beaten light. Beat these ingredients together for several minutes, strain the cream through a fine hair sieve, and when wanted beat it constantly with a brisk movement.

OATMEAL PORRIDGE.

Allow one cupful of oatmeal to one quart of boiling water, and one teaspoonful of salt. Sift the meal in the boiling water with one hand, stirring with the other. Boil from half to three-quarters of an hour.

OATMEAL GEMS.

Take one cup of oatmeal and soak it over night in one cup of water; in the morning add one cup of sour milk, one teaspoon of saleratus, one cup of flour, a little salt; they are baked in irons as other gems and muffins; if on first trial you find them moist and sticky, add a little more flour, as some flour thickens more than others. Or use sweet milk and baking-powder.

FRIED CORN BREAD.

Take pieces of cold corn bread, and crumble them up fine; put them in a saucepan, pouring in a little hot water, just to moisten; add butter, pepper, and salt; mix and warm up. This makes a nice dish for lunch, and is a good way to save pieces of corn bread left.

FRENCH TOAST.

1. Take three eggs, beat well, and add one-half teacupful of milk; dip into this mixture slices of bread, and fry them in butter till slightly browned; serve piping hot.

2. For a family of five, take five slices of bread (the longer the bread has been baked the better), and have ready a bowl of water, into which a pinch of salt has been dropped; take a piece of butter the size of a walnut, and thoroughly grease the bottom of a frying-pan; then beat five eggs to a froth; dip each slice of bread into the water, then into the egg, and place it flat on the bottom of the frying-pan; pour over the bread the remaining egg which was left in the bowl; set the frying-pan over the fire, carefully turning the bread over when it becomes a light brown; pepper and salt to taste, and rest assured that as often as it is brought on the table, just so often will your dinner be praised.

GRAHAM MUFFINS.

Set the iron gem-pans on the stove to heat; beat one egg light in a basin; add one teacupful sour milk, and two tablespoonfuls sugar; stir well together; add a mere pinch of salt; stir in graham flour to make a rather stiff batter; mix thoroughly with the addition of one tablespoonful melted butter; and, lastly, stir in one third teaspoonful soda, dissolved in a teaspoonful of hot water; the latter, when ready to drop into the well-heated and greased gem-pans, should be so thick that it will not run from the spoon, but just drop nicely. This will make one dozen excellent gems.

LIZZIE'S CREAM MUFFINS.

One pint of milk, one pint of flour, three eggs (yolks and whites beaten separately), a little salt, one teaspoonful melted butter; put in gem-pans, and bake in a pretty hot oven twenty minutes. If made and baked right, these cannot be excelled.

PARKER HOUSE ROLLS.

One quart of flour; two tablespoonfuls of sugar, two tablespoonfuls of butter rubbed into the flour, one-half cup of yeast, one pint of warm milk; stir this up at night, and put it to rise; in the morning stir in flour enough to have it knead without sticking, and then put it back in the same dish to rise again, and when risen light and nice, make it out into rolls; put them in the tin you wish to bake them in, and let them be in a moderately warm place until tea-time; then, if they are not risen enough, put them near the stove a few minutes until they do rise, then bake in a quick oven.

ROLLS.

Boil six potatoes in two quarts of water, and when done pour and press the whole through the colander; when cool, but not cold, add flour to make a stiff batter; add half a cup of yeast or one-half cake of compressed yeast, and set to rise; when light, add half a cup of lard and butter mixed, a tablespoonful of sugar, a teaspoonful of salt, and flour to make a soft dough; knead well and set again to rise; when light, knead down again, and repeat three or four times; an hour before they are needed, cut in small pieces, roll out, spread with melted butter, and fold over, laying them in a pan so that they will not touch each other; set them in a warm place, and when light, bake quickly. Or make into oblong rolls without spreading and folding, and just before putting them into the oven, gash deeply across the top with a sharp knife.

RUSK.

Take four cups of dough, a cup of sugar, half a cup of melted butter, and three eggs; mix, and add flour as needed; let it rise; when light, knead well and make into biscuit, and set to rise again; add a few currants, if desired, when light; glaze the tops with sugar and water; sift over some dry sugar, and bake.

DELICIOUS RICE WAFFLES.

Take one quart of sweet milk two coffee-cups of boiled rice, and three-quarters of a cup of wheat flour; warm the milk, stir in the above-named articles, add half a teacup of home-made yeast, two tablespoonfuls of distillery yeast, and half a teaspoonful of salt; make at 12 o'clock to use for tea at 6; set in a warm place; when ready to cook, add two eggs well beaten; bake in waffle-irons.

SNOW BALLS.

One cup sugar, one-half cup butter, whites of five eggs, flour to make a batter, and bake in small tins or gem-pans.

FRITTERS.

1. Two eggs, two teaspoonfuls sour milk, one teaspoonful soda, four tablespoonfuls butter, and flour to make a stiff batter; fry in hot lard, and serve with sweet sauce.

2. Take three eggs to each pint of rich sweet milk, a pinch of salt, and flour to make a batter stiff enough to drop from a spoon into boiling lard. Or, use a teacupful of newly-fallen snow, instead of the eggs, and fry immediately.

FRITTER BATTER.

Two cups of flour (sifted), teaspoonful of baking-powder, salt, and two or three eggs, beaten separately; to this batter add any fruit desired, cut in small pieces; drop by spoonfuls into boiling hot lard; drain in a colander, and dust over with fine sugar, and serve quickly.

HOMINY FRITTERS.

To one cup of cold boiled hominy add one-half cup of milk, and when well mixed add one cup of flour, one or two eggs, a saltspoonful of salt, and one teaspoonful of baking powder, stirred in last in a little of the flour; have plenty of boiling lard in a frying-pan, enough to float the fritters; drop in from a spoon; fry till a good brown color. If these directions are faithfully followed, we can promise you some fritters that will delight all who partake of them.

OATMEAL GRUEL.

Take two ounces of oatmeal, and one and one-half pints of water; rub the meal in a basin with the back of a spoon in a small quantity of water, pouring off the fluid after the coarser particles are settled, but while the milkiness continues; repeat the operation until the milkiness disappears; next put the washings into a pan, stir until they boil, and a soft, thick mucilage is formed; sweeten to taste.

SAVORY BISCUITS.

Take twelve eggs, their weight in powdered sugar, and half their weight in fine flour; beat up the yolks with the sugar, adding a little grated lemon peel and orange flower water; whip the whites separately into a stiff froth, mix with the other, then stir in the flour, and beat the whole together; butter a mold, and put in your mixture; bake in a moderately warm oven. These biscuits are very light and delicate.

DYSPEPSIA BREAD.

One pint bowl of graham flour, dissolve one-half teaspoonful of soda in two-thirds of a cup of home-made yeast, and add to the mixture one teacup of molasses; pour in sufficient warm water to make it somewhat thinner than flour bread.

PUFFETS.

One quart of flour, one-half teaspoonful of salt, butter the size of an egg, two eggs, two tablespoonfuls white sugar, one pint of milk, and three teaspoonfuls of baking powder. Rub butter into the flour, beat the eggs separately, adding the whites last. Bake in gem-pans in a hot oven.

RICE MUFFINS.

One pint of boiled rice, one pint of milk, five eggs, one-half cup of butter and lard mixed, one pint of sponge, and a little salt. Beat the rice, butter, and yolks of the eggs together, then add sponge and milk, flour enough to make a stiff batter. Let it rise very light, beat the whites of the eggs, and stir in just before putting into the oven.

RICE BREAD.

Take a plate of boiled rice warm enough to melt a lump of butter the size of a walnut, beat two eggs separately, mix with them one and one-half cups of flour, and milk enough to make a thick batter. Grease the pans, and bake like bread or muffins.

RICE CROQUETTES.

Take cold boiled rice, add three eggs, with sugar and lemon peel to your taste; make into oval balls; rub with bread crumbs, dip in egg, fry in butter; when done sprinkle sugar over them.

APPLE PANCAKES (VERY NICE).

Three pints of milk, eight eggs, and flour enough to make a thick batter, teaspoon of salt; add six or eight apples, chopped fine, and fry in lard.

SPANISH PUFFS.

Put into a saucepan a teacupful of water, a tablespoonful of powdered sugar, half a teaspoonful of salt, and two ounces of butter; while it is boiling add sufficient flour for it to leave the saucepan; stir in one by one the yolks of four eggs; drop a teaspoonful at a time into boiling lard; fry them a light brown. Eat with maple syrup.

CORN STARCH PUFFS.

Four eggs beaten separately, one cup of sugar, one cup of corn starch, one-half cup of butter, one teaspoonful of lemon in the butter and sugar, two teaspoonfuls of baking powder mixed in the corn starch.

BREAKFAST PUFFS.

One pint of milk, one pint of flour, two eggs, a lump of butter the size of an egg, and a pinch of salt; put the flour after sifting in a pan, and the butter in the middle of the flour, break in the eggs, and work the butter and eggs thoroughly into the flour, then gradually add the milk until you have a smooth batter. Bake them in French roll pans. They take but a few minutes to bake.

FLANNEL CAKES.

Three eggs, one quart of sweet milk, about one quart of flour, a small teaspoonful of salt, two tablespoonfuls of Craig's baking powder; beat the yolks and half of the milk, salt, and flour together, then the remainder of the milk; at last the whites of the eggs, well beaten. A teacup of boiled rice is an improvement.

OYSTER FRITTERS.

One and one-half pints of sweet milk, one and one-fourth pounds of flour, four eggs (the yolks must be beaten very thick), to which add milk and flour; stir the whole well together, then beat whites to a stiff froth, and stir them gradually into the batter; take a spoonful of the mixture, drop an oyster into it, and fry in hot lard; let them be a light brown on both sides.

FRITTERS.

1. One cup of milk, one cup of flour and three eggs.
2. Two eggs, one cup of milk, a little salt, and flour enough to make a stiff batter; drop into boiling lard, and eat hot with syrup or sweetened cream.

APPLE FRITTERS.

1. Three eggs, one cup of flour one of milk; bake on a griddle, a little thicker than flour cakes. Pare the apples, cut in thick slices, and bake in the oven; while hot, lay a piece of apple on each fritter; sprinkle a little sugar over the top of each apple; serve.

2. Four eggs to one quart of sweet milk, one teaspoon of soda, two teaspoonfuls of cream tartar, flour; pare and cut apple in thin slices, and mix into the batter.

CREAM FRITTERS.

One and one-half pints of flour, yolks of four eggs two teaspoonfuls of baking powder, shortening of lard and butter together the size of a hickory nut, milk enough to make a thick batter; drop in hot lard, and fry. Eat with butter and sugar, or dip pieces of apple into the batter before frying.

EGG WAFFLES.

One pint of milk, one-half cup of melted butter, and flour to make a soft batter, four eggs beaten separately; beat all thoroughly, and add two teaspoonfuls of baking-powder.

HOW TO COOK OATMEAL.

Oatmeal is seldom cooked sufficiently. For the coarser oatmeals (which are by far the best for mush) measure five or six parts water (preferably soft)—yes, measure it, and then you will have it alike every time and not be at the trouble of watching it to see if it is of right consistency and adding more meal. As soon as the water boils, pour in one part meal. These coarse meals do not require stirring up. Let it boil up smartly until it sets or is evenly diffused through the water, then set it back where it will not boil so fast, and, after half an hour, place it where it will hardly simmer. Let it cook half an hour at least, and two hours if possible. If the time is limited, put it to soak beforehand, and stir it when heating up. After that it requires no stirring. The slimyness often complained of is due to the constant stirring which some cooks practice. The surest way to avoid scorching is to cook it in a double kettle, or in a tin dish set into a kettle of boiling water, then all the attention it requires is to keep water in the kettle beneath and to see that it boils. Disturb as little as possible when dishing, and allow it to stand a few minutes before serving. With the Scotch and other fine oatmeals, the process is much the same, only they require much stirring while setting, and the proportion of meal is much greater after that. It is particularly important not to stir them until served. The time required to cook them is less, but an hour is none too much to get the best results from the Scotch (or Canadian, as it is sometimes called). But no amount of cooking will make them equal to the coarser kinds in delicacy of flavor. A coffee cup of oatmeal will suffice for five or six persons, as the main dish for breakfast.

OATMEAL MUSH IMPROVED.

Much better than the old way of stirring the oatmeal into boiling water is the new way of cooking it in a farina-kettle. If no farina-kettle or steam-cooker is at hand, one may always be improvised in this way: Set a stone jar or a tin pail, containing the food to be cooked, into a kettle of water, putting a couple of sticks under the jar to keep it from coming in contact with the bottom of the kettle.

PUDDINGS.

In boiling pudding, have plenty of water in the pot boiling when the pudding is put in, and do not let it stop; add more as it is needed. Turn the pudding frequently. If a cloth is used, dip the pudding when done into a pan of cold water, so that it can be removed easily.

In using molds, grease well with butter, tie the lid closely, and set in a pot with very little water, and add more as needed.

Fruit sauces are nice with blanc-mange and corn-starch puddings.

Fresh red cherries, stewed, sweetened, and passed through a sieve, and slightly thickened with corn starch, make a good sauce.

Beat the eggs separately.

If a mold is used for boiling, be sure to have it well greased.

A bag or cloth should be wrung out of hot water and well floured.

In boiling, always put the pudding into boiling water, enough to cover.

Boiled and steamed puddings require nearly twice as much time as baked.

APPLE DUMPLINGS.

Use good-sized rather tart apples, pare and remove the cores; envelope each separately in puff-paste, and tie it in a piece of cloth; boil or steam for one hour; before serving, remove the cloths, cut a piece from each, and put in some sugar and fresh butter; replace the piece of paste, and sprinkle with powdered sugar; if preferred, they may be served with liquid sauce or sweetened cream.

APPLE ROLL.

One pound flour, one-fourth pound of butter, mix with sufficient water to make a not very stiff paste; pare and slice rather thick some tart apples, roll out the paste as for pie-crust, and spread the sliced apples to cover it, sprinkle on a little flour, and roll up as tightly as possible without breaking the paste; cook it in a steamer, or wrap in a cloth and boil for an hour; serve by cutting across in thin slices, with sauce of butter and sugar.

BROWN-TOP PUDDING.

Take slices of any kind of rich cake without fruit, make a custard of four eggs, one quart of milk, sugar, and flavor to taste; pour over the cake, which will rise to the top; bake like custard.

BLACKBERRY PUDDING.

1. Put the berries into a preserving kettle, and mash with sugar

enough to make sweet; set **over the** fire, and when it begins to simmer stir in very gradually two teaspoonfuls of flour to a quart of fruit; stir until well cooked, and **eat** either hot or cold with cream; raspberries may be used in the same way.

2. Butter and lard together the size of an egg, one cup of sugar, one egg; beat sugar, butter, lard, and egg together, one cup of sweet milk, two teapoonfuls of baking powder; stir thick with berries.

BATTER FRUIT PUDDING.

Butter thickly a pudding-dish that will hold a pint and one-half; fill it nearly full of good baking apples cut up fine; pour over them a batter made with four tablespoonfuls of flour, three eggs, and one-half pint of milk; tie a buttered and floured cloth over the dish—which ought to be quite full—and boil the pudding one and a quarter hours; turn it out into a hot dish, and strew sugar thickly over it.

CHARLES' PUDDING.

One cup of sugar, one tablespoonful of melted butter, one cup sweet milk, one egg, one and one-half teaspoonfuls of baking powder; mix with one pint of flour; bake one-half hour, and eat hot with sweet sauce.

DYSPEPTICS' PUDDING.

Boil a cup of rice until it is done soft, then take two eggs, a cup of sugar, and one of milk, and stir all together and add to the rice; pare six good cooking apples, slice small, and place in bottom of pudding-dish, and pour the rice custard over them; place in a moderate oven long enough to bake the apples. To be eaten warm, either with or without cream.

DELICIOUS PUDDING.

Two cups of fine bread crumbs, one and one-half cups white sugar, five eggs, one tablespoonful butter, one quart fresh milk, one-half cup jelly or jam; rub the butter and one cup of the sugar together; then add the beaten yolks of the eggs; beat all to a cream; then add the bread crumbs, which have previously been soaked in the milk; bake in a pudding-dish (not filling it more than two-thirds full) until the custard is "set;" then draw it to the mouth of the oven, and spread over the jelly or jam; then cover this with a meringue made of the beaten whites and half a cup of sugar; put back in oven, and allow it to remain until the meringue begins to color; to be eaten cold with cold cream. This is truly delicious.

INDIAN PUDDING.

Take two quarts of sweet milk, scald one of them, add fourteen tablespoonfuls (level full) of Indian meal, one teacupful of chopped sweet apple, either dried or green, and salt and molasses to taste; bake three hours.

AUNT KITTIE'S SUET PUDDING.

One cup molasses, one cup suet, one cup raisins, one cup milk, two teaspoonfuls baking powder; add flour till very stiff to beat with a spoon; put in a steaming pan or floured bag, and steam *constantly* for three hours.

LEMON PUDDING.

1. One pint of white sugar, one-quarter of a pound of butter, three lemons, four wine-glasses of water, the yolks of four eggs; cook down thick, and pour over sponge cake sliced in a pan; beat the whites of four eggs, with two tablespoonfuls of white sugar to each white of egg, and put over the top of the pudding; let it remain in the stove just long enough to become a light brown.

2. One large lemon or three small ones, half a pound of sugar, half a pound of butter, one coffeecup of cream or milk, six eggs, three tablespoonfuls of grated cracker or bread crumbs. Beat the butter and sugar to a cream, grate the rind of a lemon, add juice and yolks of eggs and crackers, then the beaten whites of eggs and lemon. Sauce for the above: Mix well three tablespoonfuls of butter, add one and one-half cups white sugar, then two eggs well beaten, and one gill of milk; put in a small bucket in a kettle of hot water, and let it thicken. Flavor with vanilla or lemon.

3. Four eggs, four lemons, bread crumbs to thicken, one cup of suet, one-half cup of milk, sugar to sweeten. Steam three hours.

4. Beat the yolks of two eggs light; add two cupfuls of sugar; dissolve four tablespoonfuls of corn starch in a little cold water; stir into it two teacupfuls of boiling water; put in the juice of two lemons, with some of the grated peel. Mix all together with a teaspoonful of butter. Bake about fifteen minutes. When done, spread over the top the beaten whites of the eggs and brown.

5. One lemon, grated, one-half cup sugar, one cup of suet chopped fine, four eggs beaten separately, one cup of milk, one-half cup of flour, two cups of bread-crumbs, two teaspoonfuls baking-powder. Soak the bread-crumbs in the milk, add eggs and sugar, then suet, and beat thoroughly together; then add lemon and flour. Steam or boil in a mold two and one-half hours. Eat with sauce.

6. Line a pudding-dish with a nice pie-paste; make a custard of a pint and a half of milk, yolks of two eggs; two tablespoonfuls of flour or corn-starch, three-quarters of a cup of sugar, and the grated rind and juice of a lemon; pour in the dish and bake; when done, spread whites, beaten, over the top, and brown.

POVERTY PUDDING.

Put a layer of apple-sauce in a buttered pudding-dish, then a layer of cracker or bread-crumbs, sprinkled with bits of butter and seasoned with spice to taste, then a layer of sauce, and so on, the upper layer being of crumbs; lay bits of butter on the top and bake; eat with cream.

ENGLISH PLUM PUDDING.

Nine eggs beaten to a froth, add flour sufficient to make a thick batter free from lumps; add one pint new milk, and beat well; add two pounds of raisins, stoned, and two pounds of currants, washed and dried, one pound of citron, sliced, one-quarter pound bitter almonds, divided, three-fourths of a pound brown sugar, one nutmeg, one teaspoon of allspice, mace, and cinnamon, three-fourths of a pound beef suet chopped fine; **mix** three days before cooking, **and** beat well again; add **more milk if required.** If made into two **puddings, boil** four hours.

PLUM PUDDING.

1. One pound of raisins, stoned, one pound of currants washed and dried, one pound of rich beef suet minced, one pound of stale bread-crumbs, one pound of flour. Mix the bread-crumbs, flour, and suet together; beat six eggs well, and add to them a pint of sweet milk, a teaspoonful of soda in the milk; beat the eggs and milk with the suet and flour for some time, then stir in the currants and raisins, mixing well as you proceed. Mix in also one-fourth of a pound of candied orange and lemon peel cut in small pieces, one ounce of powdered cinnamon, one-half ounce of powdered ginger, one grated nutmeg, and a little salt. Either bake or boil, according to taste; bake nearly two hours; if boiled, pour into a cloth, tie the cloth, allowing a little room to swell, and boil for six hours. It is better boiled. Serve with vanilla sauce.

2. Take half a pound of wheat flour, half a pound of raisins stoned and chopped, and the same of currants picked, washed, and dried; use milk enough to stir easily with a spoon, add half a pound of suet chopped fine, and four well-beaten eggs, and a large teaspoonful of mace, cinnamon and allspice; mix all well together, and boil it for two hours and a half in a cloth or tin; serve with butter or sugar, or wine sauce. Plum pudding, if cold, may be warmed in a pan with some of the sauce.

PINEAPPLE PUDDING.

Line a pudding-dish with slices of cake; slice thin a pineapple, and place a layer on the cake in the bottom of the dish, sprinkle with sugar, then more pineapple, and so on until the dish is full; cover with slices of cake, and over the whole pour a cup of water; cover and bake slowly for nearly two hours.

QUEEN OF PUDDINGS.

One pint of bread-crumbs, one quart milk, one cup sugar, butter size of an egg, yolks of four eggs; flavor with lemon, and bake as custard; beat the whites of four eggs to a froth, mix with a cup of powdered sugar and juice of a lemon; spread a layer of fruit jelly over the custard while hot; cover with the frosting, and bake until slightly brown. To be eaten with cold cream, or warm, with any sauce that may be preferred.

RYE MINUTE PUDDING.

Heat milk to the boiling-point, salt to taste, and stir in gradually rye flour, to make a thick mush; cook about fifteen minutes, and eat with sugar and cream.

PUDDINGS.

BATTER PUDDING.

1. One egg, one cup sugar, two and one-half flour, three teaspoonfuls baking-powder, two tablespoons melted butter, few dried currants; steam three-quarters of an hour; to be eaten with sauce. One-half meal is better, we think.

2. Six eggs, six tablespoonfuls flour, one quart milk, a little salt, and half a teaspoonful of soda, or a teaspoonful of baking-powder; bake in a buttered pan for twenty minutes.

BAKED INDIAN PUDDING.

1. Into one quart of boiling milk, stir a half pint of corn meal; when cold, add one-half cup of sugar, tablespoonful of butter, one cup of raisins, and four eggs well beaten; mix well, and bake an hour and a half.

2. Boil one pint of milk; while boiling stir in one large tablespoonful of Indian meal, cool a little and add three eggs well beaten, one pint of cold milk, one tablespoonful of flour, one-half cup of sugar, one cup of molasses, one teaspoonful of ginger, one of cinnamon, a little salt; bake an hour and a half.

3. For a two-quart pudding use two teacups meal; moisten the meal with cold water, then pour over it one pint boiling water; add one tablespoonful of butter, two teacups of sugar, one cup of raisins, three eggs, well beaten before adding, and fill up with sweet milk; season with whatever spice is preferred; bake slowly half an hour or more.

BOILED INDIAN PUDDING.

One and one-half cups sour milk, two eggs well beaten, one small teaspoonful saleratus dissolved in the milk; then sift in dry corn meal until of the consistency as if for griddle-cakes—perhaps a little thicker; stir in a teacup of dried fruit—cherries are the best; put in a bag and boil one hour. For sauce, sweetened cream flavored with nutmeg.

BROWN BETTY.

Grease a pudding-dish; put into this a layer of nice cooking apples sliced, then a layer of bread crumbs, with sugar sprinkled over, and small bits of butter. For three apples use one cup of bread crumbs, one-half cup sugar, and a piece of butter the size of an egg. Put a layer of bread crumbs on top; bake. It is nice either with or without cream.

HEN'S NEST.

Make blanc mange; pour in egg-shells and set to cool; when cold break the egg-shells, place in a glass dish, cut strips of lemon peel, let them boil in a syrup of sugar and water till they are tender, and sprinkle them over the egg shapes, and make a custard and pour over all.

GOOSEBERRY CREAM.

Take a quart of gooseberries, and boil them very quick in enough water to cover them; stir in half an ounce of good butter, and when they become soft pulp them through a sieve; sweeten the pulp while it is hot, and then beat it up with the yolks of four eggs; serve in a dish or glass cup.

LIQUID SAUCE FOR PUDDINGS.

One cup of sugar and one-third cup of butter rubbed to a cream; then stir in the well-beaten white of an egg; flavor with lemon or nutmeg; add one cup of boiling water, and mix just before bringing to the table.

CRACKED WHEAT.

This excellent dish is often spoiled by very good cooks, who think they must stir it all the time to keep it from burning. Too much stirring makes it like paste; putting in more water when nearly done has the same effect. One-third of wheat by measure to two-thirds of water, soft if you have it, will make it about right; the water should be cold when the wheat is put in; it should cook slowly and be covered closely. In this way scarcely any stirring will be found necessary. There is a deliciousness in this dish, when cooked as above, which is never found if stirred while cooking. The same may be said of oatmeal, only the latter should be quickly stirred into *boiling* water; cover closely, and let cook for about twenty minutes. Wheat may be cooked about the same time, although it bears cooking longer.

ROLEY-POLEY.

Make a good biscuit dough, and roll about three-quarters of an inch thick, and spread with berries, preserves, or slices of apple; roll up, and tie in a cloth; boil or steam an hour and a half.

SNOW PUDDING.

One-half box gelatine soaked ten or fifteen minutes in four tablespoonfuls of cold water; then add a pint of boiling water, the juice of two lemons, and one cup of sugar; strain it, and set away to cool; when cool—not stiff—add the well-beaten whites of three eggs, mix thoroughly, and pour into a mold and cool.

SUET PUDDING.

One cup of suet chopped fine, one cup of raisins, one cup currants, one cup molasses, one cup milk, two and one-half cups flour, teaspoon baking powder, one-half teaspoon cinnamon, nutmeg, and a little candied lemon chopped; steam or boil from two to three hours.

MRS. ELLIS' ENGLISH PLUM PUDDING.

One pound of raisins, one pound of currants, half a pound of citron, one pound beef suet, ten eggs, one pound of sugar, one pint of bread crumbs soaked in milk, a little salt, a nutmeg or mace, flour added to make it stiff enough for the spoon to stand up straight; boil constantly five hours.

MOCK STRAWBERRIES.

Cut choice apples and ripe peaches—one apple to three peaches—into pieces about the size of a strawberry, place in alternate layers, and

PUDDINGS.

sprinkle the top thickly with sugar and pounded ice; let it stand two hours; mix thoroughly, and set aside for an hour longer.

EXTRA NICE DESSERT DISH.

Make a sponge cake, consisting of three eggs, one cup white sugar, one cup flour, two teaspoonfuls baking powder, and three tablespoonfuls boiling water; this will make three cakes on round tins, sufficient for a dessert for eight; then make a boiled custard, consisting of one quart of milk, two large eggs, and three tablespoonfuls of white sugar; pour it over the cake; take one-half pint of thick cream and whip it to a stiff froth; sweeten and season to suit the taste, and spread it smoothly over the whole; let it cool thoroughly by setting it on ice or otherwise.

STRAWBERRY SAUCE.

Beat a coffeecup of sugar and piece of butter size of an egg to a cream, and add two cups of strawberries, mashed, and the beaten white of an egg. A nice sauce can be made of raspberries, cherries, and other fruits as above, or by simply taking the juice, sweetening it, and thickening with a little corn starch.

FOAM SAUCE.

One teacupful of sugar, two-thirds of a cup of butter, one teaspoonful of flour, beat smooth, place over the fire, and stir in three gills of boiling water; a little lemon, vanilla, or orange adds much to the sauce; to be eaten with sponge cake or puddings.

LEMON SAUCE.

Beat two tablespoonfuls of butter and nearly a pound of sugar until light; add the juice and part of the rind of two lemons and two eggs; beat well, and stir into it two cups of boiling water, and boil a few moments.

CREAM PUDDING SAUCE.

Beat half pound light sugar and butter the size of an egg until light, and then add about half a cup of cream; stir in it a half cup of boiling water and boil; flavor to taste just before sending to the table.

COCOA SAUCE.

Half pound of sugar and two ounces of butter beaten until light; tablespoonful of flour, milk of a cocoanut, and a tablespoonful of nut grated; boil only enough to cook the flour.

APPLE TRIFLE.

Scald as many apples as, when pulped, will cover the dish you design to use to the depth of two or three inches; before you place them in the dish add to them the rind of half a lemon grated fine, and sugar to taste; mix half a pint of cream and the yolk of an egg; scald it over the fire, keeping it stirring, and do not let it boil; add a little sugar, and let it stand till cold, then lay it over the apples, and finish with the cream whip.

APPLE CREAM.

Six apples stewed and mashed to pulp; when the apples are cold add six eggs beaten very light, and five tablespoonfuls of sugar; whisk until stiff, and serve with sweetened cream flavored to taste.

APPLE FLOATING ISLAND.

Stew eight or nine apples; when soft pass through a colander, and season to taste with sugar and spice; beat to a froth the whites of five eggs, and mix with the apples, adding a little rose water; sweeten some cream, and place the mixture upon it.

CHARLOTTE RUSSE.

1. Boil one ounce of gelatine in one pint of milk; beat four eggs and nearly a cup of sugar together until light, and pour over them the gelatine and milk; whip a pint of cream, which must be very cold, to a stiff froth, and add the above mixture; flavor with vanilla; line a mold or dish with thin slices of sponge-cake or lady-fingers, and pour in the mixture and set on the ice.

2. One ounce of gelatine dissolved in a pint of boiling milk; put into a pint of cream a cup and a half of sugar and vanilla to flavor, and whip to a froth; mix with the gelatine, adding the whites of the eggs beaten light; pour into a mold or dish lined with sponge cake, and set on the ice till needed.

DRIED PEACH SAUCE.

Pick over and wash thoroughly; cover with hot water and leave all night; stew until very soft, and when done pass through a colander; sweeten to taste, and then boil up once.

ORANGE FLOAT.

Put one quart of water, one cup of sugar, and pulp and juice of two lemons on the fire; when boiling thicken with four tablespoonfuls of corn starch, and boil ten or twelve minutes, stirring constantly; when cold pour it over some peeled and sliced oranges, and spread the beaten whites of two eggs, sweetened and flavored with a few drops of lemon juice.

RASPBERRY BLANC-MANGE.

Stew fresh raspberries; strain off the juice, and sweeten to taste; put over the fire, and when it boils stir in corn starch wet in cold water, allowing two tablespoonfuls to a pint of juice; stir until cooked, and pour into molds to cool. Strawberries and cherries are very nice; eat with sweetened cream or boiled custard.

CHOCOLATE ICE CREAM.

Scald a pint of new milk, and add gradually a cup and a half of sugar, two beaten eggs, and two-thirds a cup of grated chocolate rubbed smooth in a little milk; beat and set over the fire until thick, stirring continually; take off and add tablespoonful of dissolved gelatine; when cold put in the freezer; when it begins to set add two cups of cream, and two cups of cream whipped to a froth.

LEMON CUSTARD.

Beat one pound of sugar and a quarter of a pound of butter together until light; add four eggs also beaten light, and two rolled crackers, one cup of milk, and the grated rind and juice of lemon.

LEMON ICE CREAM.

Squeeze any quantity of lemons desired; make the juice thick with sugar; stir it into cream, allowing nearly three quarts to a dozen lemons, and freeze.

LEMON ICE.

One gallon of water and four pounds of sugar, well boiled and skimmed; when cold, add the juice of a dozen lemons, and the sliced rind of eight, and let infuse an hour; strain into the freezer without pressing, and stir in lightly the well beaten whites of twelve eggs.

ORANGE ICE.

Boil a cup and a half of sugar in a quart of water, skimming when necessary; when cold add juice of half a dozen oranges; steep the rinds in a little water, and strain into the rest; add the rind and juice of a lemon, and strain into the freezer and freeze like ice cream.

PEACHES AND CREAM FROZEN.

Peel and quarter the peaches; mix with sugar and cream; line a Charlotte mold with some of the quarters and fill; freeze solid.

Line a mold with ice cream, and fill the center with berries or sliced fruit; cover with ice cream; cover closely and pack in ice for half an hour. The fruit must not be frozen.

CREAM TAPIOCA.

Soak a cup of tapioca all night in milk enough to cover; in the morning add nearly a cup of sugar and the yolks of three eggs beaten; put a quart of milk in a pail and set into a kettle of water on the fire; when the milk boils add the tapioca, and let it boil until thick; take from the fire; add flavor to taste, adding also the whites of the eggs beaten stiff.

PINEAPPLE PUDDING.

To the beaten yolks of five eggs, add half a pound of grated pineapple and good cupful of fine sugar, little salt, and nearly a cup of boiled cream; set into a kettle of boiling water, and stir until it begins to thicken; set into an ice cream freezer, and when cold add half a pint of cream whipped; put in a mold until cold, and serve with cream.

SNOWBALLS.

Boil a cup of rice in water without breaking the grains; pare and core some good cooking apples; spread some of the rice on pudding-cloths, just large enough to cover an apple; set an apple in the center of the rice carefully, and boil and steam for an hour; when done serve with a nice lemon sauce.

LEMON CUSTARD.

Beat two cups of sugar and half a cup of butter until light; then add four well-beaten eggs, two grated crackers, the grated rind and juice of two lemons, and half a pint of milk.

RICE CHARLOTTE.

Boil one cup of rice in one quart of milk, with sugar and seasoning to taste; when soft set to cool, and then add a pint of whipped cream; put into a mold alternate layers of rice and peaches, either fresh or preserved, and set on the ice until stiff.

RICE CREAM.

Boil a cup of rice in sweet milk until soft, adding sugar and salt to taste; pour into cups, and, when cool, turn out into a dish, scoop a little piece out the top of each, and fill the space with jelly; beat a cup of cream until stiff, sweeten and season, and pour over the rice.

LEMON JELLY.

Soak a half box of gelatine in a cup and a half of warm water; when the gelatine is dissolved, add a cup of sugar, the juice of three lemons, and a cup and a half of boiling water; add the white of an egg, beaten light, and let come to a boil; strain into a mold and set away to cool.

JELLIED GRAPES.

Take about one-half a cup of tapioca, two cups of grapes, three tablespoonfuls of sugar, and a little more than a half-cup of water; sprinkle the tapioca and grapes together in a pudding-dish; pour over the water, cover closely, and bake very slowly for an hour and a half; eat warm with sauce, or cold with cream.

APPLE CUSTARD.

Stew until tender, in a very little water, a dozen apples; flavor with the grated rind of a lemon; rub them through a sieve, and to three cups of the strained apple, add nearly two cups of sugar; leave it until cold; beat five eggs very light, and stir alternately into one quart of rich milk with the apples; pour into a pudding-dish and bake. To be eaten cold.

COTTAGE PUDDING.

Three cupfuls of flour, or sufficient to make the batter; one tablespoonful butter, one cupful sugar, two eggs, one cupful milk, half a teaspoonful soda, one teaspoonful each of cream of tartar and salt; mix the cream of tartar with the flour; beat the whites of the eggs; put the butter, sugar, and yolks of the eggs together; then work in the milk, soda, and salt, adding gradually the flour and whites of the eggs; there should be flour enough to make a fairly stiff batter; butter a mold or dish, and bake; it may be turned out or served from the dish; to be eaten with any liquid sauce.

CHOCOLATE PUDDING.

Scald together one quart of milk and three ounces of grated chocolate, and set it aside to cool; then add nearly a cup of sugar and yolks of five eggs; bake, and when done spread whites on top, beaten stiff with sugar, and brown.

CORN STARCH PUDDING.

One quart of milk set into a kettle of boiling water; mix four ounces of corn starch, two ounces of sugar, with a little cold milk; pour into the milk when boiling, and stir until thick; just before taking from the fire add the whites of two eggs beaten to a stiff froth, and flavor.

CRACKER PUDDING.

One quart of milk, three soda crackers, one egg, a small piece of butter, spice and raisins to taste; bake.

PUDDING SAUCE.

1. Mix together the yolks of four eggs, four tablespoonfuls of sugar, one tablespoonful of flour, and two cups of milk; set on the fire, and stir constantly until thick; flavor to taste.
2. Beat one cup of butter to a cream, then stir in a large cup of brown sugar and the yolk of an egg; simmer slowly a few minutes, stirring constantly; flavor to taste.
3. Rub well together until light four large tablespoonfuls of light brown sugar and two ounces of butter; stir into a teacup of boiling water, quickly and well, until it has dissolved; on no account omit stirring constantly till well dissolved, or it will lose its lightness; add grated nutmeg to taste; serve hot.
4. One cup of sugar, yolk of one egg well beaten with the sugar, four tablespoonfuls of boiling milk; add the white well beaten.
5. Rub to a cream two cups of sugar with three-fourths of a cup of butter; flavor to taste; float the dish in boiling water until well heated; pour one-half pint of boiling water on it just before serving.

LEMON SAUCE.

1. One-half cup of butter, one cup of sugar, yolks of two eggs, one teaspoonful of corn starch; beat the eggs and sugar until light; add the grated rind and juice of one lemon; stir the whole into three gills of boiling water until it thickens sufficiently for the table.
2. One large tablespoonful of butter, one small tablespoonful of flour, one cup of sugar, grated rind and juice of one lemon.

STRAWBERRY SAUCE.

Rub half cup of butter and one cup of sugar to a cream; add the beaten white of an egg, and one cup of strawberries thoroughly mashed.

HARD SAUCE FOR PUDDINGS.

One cup butter, three cups sugar; beat very hard, flavoring with lemon juice; smooth into shape with a knife dipped into cold water.

ENGLISH PLUM PUDDING.

One pound of currants and **one** pound of raisins dredged with flour, one-half pound of beef suet, and one pound of bread crumbs, one-fourth of a pound of citron, eight eggs, one-half pint of milk, a large cup of brown sugar and **one** of molasses; **mace** and nutmeg to **taste**. It requires six or seven hours to boil; turn it several times. Beat the whites of six eggs and put in the last thing. Use currants if you like them.

IMITATION PLUM PUDDING.

Soak some dried apples all night; in the morning chop very fine, put a teacupful of them into a pint of molasses, and keep slightly warm for an hour or two; after that add one cup of chopped suet, one of water, one of chopped raisins, a pinch of salt, a teaspoonful of cinnamon, three pints of flour, and two teaspoonfuls of baking powder. Put the flour in last, and stir all together thoroughly. Boil two hours and a half in a bowl or tin pudding-mold. This may be eaten with lemon sauce, and is a good imitation of a genuine plum pudding.

BAKED APPLE PUDDING.

Six apples well stewed, quarter of a pound of butter—half of it stirred into the apple while hot—and sugar to your taste; when cold add six eggs, well beaten, to the apple. Pound and sift six crackers, butter your dish, and put in a layer of crackers and a layer of your prepared apple, and thus until you have filled your dish. Let the cracker be the upper layer, and put the remainder of your butter in small bits upon it. Bake half an hour.

EXCELLENT BAKED APPLES.

Take ten or twelve good-sized juicy apples, pare and core; butter a baking-dish, and put in it the apples; fill the cavities with sugar; take a half teacup of butter and tablespoonful of flour, rub together until smooth; to this put enough boiling water to make it thin enough to cover each apple; grate over them nutmeg; bake in a slow oven one hour or more; can be eaten with meat, or used as a dessert with cream.

APPLE OR PEACH PUDDING.

Pare and quarter fine sour apples, and half fill a gallon crock with them; take light bread dough, roll half an inch thick, cut small places for the air to escape, and spread over the apples as you would an upper crust for pie; cover and set on the back of the stove, and let it cook slowly for a short time, then move it forward, cooking in all about one-half hour. Eat with sugar and cream. Peaches can be used in the same manner.

APPLE OR PEACH DUMPLINGS.

Pare and core fine juicy apples; then take light-bread dough, cut into round pieces half an inch thick, and fold around each apple until well covered, put them into a steamer, let them rise, then set the steamer over a pot of boiling water and steam. Eat with butter and sugar, or cream. Use peaches in the same way.

BAKED APPLE DUMPLINGS.

Cook apples almost entirely whole, coring or not, as you may prefer; melt butter and sugar in a baking-pan, and having inclosed them in good paste, bake; baste them constantly.

APPLE BATTER PUDDING.

Three eggs, one coffeecupful of sour milk, one large tablespoonful of butter, three large tablespoonfuls of sugar, one-half teaspoonful of soda, and flour enough to make a batter as stiff as cake. Add quartered apples as desired.

APPLE CODDLE.

Pare and quarter tart apples, and mix them gently with one lemon for every six apples, and cook until a straw will pass through them. Make a syrup of half a pound of white sugar to each pound of apples; put the apples and lemons, sliced, into the syrup, and boil gently until the apples look clear, then take them up carefully, so as not to break them, and add an ounce or more of gelatine to the syrup, and let it boil up. Then lay a slice of lemon on each apple, and strain the sugar over them.

STEAMED DUMPLING.

Pare and quarter ripe, tart apples; place them in a deep dish, adding a little water; make a crust as you would tea biscuit, of sour cream or rich buttermilk, if you have it, if not, any of the nice baking-powder receipts will do; roll about an inch thick; place over the apples, and steam one-half an hour. Serve with sauce made of one-third butter and two-thirds sugar, stirred to a cream. This dumpling may be made of any kind of fruit, fresh or canned.

APPLE PUDDING.

Pare eight or nine juicy apples and core them whole. Put them into a pudding-dish half filled with water, cover closely and set into the oven until tender. Drain off the water, fill each apple with jelly, and season with any spice preferred. Let them stand until cool. Scald one pint of milk, into which stir one-half pound of macaroons pounded fine, a little salt, a tablespoonful of corn-starch, three tablespoonfuls of sugar. Boil all together a minute or two, and when cool beat in the whites of three eggs beaten to a stiff froth. Pour over the apples and bake twenty or thirty minutes. Eat with cream.

ALMOND PUDDING.

Turn boiling water on to three-fourths of a pound of sweet almonds; let it remain until the skin comes off easily; rub with a dry cloth; when dry, pound fine with one large spoonful of rose-water; beat six eggs to a stiff froth with three spoonfuls of fine white sugar, mix with one quart of milk, three spoonfuls of pounded crackers, four ounces of melted butter, and the same of citron cut into bits; add almonds, stir all together, and bake in a small pudding-dish with a lining and rim of pastry. This pudding is best when cold. It will bake in half an hour in a quick oven.

DELICIOUS PUDDING.

Bake a **common** sponge cake in flat-bottomed pudding-dish; when ready for **use**, **cut** in six or eight pieces; split, and spread with butter and **return them** to the dish. Make a custard with four eggs to a quart of milk, flavor and sweeten to taste; pour over the cake and bake one-half hour. The cake will swell and fill the custard.

DELMONICO PUDDING.

Stir three tablespoonfuls of **corn starch** into **one quart of** boiling milk, and let it boil two **minutes; beat the yolks of five eggs** with six **tablespoonfuls of sugar, flavor, and stir in the corn starch.** Put the whole in a dish and bake it. Beat the whites of the eggs, and stir into them three tablespoonfuls **of sugar, and when nicely done, spread on** the top and bake a light brown.

FIG PUDDING.

One-fourth pound figs chopped fine, one-fourth pound bread-crumbs, **one-fourth pound sugar (brown),** one-fourth pound suet, one-fourth **pound candied lemon-peel and citron, one** nutmeg and five eggs; **mix thoroughly, put into a mold, and boil or steam four hours.**

FLORENTINE PUDDING.

Put a quart of milk into your pan, **let it come to** a boil; mix smoothly three tablespoonfuls of corn starch **and a little** cold milk; add the yolks of three eggs, beaten, half a teacup **of sugar,** flavor **with vanilla, lemon, or** anything your fancy suggests; stir **into** scalding **milk;** continue **stirring till** the consistency of starch **(ready for use), then** put into the pan or dish you wish to serve in; **beat the whites of the eggs with a** teacup of pulverized sugar, **spread over the top; place in the oven a few minutes, till the** frosting is a pretty brown. **Can be eaten with cream, or is** good enough without. **For a change, you can bake in cups.**

GELATINE PUDDING.

One ounce gelatine, **one** pint cold **milk;** set on range and let come slowly to a boil, stirring occasionally; **separate the** yolks and whites of six fresh eggs; beat the yolks well, **and stir slowly** into hot milk; add half **a pound** of granulated sugar; when quite **cold,** stir in a quart of whipped cream, flavor with vanilla and lemon extract; have the whites of the **eggs** beaten very stiff, and stir in the last thing; **pack on** ice.

BREAD PUDDING.

One **coffeecup** bread crumbs **dried and rolled fine;** one teacup of sugar, one quart of milk, one teaspoonful ginger, **a** little salt, three eggs (saving out the whites of two). When baked spread jelly over the top, then a **frosting made** of the whites of the eggs and **one** tablespoonful **of sugar.** Return to the oven until slightly browned.

BREAD AND APPLE PUDDING.

Butter a pudding-dish, **place** in it alternate layers of bread crumbs and thinly-sliced apples; sprinkle sugar over each layer of apples; when the dish is filled let the top layer be of bread crumbs, over which two or three tablespoonfuls of melted butter should be poured. Bake in a moderately hot oven, and place two or three nails under the pudding-dish to keep from burning in the bottom. Let it bake from three-quarters to a whole hour, according to the quality of the cooking apples.

CABINET PUDDING.

The remains of any kind of cake broken up, two cups; half cup raisins, half can of peaches, four eggs, one and a half pints milk. Butter a plain pudding-mold and lay in some of the broken cake, one-third of the raisins, stoned, one-third of the peaches; make two layers of the remainder of the cake, raisins, and peaches. Cover with a very thin slice of bread, then pour over the milk beaten with the eggs and sugar. Set in a sauce-pan of boiling water to reach two-thirds up the side of the mold, and steam three-quarters of an hour. Turn out carefully on a dish, and serve with peach sauce, made as follows: Place the peach juice from the can into a small saucepan; add an equal volume of water, a little more sugar, and eight or ten raisins; boil ten minutes, strain, and just before serving add six drops of bitter almond.

CRACKER PUDDING.

Mix ten ounces of finely-powdered crackers with a little salt, half a nutmeg, three or four tablespoonfuls of sugar, and three of butter; beat six eggs to a froth, mix with three pints of milk, pour over the crackers, and let stand till soft. Then bake.

SAUCE FOR CRACKER PUDDING.

One cup of sugar, one-half cup of butter, one egg, one teaspoonful of grated nutmeg, one lemon, inside grated, three tablespoonfuls of boiling water.

COCOANUT PUDDING.

One-quarter of a pound of butter, yolks of five eggs, one-quarter of a pound of sugar; beat butter and sugar together; add a little of the cocoanut at a time, and one-half teacupful of cream. Do not bake too long, as it will destroy the flavor. Use one cocoanut. After it is baked beat the whites of the eggs with four or five tablespoonfuls of sugar. Spread over the pudding, and bake a light brown.

CHOCOLATE PUDDING.

1. Scrape very fine two ounces of vanilla chocolate, put it into a pan, pouring over it one quart new milk, stirring it until it boils, and adding by degrees four ounces of sugar, milling the chocolate until it is smooth and light; then pour out to cool; beat eight eggs to a froth, and mix with the chocolate; pour into a buttered dish, and bake three-quarters of an hour. Serve cold with sifted sugar over it.

2. One-quart of milk, fourteen even tablespoonfuls of grated bread crumbs, twelve tablespoonfuls grated chocolate, six eggs, one tablespoonful vanilla, sugar to make very sweet. Separate the yolks and

whites of **four eggs, beat** up the four yolks and two whole eggs together very **light with the sugar.** Put the milk on the range, and when it comes **to a perfect boil** pour it over the bread and chocolate; add the beaten **eggs and sugar and** vanilla; be sure it is sweet enough; pour into **a buttered dish; bake one** hour in a moderate oven. When **cold, and just before it is served, have the four whites beaten with a little** powdered sugar, and flavor with vanilla, and use as a meringue.

3. One quart of milk, twelve tablespoonfuls of bread crumbs, eight tablespoonfuls **of chocolate,** yolks **of four eggs.** Put the milk **and** bread crumbs **on** the fire; let them get **moderately** warm; beat sugar, yolks, and chocolate, and **stir** them into **the milk; one** tablespoonful of corn starch; let it get boiling hot, then turn into a dish with the whites beaten, with sugar on top, and bake a **light brown.**

4. Make a corn starch pudding **with a** quart **of** milk, three tablespoonfuls of corn starch, and three tablespoonfuls of sugar. When done remove about half, and flavor to taste, and then to that remaining in the kettle add an egg beaten very light, and two ounces of vanilla chocolate. Put **in a** mold, alternating the dark and light, and serve with whipped cream or boiled custard.

COTTAGE PUDDING.

One cup **of** sugar, butter the size of a walnut, one-half cup **of milk,** two eggs beaten separately, one and one-half cups of flour, **two teaspoonfuls baking powder.** Serve with lemon sauce.

CHERRY **PUDDING,**

Two eggs, one cupful sweet milk, **flour** enough **to make a stiff batter, two** teaspoonfuls of baking powder, **and as** many **cherries as can be** stirred in. Serve with cherry sauce.

CABINET PUDDING.

Butter a mold well, slice some citron, and cut it **in** any fancy shape and place it **tastefully on** the bottom; place some raisins to imitate flowers, stars, **etc.; put over** them a layer of sponge cake, cut in strips of any length, **and about a** half an inch thick; on the cake place **a** layer of citron, **candied fruits of** several kinds, also some raisins; then another layer **of cake, some** more fruits, and so **on,** till the mold is nearly full. Set about a pint of milk on the fire, and **take it off as** soon as it rises. Mix well in a bowl three ounces of sugar, **with three** yolks of eggs, then turn the milk into the bowl little by little, stirring and mixing the while, and pour over the cake and fruits in the mold. The mixture must be poured over in sprinkling, and it must nearly cover the whole, or within half an inch. It must not be poured over slowly, for the cake absorbing the liquor pretty fast, you would have too much of it. Place the mold in a pan of cold water so that the mold is about one-third covered by it; **set on the fire,** and as soon as it boils place the whole (pan and mold) **in** an oven at about 380 degrees Fahrenheit, and bake. It takes one hour to bake. When done, place a dish over the mold, turn upside down, remove the mold, and serve with a sauce for pudding.

PUDDINGS.

SNOW PUDDING.

Dissolve one box of gelatine in one pint of cold water; when soft, add one pint of boiling water, the grated rind and juice of two lemons; two and one-half cups sugar, whites of five eggs (well beaten). Let it stand until cold and commences to jell; then beat in the whites of eggs.

SAUCE FOR SNOW PUDDING.

One quart of rich milk, the yolks of five eggs, with two extra eggs added; add one-half cup sugar, and flavor with vanilla, as for stirred sugar.

CREAM TAPIOCA PUDDING.

Soak three tablespoonfuls of tapioca in water overnight; put the tapioca into a quart of boiling milk, and boil three-quarters of an hour; beat the yolks of four eggs into a cup of sugar; add three tablespoonfuls of prepared cocoanut; stir in and boil ten minutes longer; pour into a pudding-dish; beat the whites of four eggs to a stiff froth, stir in three tablespoonfuls of sugar; put this over the top and sprinkle with cocoanut, and brown for five minutes.

TAPIOCA PUDDING.

1. One cup of tapioca, soaked two hours on the back of the stove in one quart of water. Butter a pudding-dish well, and line the bottom with pared and cored apples; season the tapioca with a spoonful of sugar, a very little cinnamon, or nutmeg, and salt; pour it over the apples, and bake until the apples are thoroughly done. Eat with sugar and cream.
2. Take ten tablespoonfuls of tapioca, wash it in warm water, drain off the water, and put the tapioca in a pan with a quart of rich milk; set the pan over a kettle of boiling water, and stir till it thickens, then add two tablespoonfuls of butter, six of white sugar, one lemon grated (or flavor to suit the taste with good lemon or vanilla extract), remove the pan from the fire, and having beaten four eggs very light, stir them gradually into the mixture. Pour it into a buttered dish, and bake three-fourths of an hour. Serve with rich cream or custard sauce.
3. Boil one-half teacup of tapioca in half a pint of water till it melts. By degrees stir in half a pint of milk, and boil till the tapioca is very thick. Add a well-beaten egg, sugar, and flavoring to taste. Turn into your pudding-dish and cook gently in the oven three-quarters of an hour. This dish is excellent for delicate children.
4. Four tablespoonfuls of tapioca, one quart of milk, four eggs, leaving out the whites of two for frosting; three tablespoonfuls of sugar. Soak the tapioca overnight, or for several hours, in a little water. Boil the milk and turn over the tapioca. Add, when it is blood-warm, the sugar and eggs, well beaten; bake about an hour, and after it has cooled a little, add the whites of the eggs to one-half pound sugar for frosting. It answers well for a sauce, and looks quite ornamental.
5. One cup tapioca, soaked all night in water; rub fine; one quart of milk and a pinch of salt; let it come to a boil, and then add the yolks of six eggs, well beaten, and one cup of sugar, and let it boil to

the consistency of custard; add the tapioca and boil ten minutes; flavor; when cold, cover the top with the whites of the eggs, beaten with a cupful of white sugar. Set in the oven to brown.

TRANSPARENT PUDDING.

Whites of six eggs, beaten stiff, one cup powdered sugar, butter size of an egg, melted, two cups of flour and three cups of milk. Bake in a quick oven and eat with sauce.

MACARONI PUDDING.

A quarter of a pound of macaroni broken into pieces an inch long, one pint of water, one tablespoonful of butter, one large cupful of milk, two tablespoonfuls of powdered sugar, grated peel of half a lemon, a little cinnamon and salt. Boil the macaroni slowly in a pint of water (in a dish set in a kettle of boiling water) until it is tender; then add the other ingredients. Stir altogether, taking care not to break the macaroni; simmer ten minutes. Turn it out in a deep dish, and serve with sugar and cream.

MOLASSES PUDDING.

One cup of molasses, one cup of sour milk, one cup of chopped suet, one cup currants, one teaspoonful of soda, a little cloves, allspice, cinnamon, enough flour to stiffen. Steam one and a half hours.

ORANGE PUDDING.

1. Cut up oranges in small pieces to make a thick layer on the bottom of a pudding dish. Make a thick boiled custard, and when cool pour over the oranges. Use the whites of the eggs (two or three), make a a meringue of the whites, spread over the top, and slightly brown in the oven.

2. Take one pint of milk and put on the stove to scald; while it is doing so, pare and separate three or four oranges, and place them in a two-quart dish, and put one teacup sugar over them. Take the yolks of two eggs, half a teacup of sugar, one-third corn starch; beat together, and add to milk; let it scald up, then pour over the oranges; beat the whites of two eggs stiff, and a little pulverized sugar, and pour over the whole; bake until the whites are of a light brown.

3. One quart of milk, three eggs, two dessertspoonfuls of corn starch; use the yolks, corn starch, and milk, and make a boiled custard, let it stand until cold, pare and slice four oranges in a dish, with two cups of sugar, pour the custard over the oranges, stir all together, then put the whites, well beaten with a little sugar, on the top of the whole, set in the oven for a few moments to brown; let it get very cold before serving.

PEACH MERINGUE.

Put on to boil a scant quart of new milk, omitting half a teacupful, with which moisten two tablespoonfuls of corn starch. When the milk boils, add corn starch, stir constantly, and when it commences to thicken, remove from the fire; add one tablespoonful of perfectly sweet butter, let cool, then beat in the yolks of three eggs until the custard seems light and creamy, add one-half teacup of fine sugar; cover the bottom of a well buttered baking dish with ripe, juicy peaches that have been pared, stoned, and halved; sprinkle two tablespoonfuls of sugar over the fruit, pour the custard over gently, and bake in a quick oven twenty minutes; draw it out, and cover with the well-beaten whites of the three eggs; sprinkle a little fine sugar over the top, and set in the oven until brown. Eat warm with sauce or cold with cream.

PEACH PUDDING.

Set eight or ten peaches into a pudding dish, half fill with cold water, cover closely, and bake until almost done. Drain off the water, and set to cool. When cold pour over them a batter made of one quart of milk, five eggs, well beaten, eight tablespoonfuls of flour, one-half teaspoonful salt, butter size of a walnut, melted; two tablespoonfuls sugar, if preferred sweetened, and one and a half teaspoonfuls of baking powder. To be eaten with sauce.

PALACE PUDDING.

Two eggs, their weight in butter, flour, and white sugar; put the butter in a pan before the fire till half melted; then beat to a cream; beat the eggs (yolks and whites) together for ten minutes; mix gently with the butter, add the sugar, and then the flour by degrees; add a very little nutmeg and lemon peel; half fill cups, and bake in a slow oven half an hour.

PRINTERS' PUDDING.

One cup of suet chopped fine, two eggs, three tablespoonfuls of sugar, one cup of milk, one cup of raisins, one cup of currants, one nutmeg or lemon extract, two teaspoonfuls of baking powder, and flour enough to make a batter. Boil or steam two hours.

A GOOD PLAIN PUDDING.

Cover the bottom of a buttered pudding dish with pieces of bread soaked in milk, then a layer of chopped apples or berries, add sugar and spice if liked. Proceed till the dish is full, having bread at the top. Moisten all well with milk, and bake three hours, closely covered.

JELLIED RICE.

To three pints of milk put a teacup of rice and a little salt, cover it close, and let it simmer about three hours; beat it well, and put it into molds, and eat as blanc-mange.

ROYAL PUDDING.

Three-quarters of a cup of sago, washed, and put into one quart of milk; put into a saucepan, and stand in boiling water on the range until the sago has well swelled. While hot put in two tablespoonfuls of butter with one cup of white sugar. When cool add the well-beaten yolks of four eggs, put in a pudding dish, and bake from a half to three-quarters of an hour, then remove it from the oven, and place it to cool. Beat the whites of the eggs with two tablespoonfuls of powdered loaf sugar, till they are a mass of froth; spread your pudding with either raspberry or strawberry jam, and then put on the frosting; put in the oven for two minutes to slightly brown. If made in summer, be sure and keep the whites of the eggs on ice till you are ready to use them, and beat them in the coldest place you can find, as it will make a much richer frosting.

RICE PUDDING.

Soak one cupful of best rice; after soaking four hours, drain it off; place the rice in pudding dish; add one cupful sugar, and one teaspoonful of salt, and eleven cupfuls milk and spice; put in a moderate oven, and bake from two to three hours, stirring occasionally at first, if the rice settles.

RICE PUDDING WITHOUT EGGS.

One-half cup of rice, nearly one cup of sugar, one cup of raisins, and two quarts of milk. Stir frequently while baking, but do not let it get too stiff.

CREAM RICE.

Wash two tablespoonfuls of rice, and add to it half a cup of white sugar, a tablespoonful of grated nutmeg, same of salt, and one quart of milk. Set it in the oven to bake, stirring often. When the rice is dissolved, or very soft, remove any brown crust that may be on top, and stir in quickly half a teacup of corn starch, dissolved in half a cup of cold water. It will thicken instantly. It can be made the consistency of custard by placing it back in the oven for one moment. Serve with jelly, if for dessert.

SAGO PUDDING.

Two large spoonfuls of sago, boiled in one quart of water, the peel of one lemon, a little nutmeg; when cold, add four eggs, and a litte salt. Bake about one hour and a half. Eat with sugar and cream.

SAGO JELLY.

To one quart of water put six large spoonfuls of sago, the same of sugar, boil to a jelly, stir it all the time while boiling, flavor to your taste, put into molds, and eat with cream.

SUET PUDDING.

1. One teacupful of molasses, one of suet, one of sweet milk, two cups of raisins, two and one-half cups of flour, one teaspoonful of ginger, one of cinnamon, one-half teaspoonful of allspice, one-half teaspoonful nutmeg, one teaspoonful of soda. Boil or steam. Make sauce same as for plum pudding.

2. One cup of chopped beef suet, one cup of molasses, one cup of milk, three cups of flour, one egg, one teaspoonful of salt, and three-fourths of a teaspoonful of soda; mix well, and steam two hours; one cup of raisins. Serve with liquid sauce, flavored with nutmeg.

3. One pint of bread sponge, one cup chopped suet, one cup brown

sugar, one cup sweet milk, one large cup raisins, one and one-half teaspoons cinnamon, one of cloves, one of salt, one and one-half teaspoons soda, flour to make very stiff. Put in a two-quart pan, and steam two hours and a half. Do not lift the cover until done. Make any kind of sauce you like best, and serve hot.

STEAMED SUET PUDDING.

One cup of stoned and chopped raisins, one cup of finely-chopped suet, one cup of brown sugar, one cup of sour milk, one teaspoonful of saleratus, and flour to stir it quite stiff like bread. Steam three hours. Berries or currants may be used instead of raisins

PLAIN BOILED PUDDING.

One cup sour cream, one-half cup molasses, one-half cup melted butter, two and one-half cups flour, one teaspoonful soda, a little salt. Mix molasses and butter together, and beat until very light; stir in the cream and salt, and then the flour gradually, until it is a smooth batter; beat in the dissolved soda thoroughly, and boil in a buttered mold an hour and a half. To be eaten hot with sweet liquid sauce.

VELVET PUDDING.

Five eggs, beaten separately, one cup of sugar, four tablespoonfuls of corn starch, dissolved in a little cold milk, and added to the yolks and sugar; boil three pints of milk and add the other ingredients while boiling; remove from the fire when it becomes quite thick; flavor with vanilla, and pour into a baking-dish; beat the whites of the eggs to a stiff froth, add half a cup of sugar, turn over the pudding; and place in the oven and let brown slightly. To be eaten with this sauce: Yolks of two eggs, one cup sugar, tablespoonful of butter; beat well; add one cup of boiling milk, set on the stove until it comes to boiling heat, flavor with vanilla.

VERMICELLI PUDDING.

1. Into a pint and a half of boiling milk, drop four ounces of fresh vermicelli, and keep it simmering and stirred up gently ten minutes. when it will have become very thick; then mix with it three and one-half ounces of sugar, two ounces of butter, and a little salt. When the whole is well-blended, pour it out, beat it for a few minutes to cool it, then add by degrees four well-beaten eggs, the grated rind of a lemon; pour a little clarified butter over the top; bake it from one-half to three-fourths of an hour.

2. Boil in a quart of milk the rind of half a lemon, a stick of cinnamon, and four ounces of sugar, for quarter of an hour. Strain the milk, set again on the fire, adding four ounces of vermicelli. Stir it, and let it boil twenty minutes. Then pour it out, and stir in two ounces of butter, and two tablespoons of cream. Beat up the yolks of six, the whites of three eggs, and mix quickly. Pour at once into a buttered dish. Bake in a slow oven three-quarters of an hour, sift sugar over it, and serve hot with any nice pudding sauce. Flavor the sauce with vanilla.

PASTRY.

For pastry use the best of materials.

In warm weather keep the paste in the refrigerator until wanted, and bake in a hot oven.

A well-beaten egg rubbed with a bit of cloth over the lower crust of pies will prevent the juice from soaking through it.

Puff paste should always be made of sweet, solid butter.

The juice of fruit pies, if thickened with a little corn starch, will not "*boil* over."

In making a good pastry it is necessary to have the butter sweet, the lard fresh; the flour should be of the best quality, and sifted; the water for wetting as cold as possible—ice water preferable. In rolling the crust roll always one way, and bake in a quick oven.

PASTRY.

To one cup of water take one-half cup of lard, a little salt, and some flour; mix together with a knife. When stiff enough roll out on a board, spread on with a knife a layer of lard, and sift over a little flour; roll all together, and then roll out on the board again, repeating this three or four times. The entire amount of lard used for one cup of water should be about two cups.

PUFF PASTE.

1. One pound of flour, one pound of butter, one egg; mix the flour with a lump of butter the size of an egg, and the egg to a very stiff paste with cold water; divide the butter into six equal parts, roll the paste, and spread on one part of the butter, dredging it with flour. Repeat until all the butter is rolled in.

2. Take one pound of sifted flour, on which sprinkle a very little sugar; take the yolks of one or two eggs and beat into them a little ice water, and pour gently into the center of the flour, and work into a firm paste, adding water as it is necessary; divide three-quarters of a pound or a pound of firm, solid butter, as you prefer, into three parts; roll out the paste, and spread one part of the butter on half of the paste; fold the other half over, and roll out again, repeating the process until the butter is all rolled in; then set the paste on the ice for fifteen or twenty minutes, after which roll out again three times, each time rolling in the opposite direction; then put on the ice again until cold, when it is ready for use. It will keep several days in a refrigerator, but should not freeze.

APPLE TARTS.

Pare, quarter, core, and boil in a half teacup of water until very soft, ten large apples; beat till very smooth, then add the yolks of six eggs or three whole eggs, juice and grated rind of two lemons, half cup butter, one and a half cups sugar, or more if not sweet enough; beat all thoroughly; line little tart tins with puff paste, and fill with the mixture; bake five minutes in a hot oven.

SLICED APPLE PIE.

Line pie-pan with crust, sprinkle with sugar, fill with tart apples sliced very thin, sprinkle sugar and a very little cinnamon over them, and add a few small bits of butter and a tablespoonful of water; dredge in flour, cover with the top crust, and bake half to three-quarters of an hour; allow four or five tablespoonfuls sugar to one pie. Or, line pans with crust, fill with sliced apples, put on top crust, and bake; take off top crust, put in sugar, bits of butter, and seasoning; replace crust and serve warm. It is delicious with sweetened cream.

LEMON CUSTARD PIE.

Grate the rind of one lemon, squeeze the juice into one and one-half cups of sugar, butter the size of an egg, one tablespoonful of flour, and the yolks of four eggs; stir all together as for cake, and pour over it one pint of boiling milk; beat the whites separately, and stir in after it has cooled a little, then bake in a crust as you would a custard pie.

TWO-CRUST LEMON PIE.

Line your pie-dish with a good crust; roll your lemons to soften them, grate the rind of one large or two small lemons, cut the lemons in thin slices, pick out the seeds, spread evenly one layer over the crust, spread one cup of sugar over the lemon; then add one cup of paste, made by taking four tablespoonfuls of flour, wetting it with cold water the same as you would do to make starch; turn boiling water on it, stirring while cooking on the stove for a few moments, adding a pinch of salt, with the grated rind of the lemons. When thickened enough pour it over the sugar and lemon; cover with a crust, cutting slits in it to let out the air. Bake slowly.

LEMON PIE.

1. Two lemons, half cup sugar, yolks of four eggs, one quart milk, two-thirds cup of flour; whites beaten; put over the top when pie is done.

2. Three eggs, one grated lemon, one cup of sugar, one-half cup of water, two spoonfuls flour; bake; beat the whites separately, and add sugar, not quite as much as for frosting; put into the oven and brown a little.

3. Two lemons, juice, and rind grated, two cups of white sugar, one cup of cream or rich, sweet milk, two tablespoonfuls of corn starch mixed with the yolks of six eggs; bake in a rich crust; beat the whites to a stiff froth with eight tablespoonfuls of pulverized sugar; spread on the top of the pies, and brown. This will make two pies.

4. Grate two lemons, two cups of sugar, two eggs, half a cup of water, one tablespoonful of butter, one of flour. This will make half a dozen pies.

5. Grated rind and juice of one lemon, to which add nearly a cup of sugar, and piece of butter half the size of an egg; into one cup of boiling water stir one tablespoonful of corn starch beaten with the yolks of two eggs; bake with an under crust, and when done spread over the top the whites, beaten stiff, with a little powdered sugar, and return to the oven to brown.

6. One teacupful of powdered sugar, one tablespoonful of butter, one egg, juice and grated rind of one lemon, one teacup of boiling

water, one tablespoonful of corn starch mixed in a little cold water, cream, butter, the lemons and sugar together, and pour the hot mixture over them. When cold add beaten egg. Bake.

7. One cup of sugar, two tablespoonfuls of corn starch, and a cup of boiling water, butter half the size of an egg, the grated rind and juice of a lemon; cook together till clear, and when cold add the yolk of an egg. Line the plate with paste and bake, then fill, putting on the white of an egg with a little sugar for icing, then put in the oven, and brown.

MOCK MINCE PIE.

Three soda crackers rolled fine, one cup of cold water, one cup of molasses, one-half cup of brown sugar, one-half cup of sour cider or vinegar, one-half cup of melted butter, one-half cup of raisins, one-half cup of currants, one egg beaten light, one teaspoon of cinnamon, one-quarter teaspoon each of cloves, allspice, and nutmeg, five apples chopped fine.

MINCE MEAT.

1. Two pounds of lean beef boiled; when cold chop fine; one pound of suet minced to a powder, five pounds of juicy apples, pared and chopped, two pounds of raisins seeded, two pounds of sultanas or seedless raisins, two pounds of currants, one-half pound of citron chopped, three tablespoonfuls of cinnamon, two tablespoonfuls of mace, one tablespoonful of allspice, one tablespoonful of fine salt, one grated nutmeg, three pounds of brown sugar, one-half gallon of sweet cider. Mince meat made by this recipe will keep till spring.

2. Three pounds of beef chopped fine, six pounds of apples, one pound of suet chopped fine and mixed with the meat, four pounds of raisins, six pounds of currants, one pound of citron, one pound of candied lemon, and two pounds sugar, a tablespoonful of salt, two oranges, grated, and powdered cinnamon, mace, cloves, and nutmeg to taste. Add three pints of boiled cider, and set on the stove, stirring to prevent burning, until thoroughly scalded. Add enough sweet cider when using to make it moist.

CREAM PIE.

1. Place one pint of milk in tea-kettle boiler until hot (not boiling); add one cup white sugar, one-half cup flour, and two eggs, well beaten; stir rapidly until thoroughly cooked; flavor with lemon or vanilla; pour over crust, which should be previously baked. Beat the whites of two eggs to a stiff froth; add three tablespoons of powdered sugar; pour over the custard; set in oven, and allow to come to light brown. To be eaten cold.

2. Three eggs, one cup sugar, one and one-half cup flour, tablespoonful of sweet milk, two teaspoonfuls of baking powder; bake in a shallow pan. Cream: three eggs, one pint of milk, three tablespoonfuls of flour, five tablespoonfuls sugar; a little salt, flavor to taste, and boil until thick.

COCOA-NUT PIE.

Open the eyes of a cocoa-nut with a pointed knife or gimlet, and pour out the milk into a cup; then break the shell and take out the meat and grate it fine. Take the same weight of sugar and the grated nut and stir together; beat four eggs, the whites, and stir together; beat four eggs, the whites and yolks separately, to a stiff foam; mix one cup of cream, and the milk of the cocoa-nut with the sugar and nut, then add the eggs and a few drops of orange or lemon extract. Line deep pie-tins with a nice crust, fill them with the custard, and bake carefully one-half an hour.

CREAM PUFFS.

Melt one-half cup of butter in one cup of hot water, and while boiling, beat in one cup of flour, then take off the stove and cool; when cool, stir in three eggs, one at a time, without beating; drop on tins quickly, and bake about twenty-five minutes in a moderate oven. For the cream: half pint milk, one egg, three tablespoons sugar, two large teaspoons flour; boil same as any mock cream, and flavor with lemon. When baked, open the side of each puff, and fill with cream.

FRENCH PUFFS.

One pint of sweet milk, six ounces of flour, four eggs, half a saltspoon of salt; scald the milk and pour over the flour, beat until smooth, whisk the eggs to a froth, and add to the flour and milk when sufficiently cool. Have ready a kettle of boiling lard, and drop one teaspoonful of the batter at a time into the lard, and fry a light brown; sift the white sugar over them, or eat with syrup.

CREAM TARTLETS.

Make a paste with the white of one and yolks of three eggs, one ounce of sugar, one ounce of butter, a pinch of salt, and flour sufficient to make into a paste; work it lightly; roll out to the thickness of a quarter of an inch, line some patty-pans with it, fill with uncooked rice, and bake in a moderate oven until done; remove the rice, and fill with jam or preserves, and at the top place a spoonful of whipped cream.

DELICATE PIE.

To stewed apples sufficient for four pies, one-half pound of butter, six eggs beaten separately, one pound of sugar; flavor with lemon, the apples being quite cold before adding the eggs. Bake as a tart pie.

FRUIT PIE.

Line a soup plate with a rich paste, and spread with a layer of strawberry or raspberry preserves; over which sprinkle two tablespoonfuls of finely-chopped almonds (blanched of course) and one-half ounce of candied lemon peel cut into shreds. Then mix the following ingredients: one-half pound white sugar, one-quarter pound butter, melted, four yolks and two whites of eggs, and a few drops of almond essence. Beat well together and pour the mixture into the soup plate over the preserves, etc. Bake in a moderately warm oven.

When cold, sprinkle or sift a little powdered sugar over the top. A little cream eaten with it is a great addition.

GOOD PIE CRUST FOR DYSPEPTICS.

Equal parts of corn meal, graham flour, and white flour; wet up with sweet cream, and add a little salt; bake in a hot oven.

MOTHER'S LEMON PIE.

The grated rind and juice of three lemons, three tablespoonsfuls sugar, three tablespoonfuls flour, three eggs, one pint of syrup; mix well; make paste as for any pie; pour the above mixture in, and cover with a top crust. This is enough for three pies. Excellent.

APPLE PIE.

Fill the pie crust with sour, juicy apples, pared and sliced thin, put on the upper crust and bake until the apples are soft, then remove the upper crust, adding sugar to taste, a small piece of butter, and a little grated nutmeg; stir this well through the apples, and replace the crust.

APPLE CUSTARD PIE.

Two eggs, four or five apples grated, a little nutmeg, sweeten to taste; one-half pint of new milk or cream, pour into pastry.

APPLES.

Two pounds of apples, pared and cored, sliced into a pan; add one pound sugar, the juice of three lemons, and grated rind of one. Let boil about two hours; turn into a mold. When cold serve with thick cream.

WASHINGTON PIE.

For the crust use two cups sugar, one-half cup butter, three cups sifted flour, four eggs, one-half teaspoonful cream tartar. For the filling, one tablespoonful corn starch, boiled in one-half pint of milk; beat the yolk of one egg very light, and stir into the milk, flavor with vanilla, and when cold, add the other half of the milk, and the white of the egg beaten to a stiff froth and stirred in quickly; spread this between the cakes, and ice it with the white of one egg and eight tablespoonfuls of fine sifted sugar; flavor with lemon.

APPLE CUSTARD PIE.

Stew sour apples until soft, and press through a colander; use the yolks of three eggs, butter the size of an egg, with sugar and seasoning to taste, for each pie; spread whites over the top when baked.

COCOA-NUT PIE.

One and one-half cups sugar, one and one-half cups milk, three eggs, one tablespoonful butter, the rind of lemon, one cocoa-nut, finely grated; the crust should be the same as for custard pie.

RIPE CURRANT PIE.

One cup mashed ripe currants, one of sugar, two tablespoonfuls water, one of flour, beaten with the yolks of two eggs; bake; **frost the top with the beaten whites of the eggs and two tablespoonfuls powdered sugar, and brown in oven.**

GREEN CURRANT PIE.

Line an inch pie-dish with a good pie-crust; sprinkle over the bottom two heaping tablespoonfuls sugar, and two of flour (or one of corn starch), mixed; then pour in one pint greeen currants, washed clean, and two tablespoonfuls currant jelly, sprinkle with four heaping tablespoonfuls sugar, and add two tablespoonfuls cold water; cover and bake fifteen or twenty minutes.

HURRY PIE.

Take light bread, cut slices one inch thick and as large as you wish; cut off the crust; put the slices in a plate and spread a layer of fruit, either preserved or stewed over them; then put a few spoonfuls of cream over, and flavor as you choose. It is nice and handy for farmers' wives.

SUMMER MINCE PIES.

One cup raisins, chopped fine, one nutmeg, two cups water, tablespoonful cinnamon, two cups sugar, butter the size of an egg, one-half cup of vinegar, eight crackers, rolled fine; cook well together before baking.

ORANGE SHORT-CAKE.

One quart flour, two tablespoonfuls **butter, two** teaspoonfuls **baking-powder,** thoroughly mixed with **the flour;** mix (not very stiff) **with cold** water, work as little as possible, **bake, split open,** and lay sliced oranges **between;** cut in squares and serve with **pudding sauce.**

PINEAPPLE PIE.

1. Grate a pineapple; cream half its weight of butter, with its weight of sugar, and add the yolks of four eggs, beaten light, then add a cup of cream; bake with an under-crust, with the beaten whites of the eggs on top.

2. One grated pineapple, its weight in sugar, half its weight in butter, five eggs, the whites beaten to a stiff froth, one cupful of cream; cream the butter and beat it with the sugar and the yolks until very light; add the cream, the pineapple, and the whites of the eggs. Bake with an under-crust. To be eaten cold.

PIE-PLANT CHARLOTTE.

Wash and cut the pie-plant into small pieces, cover the bottom of a pudding-dish with a layer of pie-plant and sugar, then a layer of bread crumbs and bits of butter, or thin slices of bread nicely buttered, and so on until the dish is full. Allow a pound of sugar to a pound of fruit. Bake three-quarters of an hour in a moderate oven. If preferred, turn over the charlotte a boiled custard when ready for the table.

PUMPKIN PIE.

1. Cut the pumpkin into large pieces, and with the skins on; when

done scoop out the pulp, then add two quarts of milk, four eggs, two tablespoonfuls of ginger, two tablespoonfuls of cinnamon, and one teaspoonful of salt; sugar to taste.

2. A small pumpkin baked; scoop out the pulp, and add two quarts of milk, sugar to taste, one-half cup molasses, tablespoonful of salt, and ginger and cinnamon to taste.

RHUBARB PIE.

Stew rhubarb; add the grated rind and juice of a lemon, the well-beaten yolks of two eggs, and sweeten with white sugar; line pie-tins with a good crust, and fill with the rhubarb; bake until the crust is a delicious brown. beat the whites to a stiff froth; it will be necessary to add three tablespoonfuls of powdered sugar; flavor with vanilla, and spread over the tops of the pies; return to the oven until of a light brown. The eggs and lemon given are enough for two pies.

STRAWBERRY SHORT-CAKE.

1. Make a biscuit paste, only using more shortening; roll thin, and put a layer in a baking-pan, spread with a little melted butter, and dust with flour, and add another layer of crust, spread as before, then another layer of crust, untill all is used; bake in a quick oven, and when done spread strawberries between the layers, turning the upper one crust-side down, spreading with strawberries, and pour over all charlotte russe or whipped cream. Orange short-cake can be made by simply substituting sliced oranges for strawberries.

2. Make a nice soda-biscuit dough, bake in deep jelly-cake or pie-pans, split the cakes, and between the layers spread the strawberries, sprinkled with sugar. Eat with cream. Other berries or peaches sliced and put between the layers are nice.

TARTS.

Use the best of puff paste; roll it out a little thicker than for pie-crust, and cut with a large biscuit-cutter twice as many as you intend to have of tarts; then cut out of half of them a small round in the center, which will leave a circular rim of crust; lift this up carefully and lay on the large pieces; bake in pans, and fill with any kind of preserves, jam, or jelly.

CHOCOLATE DROPS.

One cup of cream, and two cups of powdered sugar; set in a vessel of boiling water, and boil until stiff; into another vessel of hot water set a half cup of grated chocolate, and let it melt; roll the sugar into balls, and dip into the chocolate, and then set away to cool.

LEMON TAFFY.

Two cups white sugar, one cup boiling water, one-quarter cup vinegar, one-half cup butter; flavor with lemon; pour in buttered plates to cool.

CHOCOLATE CARAMELS.

One-half pound chocolate, two pounds sugar, two tablespoonfuls vinegar, two teacups milk, **one lump of butter** twice the size of **an egg,** six tablespoonfuls molasses; boil until it hardens in cold water.

A PRETTY TEA DISH.

Make a short, sweetened pie-crust, **roll thin,** and partly bake in sheets; before it is quite done take from **the oven,** cut in squares of four inches or so, take up two diagonal **corners and** pinch together, which **makes them basket-shaped; now** fill with whipped cream or white of egg, or both, well sweetened and flavored, and return to the oven for a few minutes.

RAISIN PIE.

One lemon juice and yellow rind, one cup of raisins, one cup of water, one cup of rolled crackers. Stone the raisins, and boil in water to soften them.

SWEET POTATO PIE.

Scrape clean two good-sized sweet potatoes; boil; **when** tender rub through the colander; beat the yolks of three eggs light; **stir with a** pint of sweet milk into the potato; add a small teacup of sugar, a pinch of salt; flavor with a little fresh lemon, or extract will do; bake as **you** do your pumpkin pies; when done make a meringue top with **the** whites of eggs and powdered sugar; **brown a moment in** the oven.

ORANGE PIE.

1. Beat to a **cream** one-half cup sugar **with** a tablespoonful of butter, and add the beaten yolks of four **eggs, the** grated rind and juice of two oranges, and then the whites **of the eggs,** beaten stiff; bake with **one crust.**

2. Take **four good-sized oranges, peel, seed, and** cut in very small pieces; add **a cup of sugar,** and let stand; into **a** quart of nearly boiling milk stir two tablespoonfuls of corn starch, mixed **with a** little water, and the yolks of three eggs. When this is done let it cool, then mix with the oranges. Put it in simply a lower crust. Make a frosting of the whites of the eggs add one-half cup of sugar; spread it over the top of the pies, and **place for a** few seconds in the oven to brown.

3. The juice and part of **the** rind of one orange, two tablespoonfuls of corn starch, one cupful of hot water with one-quarter box of gelatine dissolved in it. Mix and bake in one or two pies. To be eaten cold.

OYSTER PATTIES.

Line small patty-pans with puff paste, into each **pan** put six oysters, bits of butter, pepper, and salt, sprinkle over a little flour and hard-boiled eggs, chopped (allowing about two eggs for six patties), cover with an upper crust; notch the edges and bake. Serve either in the pans, or remove them to a large platter.

MALBOROUGH PIE.

Six tart apples, six ounces of sugar, six ounces of butter or thick cream, six eggs, the grated peel of one lemon, and one-half the juice. grate the apples after paring and coring them, stir together the butter and sugar as for cake, then add the other ingredients, and bake in a rich under-paste only.

PEACH PIE.

Line a deep dish with soda-biscuit dough, or pie-crust rolled one-fourth of an inch thick, fill with peaches pared, sprinkled with sugar and a little flour, and, if not too juicy, add about two tablespoonfuls of water, put on the upper crust, secure the edges, and bake. Eat with cream.

CUSTARDS AND CREAMS.

APPLE MERINGUE.

Pare, slice, stew, and sweeten six tart, juicy apples. Mash very smooth, or rub through a sieve. Season with nutmeg or lemon peel. Line a generous-sized plate with an under-crust, and bake first. Whip the whites of three eggs with three tablespoonfuls of pulverized sugar, till it stands alone. Fill the crust with apple, then spread the eggs smoothly over the top. Return to the oven and brown nicely. If you put your eggs in a dish of cold water a while before breaking them, they will beat up nicer.

APPLE SNOW.

Prepare eight medium-sized apples as for sauce; after it is cold, break the white of one egg in a dish; turn your apple-sauce over it and whip with a fork thirty minutes. Care should be taken that each blemish be carefully cut away in preparing the apples, as the whiteness of the snow depends mainly on this.

APPLE PUFFETS.

Two eggs; one pint of milk; sufficient flour to thicken, as waffle batter; one and a half teaspoons of baking powder; fill teacup alternately with a layer of batter and then of apples, chopped fine; steam one hour. Serve hot, with flavored cream and sugar. You can substitute any fresh fruit or jams you like.

VELVET BLANC-MANGE.

Two cups of sweet cream, one-half ounce gelatine, soaked in a very little cold water one hour; one-half cup white powdered sugar, one teaspoonful extract of bitter almonds. Heat the cream to boiling, stir in the gelatine and sugar, and as soon as they are dissolved, take from the fire, beat ten minutes until very light, flavor by degrees, mixing it well. Put into molds wet with clear water.

FRUIT BLANC-MANGE.

Stew nice fresh fruit (cherries and raspberries being the best); strain off the juice and sweeten to taste; place it over the fire in a double kettle until it boils; while boiling, stir in corn starch wet with a little cold water, allowing two tablespoonfuls of starch for each pint of juice;

continue stirring until sufficiently cooked; then pour into molds wet in cold water, and set away to cool. To be eaten with cream and sugar.

CHOCOLATE BLANC-MANGE.

1. One-half box gelatine, well soaked. Let one pint of milk come to the boiling-point; one cup grated chocolate (not the sweetened); twelve tablespoonfuls sugar. Add the gelatine just before turning into the molds. To be eaten, when cold, with sugar and cream.

2. One ounce of gelatine dissolved in as much water as will cover it, four ounces of grated chocolate, one quart of milk; three-quarters of a pound of sugar, yolks of two eggs. Boil eggs, milk, and chocolate together five minutes then put in the gelatine, and let the whole boil five minutes longer stirring constantly. Add one teaspoonful of vanilla extract, and put in molds to cool.

3. Soak a half-box gelatine in one quart of milk. Heat the milk, and when the gelatine is dissolved, strain, then add one cup of sugar, and three tablespoonfuls of grated chocolate, and boil eight minutes, stirring all the time. When nearly cold, beat with the egg-beater for five minutes. Flavor with vanilla, and put into a mold to cool.

RICE BLANC-MANGE.

One quart of new milk, six tablespoons of coarsely-ground rice. Wash the rice and drain the water off. Just as the milk begins to boil, add the rice, a tablespoonful at a time, stirring constantly. Boil for twenty minutes, or until it becomes quite thick. Sweeten to taste; add two tablespoonfuls water and one teaspoonful of rose water.

LEMON ICE.

1. One quart of water, juice of four lemons, one pound of sugar; strain the mixture, and just before freezing, add the beaten whites of two eggs.

2. One-half pint lemon juice, one-half pint of water, one pint of strong syrup. The rind of the lemon should be rasped off before squeezing, with lump sugar, which is to be added to the juice. Mix the whole together, strain after standing an hour, and freeze. Beat up with a little sugar the whites of two or three eggs, and, as the ice is beginning to set, work this in with the spatula, which will much improve the consistency and taste. Orange ice the same

ICE CREAM.

Two quarts of good cream, one-half pint of milk, fourteen ounces of white sugar, two eggs; beat the eggs and sugar together as for cake, before mixing with the cream; flavor to suit the taste. Place the can in the freezer, and put in alternately layers of pounded ice and salt; use plenty of salt to make the cream freeze quickly; stir immediately and constantly, stirring rapidly as it begins to freeze, to make it perfectly smooth, and slower as it gets pretty stiff. As the ice melts draw off the water, and fill up with fresh layers.

CHOCOLATE ICE CREAM.

For one gallon of ice cream grate fine about one-half cake of chocolate; make ice cream as for the recipe above; flavor with vanilla, and stir in the chocolate.

STRAWBERRY ICE CREAM.

One quart of cream, one pint of strained strawberry juice, one pint of sugar; mix the sugar and juice together, then stir in the cream.

FLOATING ISLAND.

Beat the yolks of three eggs until very light; sweeten and flavor to taste; stir into a quart of boiling milk; cook till it thickens; when cool, pour into a low glass dish; whip the whites of the eggs to a stiff froth; sweeten, and pour over a dish of boiling water to cook. Take a tablespoon and drop the whites on top of the cream, far enough apart so that the "little white islands" will not touch each other. By dropping little specks of bright jelly on each island will be produced a pleasing effect. Also by filling wine glasses and arranging around the stand adds to the appearance of the table.

VELVET CREAM.

Two tablespoonfuls of strawberry jelly, two tablespoonfuls of currant jelly, two tablespoonfuls of pulverized sugar, whites of two eggs beaten stiff, then whip the cream, fill a wine glass one-half full of the whipped cream, and fill the glass with the above mixture beaten to a cream.

CHOCOLATE CUSTARD.

Make a boiled custard with one quart of milk, the yolks of six eggs, six tablespoonsfuls of sugar, and one-half cup of grated vanilla chocolate. Boil until thick enough, stirring all the time. When nearly cold, flavor with vanilla. Pour into cups, and put the whites of the eggs, beaten with some powdered sugar, on the top.

RUSSIAN CREAM.

One and one-half quarts rich milk, one cup sugar, one-half box gelatine, four eggs, vanilla to taste. Dissolve the gelatine in the milk; add the yolks and sugar; let it come to a boil, then remove from the fire. When cool, add whites of eggs, etc. Pour into mold. To be eaten with cream, if preferred.

PINK CREAM.

Three gills of strawberry or currant juice, mix with one-half pound of powdered sugar, one-half pint of thick cream; whisk until well mixed; serve in a glass dish.

PERSIAN CREAM.

Dissolve gently one ounce of gelatine in a pint of new milk, and strain. Then put it in a clean saucepan, with three ounces of sugar, and when it boils stir in one-half pint of good cream; add this liquid, at first by spoonfuls only, to eight ounces of jam or rich preserved fruit; mix them very smooth, and stir the whole until it is nearly cold, that the fruit may not sink to the bottom of the mold; when the liquid is put to the fruit and stirred until nearly cold, whisk them briskly together, and last of all throw in, by very small portions at a time, the strained juice of one lemon. Put into a mold, and let it stand at least twelve hours in a cold place before serving.

LEMON CREAM.

Take one lemon and grate it up fine, one cup of sugar, three-fourths of a cup of water, one cup of butter, and three eggs. Take the lemon, sugar, butter, and water, and put them in a pan, and let it come to a boil. Have the eggs well beaten, and stir in while boiling; let it thicken, then take off and cool. Nice for traveling lunch and picnics.

SOUFLEE DE RUSSE.

Three pints of milk, four eggs, one-half box of gelatine, sweeten and flavor to taste. Boil as custard. As it is taken from the fire stir in the whites beaten to a stiff froth. Pour into molds, and when cold, eat with cream.

SPANISH CHARLOTTE.

Place crumbs of stale cake or rolled crackers on the bottom of a pudding-dish, and put a layer of any kind of jelly or fruit over them. Continue them alternately until the dish is nearly full, making the crumbs form the tip. Pour a custard over it, and bake. Serve with sauce.

CHOCOLATE CREAM CUSTARD.

Scrape a quarter of a pound of the best chocolate; pour over it a teacup of boiling water, and let it stand by the fire until dissolved. Beat eight eggs light, leaving out the whites of two, and stir by degrees into a quart of rich milk alternately with the chocolate and three tablespoonfuls of sugar. Put the mixture into cups, and bake immediately.

BOILED CUSTARD.

Allow five eggs to one quart of milk, a tablespoonful of sugar to each egg; set the milk in a kettle of boiling water until it scalds; then, after dipping a little of the milk on to the eggs and beating up, turn into the scalded milk, and stir until it thickens. Flavor to taste.

BAKED CUSTARD.

One quart of milk, five eggs, a pinch of salt, sugar and flavor to taste; boil the milk; when cool stir in the beaten eggs and sugar, pour into cups, set them in pans of water, and bake; if it is baked too long will become watery.

LEMON CUSTARD.

Four eggs leave out the white of one, one cup of sugar, one cup of cold water, one grated lemon, a small piece of butter, one tablespoonful of corn starch; bake as custard; after it is baked cover it with the beaten white and pulverized sugar, return to the oven; bake a light brown.

COFFEE CUSTARD.

One-half pint of rich cream, one-half cup cold coffee, four eggs, sugar to taste.

FLOATING ISLAND.

One quart of milk, five eggs, and five tablespoonfuls of sugar; scald the milk, then add the beaten yolks, first stirring into them a little of the scalded milk, to prevent curdling; stir constantly until of the right consistency; when cool, flavor; let it get very cold, and before serving beat up the whites of the eggs to a stiff froth, and stir into them a little fine sugar and two tablespoonfuls of currant jelly; dip this on to the custard.

ALMOND CUSTARD.

One pint of new milk, one cup of pulverized sugar, one-quarter pound of almonds, blanched and pounded, two teaspoonfuls rose water, the yolks of four eggs; stir this over a slow fire until it is of the consistency of cream, then remove it quickly, and put into a dish. Beat the whites with a little sugar added to the froth, and lay on top.

INDIAN CUSTARD.

Heat two quarts of milk, then stir in one cup of molasses, a small cup of fine corn meal, two beaten eggs, and a little salt. Cook slowly one hour. If it seems too thick, thin it with a little cold water.

IRISH MOSS.

Soak a scant handful of Irish moss in strong soda water until it swells; then squeeze the moss until it is free from water, and put in a tin bucket which contains six pints of sweet milk. Set the bucket in a large iron pot which holds several pints of hot water; stir seldom, and let it remain until it will jell slightly by dropping on a cold plate. Strain through a sieve, sweeten, and flavor to taste. Rinse a mold or a crock with tepid water, pour in the mixture, and set it away to cool. In a few hours it will be palatable. Eat with cream and sugar; some add jelly.

LEMON JELLY.

1. One box gelatine; pare five lemons thin, and squeeze out the juice; break up one small stick of cinnamon and a little orange peel, one and one-half pints of sugar; then pour on one pint of cold water, and let it soak for three hours. Put in the kettle with three pints of boiling water, stirring until the gelatine is dissolved; then let it simmer for about half an hour. Strain through a bag into jelly molds, and let it cool.

2. One pound of sugar, one-fourth of a pound of butter, six eggs, juice of two lemons, and rind of three lemons. Beat thoroughly together; cook until as thick as boiled custard.

A DISH OF SNOW.

Grate a cocoa-nut, leaving out the brown part. Heap it up in the center of a handsome dish, and ornament it with fine green leaves, such as peach or honeysuckle. Serve it up with snow cream, made in this way: Beat the whites of five eggs to a stiff froth, add two large spoonfuls of fine white sugar, a large spoonful rose water or pineapple. Beat the whole well together, and add a pint of thick cream. Put several spoonfuls over each dish of cocoa-nut.

APPLE FLOAT.

One cup of pulverized sugar, one cup of cream beaten to a stiff froth, five eggs beaten light, one lemon, four large apples grated, three tablespoonfuls of gelatine dissolved in warm water. Fills one quart bowl.

STRAWBERRY CHARLOTTE.

Make a boiled custard with one quart of milk, yolks of six eggs, and three-quarters of a cup of sugar, flavored to taste. Line a glass dish with slices of sponge cake dipped in sweet cream, lay upon ripe strawberries, sweetened to taste, then a layer of cake and strawberries as before. When the custard is cold pour over the whole. Then beat the whites of the eggs to a stiff froth, add a little sugar, and put over the top. Decorate with some ripe berries.

LEMON BUTTER.

For tarts: One pound pulverized sugar; whites of six eggs, and yolks of two; three lemons, including grated rind and juice; cook for twenty minutes over a slow fire, stirring all the while.

APPLE BUTTER.

Take tart cooking apples, such as will make good sauce. To three pecks, after they are peeled and quartered, allow nine pounds of brown sugar and two gallons, or perhaps a little more of water. Put the sugar and water in your kettle, and let it boil, then add the apples. After they begin to cook, stir constantly till the butter is done. Try it by putting a little in a saucer, and, if no water appears around it, the marmalade is ready for the cinnamon and nutmeg "to your taste."

ORANGE DESSERT.

Pare five or six oranges; cut into thin slices; pour over them a coffee-cup of sugar. Boil one pint of milk; add, while boiling, the yolks of three eggs, one tablespoon corn starch (made smooth with a little cold milk); stir all the time; as soon as thickened, pour over the fruit. Beat the whites of the eggs to a froth; add two tablespoonfuls of powdered sugar; pour over the custard, and brown in the oven. Serve cold.

FROZEN PEACHES AND CREAM.

Choose nice ripe peaches, but perfectly sound; peel and slice them; mix them with sugar and cream to taste. Freeze.

AMBROSIA.

A layer of oranges, sliced, then sugar, then a layer of cocoa-nut, grated; then another of oranges, and so on until the dish is full.

FROZEN PEACHES.

Take two quarts of rich milk, and two teacupfuls of sugar, mix well together, and put into a freezer with ice and salt packed around it. Have ready one quart of peaches, mashed and sweetened. When the milk is very cold, stir them in and freeze all together. Strawberries can be used in the same way, but will require more sugar.

FROZEN STRAWBERRIES.

Take nice ripe strawberries, put them into a bowl and mash them. Make them rather sweeter than for the table. Let them stand until juice is drawn out then freeze. Serve with cream or ice cream.

CHARTREUSE D'ORANGES.

Make a very clear orange jelly, with one and a half pints of water, six oranges, sugar to taste, one and one-half ounces of gelatine; divide three or four oranges into quarters, and with a sharp knife, remove every vestige of skin of any sort—also the seeds; have two plain molds, one about one and a fourth inches more in diameter than the other, pour a very little of the jelly at the bottom of the large mold, place in this a layer of orange quarters (if too thick, split in two lengthways), cover with more jelly, but only just enough to get a smooth surface; set on ice to set; when it is quite firm, put in the small mold inside of the larger one, taking care to place exactly in the middle, so that the vacant place between the two molds be exactly of the same width; in the vacant place, put more orange quarters, filling up with the jelly, until the whole space is filled up; place the mold on ice, and proceed to whip one pint of cream with one-half ounce of dissolved gelatine and some sweetened orange juice, which must be added to it a very little at a time, else the cream will not rise in a froth; when the cream is ready, and the jelly set, remove the inner mold by pouring warm water into it, and fill up the space of the chartreuse with the whipped cream. Set on ice for an hour, turn out, and serve.

BAKED PEARS.

Place in a stone jar first a layer of pears (without paring), then a layer of sugar, then pears, and so on until the jar is full. Then put in as much water as it will hold. Bake three hours.

CHARLOTTE RUSSE.

Beat the yolks of four eggs, and stir them into one pint of scalding milk. Boil like custard and set away to cool. Pour a large cup of warm water over a half box of gelatine, set it in the stove, but do not let it get hot; beat the whites of the eggs very light, and add enough pulverized sugar to make stiff; then whip one pint of good cream and stir into the custard; then the whites flavored with vanilla; then the gelatine well dissolved. Mix thoroughly and set away to cool (about two hours). Line your dish with either sponge cake or lady fingers, and fill with the mixture. Let it stand five or six hours.

TUTTI FRUTTI.

One quart of rich cream, one and one-half ounces of sweet almonds, chopped fine; one-half pound sugar; freeze, and, when sufficiently congealed, add one-half pound of preserved fruits, with a few white raisins chopped, and finely-sliced citron. Cut the fruit small, and mix well with the cream. Freeze like ice cream; keep on ice until required.

CAKES.

Use the best materials, and have everything ready before you begin mixing the materials. Always sift the flour, adding to it the baking-powder and mixing well. If it is summer weather, lay the eggs in cold water for a few minutes, and beat yolks and whites separately, very thoroughly. Mix butter and sugar to a cream, then add sugar, then the yolks of the eggs, then the milk and flour alternately in small quantities, then the whites.

If fruit is used flour it well, and add the last thing.

Bake slowly at first.

Cookies, jumbies, ginger-snaps, etc., require a quick oven; if they become moist or soft by keeping, put again into the oven a few minutes.

While the cake is baking no air must be permitted to get into the oven, unless when necessary to look at the cake, as it is apt to make it fall. The heat of the oven should be even and regular. When cake is done, it can be tested by sticking a clean straw into it. If nothing adheres to the straw, the cake is done.

SOFT FROSTING.

Ten teaspoonsfuls of fine sugar to one egg; beat one-half hour.

SUTTI FRUITTI FROSTING.

One-half teacupful of water, three cups of sugar, whites of two eggs; boil sugar and water until very thick and waxy; beat the white of eggs to a stiff froth, and pour the syrup over them, beating all till cool. Then add one-half pound of almonds, chopped fine; one small half teacup of large white raisins, and a little citron sliced thin. Very nice for sponge cake.

CHOCOLATE FROSTING.

One cake (or one-half pound) French vanilla, sweet chocolate, grated, one-half cup granulated sugar, three-fourths of a cup of sweet milk, one tablespoon butter, a little salt. Boil twenty minutes, stirring constantly; take from the fire and pour into a dish. When near cool, add one tablespoon of vanilla; spread on the cake. If the mixture is thicker than jelly, thin it with milk. This quantity will ice two cakes, three layers each. The best cake is gold cake, baked in jelly tins.

ALMOND FROSTING.

Blanch some sweet almonds, and when cold pound in a mortar until pulverized; mix the whites of three eggs and three-fourths of a pint of powdered sugar; flavor with vanilla, and add the almonds.

GELATINE FROSTING.

Dissolve a tablespoonful of gelatine in half cup of boiling water, and strain; thicken with powdered sugar, and flavor.

HICKORY-NUT FROSTING.

Allow one cup of sugar to the white of one egg; beat until very light, and add the hickory-nut after chopping very fine.

APPLE CAKE.

The grated rind and juice of one lemon, one sour apple, pared and grated, and one cup of sugar, boiled together for five minutes, make a jelly, which is to be spread between the layers of the following cake, to make which take: One cup of sugar, butter, the size of an egg, one cup flour, one teaspoonful baking powder; bake in four layers.

ALMOND COOKIES.

Two pounds of butter, three pounds of sugar, one pound of shelled almonds, one dozen eggs, one teaspoonful of ground cinnamon one-half teaspoonful of soda, a cup of boiling water, one lemon grated; mix butter, sugar, yolk of eggs, lemon, cinnamon, and hot water; beat the whites, take three parts, mix also one-half of the almonds, and as much flour as it will hold; roll them, and brush with the whites of eggs. Before putting in the almonds and sugar, almonds must be scalded, dried, and cut fine. Bake in a moderate oven.

BOILED ICING.

1. One and one-half cups of sugar; put to this two tablespoonfuls of water. Let it boil on back of stove until it is waxy, or stringy; then add whites of two eggs.

2. Whites of four eggs, beaten stiff; one pint of sugar, melted in water, and then boiled; add to it the eggs, and beat until cold.

CHOCOLATE ICING.

One-half cake of chocolate grated fine, two-thirds of a cup of sugar, one-half cup of milk or cream; boiled and stirred to a paste.

2. Take the whites of two eggs, one and one-half cups of powdered sugar, and six large tablespoonfuls of chololate.

ICING.

1. Two and a half cups sugar, two-thirds of a cup of a water; boil together until it candies; then add the whites of three eggs, slightly beaten, stirring briskly for fifteen minutes, or until it seems perfectly smooth and white; then add the juice of one lemon. This is sufficient for one large white mountain cake, of eight or nine layers, covering also top and sides.

2. Beat the whites of four eggs with one pound of powdered sugar sifted, with one-half a tablespoon starch, and one-fourth of an ounce of fine gum-arabic. Stir it well.

ICING FOR CAKE.

1. Beat the whites of four eggs with one pound of powdered sugar,

one teaspoonful each of corn starch and sifted white gum-arabic, and the juice of one lemon.

2. Beat the whites of six eggs with one pound each of powdered sugar and blanched and pounded almonds; a little rose-water should be added to the almonds during the process of pounding; lay on with a knife, and harden in a cool oven. The eggs must be beaten to a stiff froth.

BLACK CAKE.

1. One pound of flour, one and one-half pounds of brown sugar, one pound of butter, twelve eggs, or leave out part of the eggs; use the same quantity of molasses. One teaspoon of soda, three pounds of currants, four pounds of seeded raisins, one pound of citron, two nutmegs, one teaspoon of ground cloves and cinnamon each. Bake in a large loaf three or four hours.

2. One pound browned flour; one pound brown sugar, one pound citron; two pounds currants, three pounds stoned raisins, three-quarters pound of butter one teacup of molasses, two teaspoonfuls mace, two teaspoonfuls cinnamon, one teaspoonful cloves, one teaspoonful soda, twelve eggs.

3. One pound sugar, one pound butter, one pound flour, three pounds raisins, three pounds currants, one-half pound citron, ten eggs, two teaspoonfuls cinnamon, one teaspoonful cloves, two teaspoonfuls nutmeg; brown the flour to darken the cake.

BREAD CAKE.

1. Four cups dough, two cups sugar, one cup butter, one cup cream; two eggs, one teaspoonful saleratus. Mix with the hands, and add a little flour, also fruit and spices to suit the taste, and let it rise well before baking.

2. Two cups of light dough, one and one-half cups of sugar, one of butter, half cup of milk, two eggs, soda or baking-powder, nutmeg. If too thin, stir in a little flour.

COFFEE-CAKES.

1. Three eggs well beaten, two cups brown sugar, one cup butter, one cup of milk, one teaspoonful of soda, two teaspoonfuls of cream of tartar. Work this to a stiff dough, and roll out to about half inch in thickness. Sift ground cinnamon over evenly, then roll up like roll jelly cake. Cut slices about a half inch thick from the roll, drop into granulated sugar, and bake thoroughly with sugared side up.

2. One pint warm milk, one coffee cup melted lard, one-half cup yeast; put in enough flour to make a stiff sponge, and set over night; in the morning add two coffecups sugar, four eggs, one teaspoonful cinnamon; mold and set to rise again, after which roll one-half inch thick on a warm board; cut with small cutter, and fry; roll in pounded sugar, and place on separate plates till cool.

BREAKFAST COFFEE-CAKES.

Three cups bread sponge, one-half cup butter, little sugar, one egg. Roll thin as bakingpowder biscuit. Cut out with tumbler or cake-cutter, sprinkle over a little sugar, cinnamon; and little bits of butter.

CORN STARCH CAKE.

1. One and one-half cups sugar, whites of six eggs, one-half cup sweet milk, one and one-half cups flour, one-half cup corn-starch, one-half cup butter, two teaspoonfuls of cream tartar, and one teaspoonful of soda; lemon to flavor. After all is well mixed, add one-half cup cold water.

2. Four eggs, whites only; one cup of powdered sugar, one-half cup of butter, two-thirds cup of corn starch, one-half cup sweet milk, one cup flour, two teaspoonfuls baking powder, lemon or rose-water flavoring. Cream the butter and sugar thoroughly, either with the hand or silver spoon; mix the corn starch with the milk, and add. Then add the eggs, beaten stiff, next the sifted flour, into which the baking powder has been stirred.

CREAM PUFFS.

One-half pint cold water, into which rub smooth six ounces of flour; put it into a spider with four ounces of butter, and stir it continually over a fire not too hot till it is thoroughly cooked. It will resemble a lump of putty and cleave off the spider like a pancake. Cool this lump and add four eggs. Beat well, and then drop on a buttered tin in neat, compact little "dabs;" far enough apart not to touch when they rise. Have the oven about as hot as for cookies. and in turning them lift up the tin. If you shove them before they are set you will have pan-cakes. They should be hollow balls. Bake them long enough so they will not fall when removed, and cool them on brown paper as quickly as possible, so they won't sweat. To fill them take one-half pint milk, two beaten eggs, one-quarter cup of flour or corn starch wet smoothly, one cup sugar, lemon or vanilla flavor; cook it in a tin pail in a kettle of hot water, and stir it so it will be smooth. When both are cold, open the puff with a sharp knife, just a little slit on the side, and fill in one tablespoonful of custard.

CITRON CAKE.

1. One cup butter, three cups of sugar, one cup of milk, three cups of flour, half cup of corn starch, two teaspoonfuls baking powder, one cup candied citron, and whites of twelve eggs.

2. Six eggs, four cups of flour, two and one-half cups of sugar, two cups of citron, cut in little slips; two teaspoons baking powder, one cup sweet milk, one cup butter.

3. Whites of twelve eggs, two cups of butter, two cups of sugar, four and one-half cups of flour, one-half cup of milk, three teaspoonfuls baking-powder, and one pound of citron.

CHOCOLATE CAKE.

1. Make as for nice cup cakes, bake in jelly cake tins. Icing: Boil together for a few minutes three cups of sugar, and one cup of boiling water; pour this syrup into half a cake of chocolate grated; add whites of three eggs, beaten stiff. Put this icing between layers of cake and on top.

2. Two cups sugar, two-thirds cup of butter, one cup sweet milk, three cups flour, three eggs, two teaspoons baking-powder; lemon ex-

tract. Bake as jelly cakes. Caramel: The whites of three eggs beaten very stiff; two cups sugar boiled until almost candy; pour very slowly on the whites, beating them quite fast; one-half cake chocolate, grated; vanilla extract; stir until cool, then put between each cake and over the top and sides.

3. One cup butter, three cups brown sugar, one cup milk, four cups of flour, yolks of seven eggs, two teaspoonfuls of baking-powder, and cup of chocolate; bake in layers; make another cake with whites of the eggs, as given in the preceding recipe, and put together with frosting in alternate layers.

4. Three-fourths cup butter, two cups sugar, one cup milk, two cups flour, one of corn starch, two teaspoonfuls baking-powder, and whites of seven eggs; bake in a long, shallow pan; take half cup of milk, butter the size of an egg, cup brown sugar, quarter pound of chocolate; mix and boil until stiff, then add tablespoonful vanilla, spread on the cake, and set in the oven until dry.

CAKE WITHOUT EGGS.

One and a half cups sugar, half-cup of butter, one cup of milk, three cups flour, two teaspoonfuls baking-powder, one cup chopped raisins, well floured, and added the last thing before putting into the oven; spices to taste.

CREAM CAKE.

1. CAKE: Pour a cup of boiling water over a cup of butter, add immediately two cups of flour; stir until smooth, and set away to cool; when cold, add five eggs, and stir until well mixed; add a very little soda; butter a pan; drop in the mixture, a tablespoonful in a place, and bake in a quick oven.

CREAM: One pint milk; when boiling add half cup of flour, half-cup sugar, and two eggs mixed; stir until thick as cream, then flavor with lemon or vanilla. Remove the tops from the cakes; fill the hollows with the cream and then replace.

2. CAKE: One cup of white sugar, two eggs well beaten, one tablespoonful of butter, one half-cup of sweet milk, one-half-teaspoonful of soda and one of cream of tartar, one and one-half cups of flour; add a little salt, beat thoroughly, and bake quickly in five or six round tins.

CREAM: One and a half cups of sweet milk, one heaping tablespoonful of flour, rubbed smooth in the milk, one beaten egg, half a cup of white sugar; boil the whole together, stirring all the time, until quite thick; when cold, flavor with lemon, or any extract preferred, and spread between each layer.

3. One cup white sugar, one and one-half cups flour, three eggs beaten separate and very light, two tablespoons water, one teaspoon baking-powder. Bake in two cakes. Cream: One pint of milk, one cup sugar, one-half cup butter, three eggs, two tablespoons flour; lemon extract. Cut each cake, and fill with the cream.

COOKIES.

1. Two cups sugar, one cup butter, one cup milk, three eggs, flour

enough to make a soft dough, two teaspoonfuls baking-powder; roll thin; sift over with sugar and bake.

2. Two cups white sugar, one cup of sweet milk, two spoons of baking powder, nutmeg; flour enough to roll out; better if rolled out thin, and a hot oven to bake in.

3. Whites of two eggs, one large cup of milk, one cup of sugar, one half-cup butter, two teaspoonfuls baking-powder, flavor with vanilla, rose, or nutmeg; flour enough for thick batter; beat thoroughly; drop in buttered pans, dust granulated sugar on top and bake with dispatch.

4. One cup butter, two cups sugar, four eggs, four cups flour, three tablespoons milk, three teaspoons baking-powder. Rub the flour and butter thoroughly together, cream the butter and sugar, beat the eggs separately; add to the above with a little nutmeg and cinnamon, or any seasoning preferred. Sift in the flour and baking-powder, and add enough flour to mold, and roll out. These cookies will keep fresh two weeks, and if the milk is left out, a month.

5. One cup sugar, one half-cup lard or butter, one-half cup sour milk, one-half teaspoonful soda, just flour enough to roll, baking quickly. Add any flavoring you wish. No eggs are required. These are very nice if grated or prepared cocoa-nut is added.

6. One cup sour cream, one cup butter, two cups sugar, two eggs, one teaspoon soda; flour; and flavoring to suit.

7. One cup butter, two of sugar, two eggs, a teaspoonful of saleratus, dissolved in a cup of milk or water, a grated nutmeg, sufficient flour to make stiff to roll out.

MRS. CALDWELL'S COOKIES.

One cup of butter, one cup of sugar, one cup of molasses, two eggs, two teaspoonfuls soda, two teaspoonfuls ginger, flour to mix soft and roll them.

COCOA-NUT COOKIES.

1. One cup of butter, two cups of sugar, two cups of grated or prepared cocoa-nut, two eggs, flour enough to make a stiff batter, and teaspoonful of soda; drop on buttered paper in pans.

2. One and one-half cups of sugar, one cup butter (nearly), two eggs, one cup grated cocoa-nut, one-half cup milk, one-half teaspoonful soda, one teaspoonful vanilla; cut out and sprinkle with granulated sugar.

CORN GEMS.

Two cups of corn meal, two cups of flour, two cups of sweet milk, two eggs, three heaping teaspoonfuls of baking-powder, one-half cup of butter, one-half cup of sugar. Bake in gem-pans.

COCOA-NUT CAKE.

1. After using the whites of ten eggs for snow cake, take the yolks, one and one-half cups sugar, two-thirds butter, two-thirds sweet milk, two cups flour, one teaspoon soda, one cream tartar, whites of four or five eggs for frosting; sprinkle cocoa-nut upon each layer of frosting.

CAKES.

2. **Two** eggs, two tablespoonfuls butter, one cup sugar, half cup milk, two cups flour, two cups cocoa-nut, soaked in milk, two teaspoons baking-powder.

3. Two eggs, one cup of white sugar, one-half cup of sweet milk, one-quarter cup butter, one and one-half cups of flour, one and one-half tablespoonfuls baking powder. Bake in a moderate oven in pans one inch deep. To prepare the desiccated cocoa-nut, beat the whites of two eggs to a stiff froth, and one cup of pulverized sugar and the cocoa-nut, after soaking it in boiling milk. Spread the mixture between the layers of cake and over the top.

ICE CREAM CAKE.

Two cups white sugar, one cup butter, one cup sweet milk, whites of eight eggs, two teaspoonfuls cream of tartar, one teaspoonful soda, three and one-quarter cups winter wheat flour, if spring wheat flour is used, four cups. Bake in jelly pans. Make an icing as follows: Three cups of sugar, one of water; boil to a thick clear syrup, and pour boiling hot over the whites of three eggs; stir the mixture while pouring in; add one teaspoonful citric acid, flavor with lemon or vanilla, and spread each layer and top.

CUP CAKE.

One cup of butter, one cup of sweet milk, two cups of sugar, three eggs, four cups of flour, one teaspoonful each of saleratus, nutmeg, and cinnamon. You may add a cup of raisins and a cup of currants, if you like; either is good.

COTTAGE CAKE.

Three-fourths of a cup of butter, a cup of white sugar, one and one-half cups flour, four eggs, yolks and whites beaten separately; a tablespoonful sweet milk, one and one-half teaspoonfuls baking powder, lemon, and a little salt. Rub the baking powder into the flour.

CINNAMON CAKE.

One cup sour cream, one cup sugar, one-half cup melted butter, one egg, one-half teaspoon soda. Mix as for cookies, roll out and spread ground cinnamon over the top; then roll up as a roll jelly cake, and slice off with a sharp knife and bake. Any good cookie recipe will do.

COCOA-NUT JUMBLES.

One pound of cocoa-nut grated, three-fourths of a pound of sugar, three eggs, large iron spoonful of flour; drop on buttered pans.

DROP COOKIES.

Four and a half cups of flour, two and a half of sugar, one of milk, one of shortening (half butter and lard), three eggs, two teaspoonfuls baking powder, a very little nutmeg, and a few caraway seeds; rub the sugar and shortening to a cream, beat the eggs till very light, and stir thoroughly, after adding the other ingredients; drop on buttered tins, and bake quickly.

COCOA-NUT BISCUITS.

Ten of sifted flour, three eggs, six of grated cocoa-nut; whisk the eggs until very light, add the sugar, then the cocoa-nut; put a tablespoonful on wafer paper in form of pyramid; put the paper on tins, and bake in a rather cool oven. Keep in tin canisters.

DELICATE CAKE.

1. Two cups sugar, one cup of sweet milk, three-fourths of a cup of butter, three cups of flour, whites of eight egg, three small teaspoonfuls of baking powder, sliced citron.

2. Whites of four eggs, one cup of milk, running over; one-half cup butter, two cups sugar, two and one-half cups flour, heaping teaspoonful baking powder. This makes two loaves. If you want it very nice, use one cup of corn starch in place of one of flour.

PLAIN DOUGHNUTS.

One and one-half cups sugar, three eggs, one-half cup butter (scant), two cups milk, two spoonfuls baking powder, flour enough to roll out.

DOUGHNUTS.

1. Six cups of flour, one and one-half cups of sugar, three teaspoons of baking powder, one teaspoon of salt, butter the size of one-half an egg; mix thoroughly, then add four eggs, well beaten, and moisten with sweet milk until a soft dough. Flavor with nutmeg or cinnamon.

2. Three eggs, one cup sugar, one pint of new milk, salt, nutmeg, and flour enough to permit the spoon to stand upright in the mixture; add two teaspoonfuls baking powder, and beat until very light. Drop by the dessert spoonful into boiling lard. These will not absorb a bit of fat, and are the least pernicious of the doughnut family.

3. Set sponge for them about two or three o'clock; fry them the next forenoon. Make a sponge, using one quart of water and one cake of yeast. Let it rise until very light (about five hours is usually sufficient); then add one coffee-cupful of lard, two of white sugar, three large mashed potatoes, or two eggs (the potatoes are nicer), and a small nutmeg. Let rise again until light. Roll and cut or pull off bits of dough and shape as you like. Lay enough to fry at one time on a floured plate, and set in the oven to warm. Drop in boiling lard, and fry longer than cakes made with baking powder. If the dough is light enough, and you heat it before dropping in the lard, your doughnuts will be delicious.

4. One cup of milk, one egg, one cup of sugar, two teaspoonfuls baking powder, half teaspoonful cinnamon, and flour enough to roll out.

RAISED DOUGHNUTS.

One pint of new milk, four teaspoonfuls of sugar, one-half cup of yeast, and a little salt; stir thick with flour, and let it rise over night; in the morning add as little flour as will make the dough thick enough to roll out about an inch thick; cut in squares of an inch and a half; as you drop them into the hot fat, stretch them out longer, and fry them thoroughly. Lard and suet, in equal proportions, boiling hot, is said to be better for frying cakes than either alone.

DOLLY VARDEN CAKE.

Two cups of sugar, two-thirds of a cup of butter, one cup of sweet milk, three cups of flour, three eggs, one-half teaspoonful of soda, one teaspoon cream tartar. Flavor with lemon. Bake one-half of this in two pans. To the remainder add one tablespoon of molasses, one cup of chopped raisins, one-half cup of currants, piece of citron chopped fine, one teaspoonful cinnamon, cloves, and nutmeg. Bake in two pans, and put in sheets alternately with a little jelly or white of an egg beaten to a froth.

FRUIT CAKE FROM DOUGH.

Two cups sugar, one cup butter, one pint of dough, two eggs, one teaspoon soda, as much fruit as you wish, spices to suit taste; use flour enough to make as stiff as common fruit cake; set in a warm place to raise for one hour. Bake in a moderate oven.

FIG CAKE.

1. For the cake take one cup of butter, two cups of sugar, three and one-half cups of flour, one-half cup of sweet milk, whites of seven eggs, two teaspoons baking powder. Bake in layers. For the filling take a pound of figs, chop fine, and put in a stewpan on the stove; pour over it a teacup of water, and add one-half cup of sugar. Cook all together until soft and smooth. Let it cook, and spread between the layers.

2. One cup butter, two and a half cups sugar, one cup of milk, six cups of flour, three teaspoonfuls baking powder, whites of sixteen eggs, one and a quarter pounds of figs, cut and floured; to be added last.

FRIED CAKES.

One cup sweet milk, one egg, one handful of sugar, one tablespoonful of half lard and half butter, two teaspoonfuls baking powder, a pinch of salt; mix soft, roll out, and fry in hot lard. Very good.

FRUIT CAKE, PAR EXCELLENCE.

One pound of flour, sifted *well*; one pound of sugar, sifted *well*; one pound of butter, two pounds of raisins, three pounds of currants, half a pound of citron, half grated nutmeg, ten eggs, half teaspoonful of cinnamon, one goblet of equal parts brandy and milk. This makes a six-quart pan of cake.

GINGERBREAD.

1. Two cups sugar, one cup butter, one cup molasses, five cups flour, three eggs, one cup sour milk, two tablespoonfuls ginger, one teaspoonful soda; mix quickly and bake.

2. One pint of molasses, one glass of sour milk or cream, one tablespoonful of soda, one-half pint of melted lard; put the soda into the milk and molasses, and beat to a foam. Make the dough very soft.

3. One egg well beaten, one cup molasses, one cup sugar, one cup of butter, one cup of cold tea, two even teaspoons of soda, flour enough to mix about the consistency of cake. Better baked in two sheets than one, as when too thick the outside will be burned or too hard before it is done through.

4. Melt one-half a cup of butter in one cup of molasses and one of sugar, allowing the mixture to become hot; then add one tablespoon of ground ginger, one teaspoon of ground cinnamon, one cup of sweet milk, five cups of flour stirred in with a full half teaspoon of soda; bake in two flat tin pans or gem irons.

SOFT GINGERBREAD.

1. One cup of sugar, one cup of butter, one cup of sour cream, one cup of New Orleans molasses, four cups of sifted flour, one tablespoonful of ginger, two tablespoonfuls of soda, the grated rind of one lemon, three eggs well beaten; stir the butter and sugar together, then add eggs, milk, and flour.

2. Six cups of flour, one cup of butter, one cup of milk, either sweet or sour, two cups of molasses, one cup of brown sugar, three eggs, one tablespoonful of ginger, one teaspoonful allspice, one teaspoonful cloves, one teaspoonful of cinnamon, one teaspoonful soda dissolved in the milk; this makes two large cakes; half portion enough for a small family.

SPONGE GINGERBREAD.

1. Mix one cup of molasses, half cup of melted butter, and tablespoonful of ginger; make them quite warm, and add teaspoonful soda, then add one cup of sour milk, two eggs beaten, and flour to make like pound-cake.

2. In two cups of molasses sift two teaspoonfuls of soda and a dessertspoonful of ginger, and a teaspoonful of powdered cinnamon. Stir to a cream; then add four well-beaten eggs, one-half cup of butter, and one-half cup of lard, melted; one cup of sour milk, in which is dissolved three-fourths of a teaspoonful of soda. Mix all together; then add flour to the consistency of pound-cake.

HARD GINGERBREAD.

To one quart flour allow one pint of molasses, in which has been dissolved one dessertspoonful of soda; flavor with nothing but ginger; do not handle too much, and roll and cut in any shape desired.

GINGER DROPS.

One cup lard, one cup molasses, one cup brown sugar, three eggs, tablespoonful ginger, one tablespoonful soda dissolved in a cup of boiling water, five cups of flour; drop in tablespoons on buttered paper in pans.

GINGER POUND CAKE WITH FRUIT.

Three-fourths pound sugar, three-fourths pound butter, two pounds flour, six eggs, one quart molasses, one-half pound currants, one-fourth pound raisins, three tablespoonfuls ginger, one teaspoonful cloves, two teaspoonfuls cinnamon, three teaspoonfuls baking-powder, **three table-spoonfuls** milk; mix all well, and bake one hour.

GOLD AND SILVER CAKE.

One teacup white sugar, one-half teacup butter, whites of four eggs. two-thirds teacup sweet milk, two teacups flour, two teaspoons baking-powder; flavor. Gold Cake: Same as above, using the yolks of the four eggs, and adding one whole egg.

GINGER-SNAPS.

1. One cup sugar, one of molasses, one of lard or butter, two eggs, one teaspoonful of ginger, one of cinnamon, one tablespoonful of soda, one of vinegar, a little salt; dissolve the soda in a little warm water; add the vinegar to the soda; let it foam well, then add to the dough; mix hard, roll thin; bake quick.

2. Boil together one pint of molasses (sorghum is excellent for this), one teacupful of shortening (some consider beef suet the "snappiest)," a pinch of salt, a tablespoonful of ginger; let it really boil for about two minutes, then set aside to cool; when cool, add two level teaspoonfuls of soda, and beat all together, thoroughly; add flour to make a dough as soft as you can roll out very thin; cut into shapes, and bake in a hot oven, not too hot, as they scorch very easily.

3. Two cups of molasses, one cup of brown sugar, one cup of butter or lard, one tablespoonful ginger, one teaspoonful of soda, dissolved in a very little hot water; mix very thick, and roll thin.

4. One-half teaspoonful each, of salt, soda and ginger, three tablespoonfuls of boiling water, three tablespoonfuls of melted lard; put in a teacup, and fill up with New Orleans molasses. Roll very thin, and as soft as you can. Bake in a quick oven. They will keep for weeks.

5. One full cup of shortening, two cups of brown sugar, two of molasses; boil together a short time, and then let cool. Sift four cups of flour with one-half tablespoonful of ground cloves, one-half tablespoonful of cinnamon, one tablespoonful of allspice, two of ginger, one nutmeg, last of all, one teaspoonful of soda, dissolved in hot water; then let cool. It is better to use one part butter. Make in small rolls with the hand, then cut in pieces the size of a hickory nut, giving them plenty of room in the pans to spread. Bake in a moderate oven. Let them cool before taking out the pans.

6. One coffeecup New Orleans molasses, one cup butter, one cup sugar; place them on the stove, and let it come to a boil, then take off immediately, and add teaspoon soda, and a tablespoon of ginger. Roll thin and bake quickly.

GINGER COOKIES OF ATTRITION FLOUR.

One cup New Orleans molasses, one-half cup sugar, one-half cup butter, one-half cup water, one egg, one heaping teaspoon soda stirred into the molasses, and one heaping teaspoon ginger. Mix till smooth, roll thin, and bake quick.

GRAHAM COOKIES.

Two cups sugar, **one cup sour cream, one-half teaspoonful soda;** mix quickly, roll, and bake. These require less heat and more time in baking than when white flour is used.

GINGER COOKIES.

One cup of molasses, one egg, one-half cup brown sugar, one-half cup butter, one teaspoon soda, one tablespoon ginger; flour to roll.

GOLD CAKE.

The yolks of eight eggs, one whole egg, one-half cup of butter, one and one-half cups of sugar, three-quarters of a cup of milk, two cups of flour, one teaspoonful of cream tartar, one-half teaspoonful of soda.

GENTLEMAN'S FAVORITE.

One-half cup of butter, two cups of sugar, beaten to a cream, seven eggs, beaten separately, two tablespoonfuls of water, two cups of flour, two teaspoonfuls of baking-powder. Bake in jelly-cake pans in a quick oven. Jelly: One egg, a cup of sugar, three grated apples, and one lemon. Stir until it boils and becomes thick. Let it cool before putting on the cake.

SOFT GINGER COOKIES.

Two teacups New Orleans molasses, one teacup of melted lard, one teacup of boiling water, four teaspoonfuls of soda, bought in bulk, one teaspoonful of ginger. Pour the boiling water on the soda; do not knead too stiff. Bake with steady heat.

CHEAP GINGER COOKIES.

One cup molasses, one cup brown sugar, one cup warm water, one cup lard, two tablespoons ginger, one tablespoon soda (dissolved in water), one teaspoon powdered alum, put in last. Mix soft; bake quickly.

HICKORY-NUT COOKIES.

One cup of butter, two cups sugar, four cups of flour, one-half cup of sour milk, one cup of chopped nuts, and one small teaspoonful of soda, three eggs; dip in sugar.

HICKORY-NUT CAKE.

Two teacups of sugar, one-half cup of butter one cup of thin cream, three and one-half cups of flour, three teaspoonfuls of baking-powder, sifted through flour, six eggs beaten separately, one pint of chopped hickory nuts.

HONEY CAKE.

One cup of butter, two cups of honey, four eggs well-beaten, one tablespoonful essence of lemon, half a cupful of sour milk, one teaspoonful soda, flour enough to make it as stiff as can well be stirred; bake at once in a quick oven.

HONEY CAKES.

Mix a quart of strained honey with half a pound of powdered sugar, half a pound of fresh butter, and the juice of two oranges or lemons; warm slightly, just enough to soften the butter; beat the mixture very hard, adding a grated nutmeg; mix in gradually two pounds or less of flour, make into dough stiff enough to roll out easily; beat it well all over with rolling-pin; roll half an inch thick; cut with a tumbler dipped frequently in flour; lay them on shallow tins, slightly buttered, and bake well

IMPERIAL CAKE.

One pound sugar, one pound flour, three-fourths of a pound butter; one pound almonds, blanched and cut fine, one-half pound citron, one-half pound raisins, rind and juice of one lemon, one nutmeg, ten eggs.

ICE-CREAM CAKE.

1. One cup of butter, two cups of sugar, one cup of milk, three cups of flour, whites of five eggs, three teaspoonfuls of baking-powder; bake in thin layers; three small cups of sugar, dissolve in a little water and boil until done for candy; cool a little, and pour over the unbeaten whites of eggs, and heat together a half an hour.

2. Make a sponge cake as follows; four eggs beaten separately, one cup of sugar, one cup of flour, and one teaspoonful of baking-powder; bake in layers, and let them get cold; take two cups of sweet cream, and beat until light; sweeten and flavor with vanilla; pour hot water over a pound of almonds to remove the skin, chop fine, and then mix with the cream; spread thickly between the layers of cake.

JELLY ROLL.

Four eggs, one cup of sugar, one cup of flour, one teaspoonful baking-powder, pinch of salt; spread thin on long tins; flavor the jelly and spread on while hot and roll up.

JUMBLES.

1. Three-fourths of a cup of butter, one and a half cups of sugar, three eggs, three tablespoonfuls of milk, flour to roll, and teaspoonful of baking-powder, roll; sprinkle with granulated sugar, gently roll it in; cut out, with a hole in center, and bake.

2. Two cups of sugar, one cup of butter, four teaspoonfuls of sweet cream, one teaspoonful of cream tartar, one-half teaspoonful soda; knead with flour just stiff enough to roll. After they are cut, dip one side in fine sugar; three eggs.

3. One pound of white sugar, three-fourths of a pound of butter, five eggs, leaving out the yolks of two, and nearly two pounds of flour; spice if you like. Roll thin, and sprinkle granulated sugar over them before baking.

4. One and a half cups sugar, one-half a cup of butter, two eggs, one-half teaspoon soda, one of cream of tartar (dissolved in a little sweet milk), flour enough to make like pie crust. Bake in waffle-irons. Fill the little holes with light and dark jelly, alternately.

LADY FINGERS.

Four ounces of sugar, four yolks of eggs, mix well; three ounces of flour, a little salt. Beat the four whites to a stiff froth, stir the whites into the mixture a little at a time until all is in. Butter a shallow pan. Squirt through a confectioner's syringe or a little piece of paper rolled up. Dust with sugar, and bake in a not too hot oven.

LEMON JELLY CAKE.

Cake: One cup sugar, one egg, butter size of an egg, one cup milk, three cups flour. Jelly: Rind and juice of one lemon, one egg, one cup sugar, three teaspoonfuls corn starch, one cup hot water; mix, and let it boil up once.

LEMON CREAM CAKE.

Take three eggs, two cups of sugar, one tablespoonful of melted butter, one and one-fourth cups of milk, three teaspoonfuls of baking powder, enough flour to thicken; bake in jelly cake pans.

LEMON CREAM FOR CAKE.

Two lemons grated, rind and all, one-quarter pound of butter, one-half pound of sugar, six eggs; beat the eggs very light; heat the butter, sugar, and lemon, stir in eggs slowly; let the mixture boil a few minutes, stirring constantly; when cold, spread on the cakes as you would jelly.

MOLASSES FRUIT CAKE.

One cup molasses, one and three-quarters cup light brown sugar, one cup cold water. Boil the molasses, sugar, and butter together, and set aside to cool; flour as thick as a pound cake, then add eggs; beat this well, then add one pound raisins, one of currants and one-half of citron, with two heaping teaspoons of flour mixed through the fruit; bake nearly two hours.

MARY'S SPONGE CAKE.

Ten eggs, yolks and whites beaten separately; two cups of sugar, two cups of flour, two teaspoonfuls of baking-powder, grated rind and juice of one lemon; the flour sifted and stirred in as lightly as possible.

WHITE SPONGE CAKE.

Whites of eleven eggs, one even tumblerful of flour, one and one-half tumblerfuls of granulated sugar, one teaspoonful of cream tartar, one teaspoonful of vanilla; sift the flour three or four times before measuring. Beat the eggs on a large platter very stiff, then add the sugar and flour very lightly. This fills a three-quart pan, which must have a tube in it. Bake thirty-five or forty minutes in a moderate oven, then try with a broom straw. When done, remove from the oven, and let stand on the tube to cool. Success depends upon having the eggs very stiff, and adding the sugar and flour lightly.

MACAROONS.

One-half pound of almonds blanched, one-half pound of loaf sugar, whites of eggs, one by one. Pound the almonds in a mortar, occasionally putting in a little rose-water to moisten; add sugar. Beat the eggs until they are very stiff, then add enough of the mixture to make a paste. Take a little flour in your hands and mold into small cakes. Bake a few minutes in a moderately hot oven. The top of the oven should be the hottest.

WHITE AND YELLOW MOUNTAIN CAKE.

Two cups sugar, two-thirds cup butter, whites of seven eggs, well beaten, two-thirds cup sweet milk, two cups flour, one cup corn starch, two teaspoons baking powder. Bake in jelly-cake tins. Frosting: Whites of three eggs and some sugar, beaten together—not quite as stiff as for frosting; spread over the cake, add some grated cocoa-nut, then put your cakes together; put cocoa-nut or frosting for the top. Yellow mountain: Yolks of ten eggs, one cup butter, two of sugar, one of milk, three of flour, one teaspoon soda, two of cream tartar.

MARBLE CAKE.

1. Light part: One and one-half cups white sugar, one-half cup butter, one-half cup sweet milk, one-half teaspoon soda, one teaspoon cream tartar, whites of four eggs, two and one-half cups flour; beat the eggs and sugar together, mix the cream of tartar with the flour, and dissolve the soda in the milk. Dark part: One cup brown sugar, one-half cup molasses, one-half cup sour milk, one-half teaspoon soda, two and one-half cups browned flour, yolks of four eggs, one-half teaspoon each of ground cloves and cinnamon; ingredients mixed the same as light part. When both are prepared, put in the cake-pan alternate layers of each, or put them in spots on each other, making what is called leopard cake, until all is used, then bake as usual.

2. For white part: One cup of butter, three cups of sugar, five cups of flour, one-half cup of sweet milk, one-half teaspoonful of soda, whites of eight eggs; flavor with lemon. Dark part: One-half cup of butter, two cups of brown sugar, one cup of molasses, one cup of sour milk, four cups of flour, one teaspoonful of soda, yolks of eight eggs, one whole egg, spices of all kinds. Put in pan, first a layer of dark, then a layer of light, and finish with a dark layer.

MARBLE SPICE CAKE.

Three-quarters of a pound of flour, well dried; one pound white sugar, one-half pound butter, whites of fourteen eggs, one tablespoonful cream of tartar mixed with the flour. When the cake is mixed, take out about a teacup of batter and stir into it one teaspoonful of cinnamon, one of mace, one of cloves, two of spice, and one of nutmeg. Fill your mold about an inch deep with the white batter, and drop into this, in several places, a spoonful of the dark mixture. Then put in another layer of white, and add the dark as before. Repeat this until your batter is used up. This makes one large cake.

NUT CAKE.

1. Two cups of sugar, one of butter, three of flour, one of cold water, four eggs, baking powder, one and one-half cups kernels of hickory or white walnuts.

2. One cup butter, two of white sugar, four of flour, one of sweet milk, eight eggs (the whites), three teaspoonfuls of baking powder,

two cups hickory **nuts, picked out** of the shells, **and** cut up with a clean knife.

ORANGE CAKE.

1. Grated rind of one orange; two cups sugar, whites of four eggs and yolks of five, one cup sweet milk, one cup butter, two large teaspoonfuls baking powder, to be sifted through with the flour; bake quick in jelly tins. Filling: Take the white of the one egg that was left, beat to a frost, add a little sugar, and the juice of the orange; beat together and spread between the layers. If oranges are not to be had, lemons will do instead.

2. Peel the oranges, and chop very fine; to two oranges take one-half of a lemon, squeeze the juice, and chop the rest; one teacup of sugar. Bake a crust as for short-cake, cut open, butter well, and lay the orange between.

3. Make a silver cake, and bake in jelly-cake pans; one large orange, grated; one cup of sugar, one egg (one large, or two small ones); cook all until a jelly, and spread between the layers.

PINE-APPLE CAKE.

One cup of **butter, two** cups of sugar, one **cup of** milk, three cups of flour, whites **of six** eggs and yolks of four, **three** teaspoonfuls of baking powder well mixed through flour; bake in jelly-cake pans; grate pine-apple; sprinkle with sugar, spread between the layers; pine-apple jam may be substituted; frost the outside; beat two tablespoonfuls of the pine-apple into the frosting.

PEACH CAKE.

Bake sponge cake **in layers; cut peaches in very thin** slices, and spread upon the cake; **sweeten, flavor, and whip some** sweet cream, and spread over each layer, and **over the top.**

PORCUPINE CAKE.

One large cup white sugar, one-half cup butter, one egg, one cup sweet milk, one and one-half teaspoonfuls baking powder, two cups flour; mix above ingredients together as usual, and bake; when the cake is cold and just before serving, pour the following cream over it, after having stuck a teacupful of soft almonds over the top of it:

CREAM: Two eggs, one quart milk, **one cup** of sugar, two tablespoonfuls corn starch, one-half teaspoonful **vanilla;** dissolve the starch in a little milk, add beaten **eggs, sugar, and the rest of the** milk, **and cook as a** custard.

PUFF CAKE.

Two cups of sugar, three eggs, three-fourths cup of butter, one cup of milk, three cups of flour, two spoonfuls baking-powder; bake quickly in loaf.

POUND CAKE.

One pound granulated sugar **and** one pound flour, **both** thoroughly sifted; three-fourths pound butter (well washed), ten eggs; separate the eggs; beat sugar and butter to a smooth cream with the hand; add the beaten yolks; then add a little of both flour and white of eggs at a time, stirring briskly all the time until all is added; bake in a large pan, with cup or tube in center; a slow, steady fire is necessary.

RIBBON CAKE.

Two cups of sugar, half a cup of butter, three eggs, three-fourths cup of milk, flour to make the proper consistency, and a teaspoonful baking powder; take out one-third, and add to it a cup raisins, one of currants, citron, spice, and tablespoonful of molasses; bake in layers, and put together with jelly, while warm, having the fruit-cake in the middle.

RIBBON FIG CAKE.

WHITE PART: Two cups of sugar, two-thirds cup of butter, beaten to a cream; add two-thirds of a cup of milk, and three cups of flour, alternately, two teaspoonfuls of baking-powder, and then the whites of eight eggs, beaten light; bake in layers.

GOLD PART: Beat a little more than half a cup of butter and a cup of sugar to a cream; add the yolks of seven eggs and one whole egg, well beaten, one-half cup of milk, and one and one-half cups of flour, mixed with one teaspoonful baking-powder; season strongly with cinnamon and allspice.

Put half the gold cake into a pan, and lay on it halved figs closely; dust with a little flour, and then put on the rest of the cake, and bake; put the gold cake between the white cakes, using frosting between them, and cover with frosting.

SHORT CAKE.

Take one pound of sifted flour, quarter pound of butter, and half as much lard, very little salt, a pinch of soda, well dissolved in just vinegar enough to cover it; work all well together with ice-cold water enough to make a stiff dough; roll it into a paste half an inch thick; cut it into cakes; pick the top with a fork, bake in a quick oven.

SPICE CAKE.

1. One cup of butter, two cups of sugar, one-half cup of milk, five eggs, two cups of flour, teaspoonful each of cinnamon and allspice, nutmeg, essence of lemon, three teaspoonfuls of baking-powder.

2. One and one-half cups butter, three cups sugar, one cup sour milk, five cups of flour, five eggs, one teaspoon soda; cinnamon, cloves, nutmeg, allspice, each one teaspoon; one pound raisins. This will make the cakes of usual size, and will keep for two months.

3. One cup sugar, one egg, one-half cup of cream, one-half cup onttermilk, one small teaspoon soda, one-half teaspoon ginger, the same of cinnamon and salt.

4. One cup of butter, two cups of sugar, one cup of milk, the yolks of eight eggs, three cups of flour, three teaspoonfuls of baking-powder, one tablespoonful each of cinnamon, nutmeg, cloves, and allspice.

SILVER CAKE.

Whites of eight eggs, two cups sugar, two-thirds of a cup of butter, one-half cup of sweet milk, three cups of flour, two teaspoonfuls of cream of tartar, one-half teaspoon soda.

SNOW CAKE.

Three-fourths of a cup of butter, two cups of sugar, one cup milk, one cup corn starch, two cups flour, one and one-half teaspoons of baking-powder; mix corn starch, flour, and baking-powder together, add the butter and sugar alternately with the milk; lastly add the whites of seven eggs. Flavor to taste.

SPONGE GINGER-BREAD.

In two cups of molasses, sift two teaspoonfuls of soda and a dessert-spoonful of ginger, and a teaspoonful of powdered cinnamon. Stir to a cream; then add four well-beaten eggs, one-half cup of butter, and one-half cup of lard, melted; one cup of sour milk, in which is dissolved three-fourths of a teaspoonful of soda. Mix all together; then add flour to the consistency of pound cake.

SPANISH BUNS.

1. Four eggs, three-fourths of a cup of butter, two cups of sugar; beat butter and sugar to a cream, and eggs separately, one cup of milk, one tablespoonful of cinnamon, two cups of flour. Bake in a shallow pan, like soft gingerbread, and when done spread over the top a thin icing made of the white of one egg, a little sugar, and half a teaspoonful of cinnamon.

2. One pint of flour, one pint sugar, one cup of sweet milk, one cup of butter, four eggs, beaten separate, one tablespoon of cinnamon, one teaspoon of cloves, one teaspoon of soda, two teaspoons of cream of tartar, or three spoons of baking-powder; bake on tins, an inch thick, and, when taken from the oven, sprinkle with white sugar while hot.

SPONGE CAKE.

1. Two cups of white sugar, four eggs, beat separately; two cups of sifted flour; in which put two teaspoonfuls of baking-powder, three-fourths of a cup of hot water; be sure and pour water in last, and drop in a little at a time.

2. Take three eggs, beat three minutes, then add one and one-half cups sugar, and beat five minutes; add one teacup flour, and one teaspoonful cream of tartar, and beat three minutes; add one-half teaspoon soda, dissolved in one-half cup cold water, and another cup of flour, beat enough to mix well. Flavor and bake in a deep pan in a quick oven.

3. Four eggs, one cup of sugar; yolks and sugar beaten until very light, and whites beaten separately; one cup of flour, into which has been sifted one teaspoonful of baking-powder. Flavor to taste.

EASY SPONGE CAKE.

Three eggs beaten one minute; add one and one-half cups of sugar, beaten five minutes, one cup of flour beaten one minute; one-half cup of cold water and another cup of flour, in which has been mixed two teaspoons of baking powder, beaten one minute. Bake in a slow oven.

SEA FOAM.

Whites of ten eggs beaten to a stiff froth, one and one-half cups of sifted sugar, one cup sifted flour, one teaspoonful cream of tartar; put into rings, and bake quick.

SCOTCH SHORT-CAKE.

Take one-half pound of slightly salted butter, and one pound of flour; then mix flour and butter with hands; then add four ounces of loaf sugar, and work all into a smooth ball; then roll out until it is an inch thick; prick over with a fork, and pinch round the edges, and bake for half an hour in oven, and with a moderate fire, in a round or square pan, according to taste.

STRAWBERRY SHORT-CAKE.

First prepare the berries by picking; after they have been well washed—the best way to wash them is to hold the boxes under the faucet and let a gentle stream of water run over them into an earthen bowl—then drain and pick them into an earthen bowl; now take the potato-masher and bruise them, and cover with a thick layer of white sugar; now set them aside until the cake is made. Take a quart of sifted flour, one-half cup of sweet butter, one egg well beaten, three teaspoonfuls of baking powder, and milk enough to make a rather stiff dough; knead well, and roll with the rolling-pin till about one inch thick; bake till a nice brown, and when done remove it to the table, turn it out of the pan, and with a light, sharp knife cut it down lengthwise and crossways; now run the knife through it, and lay it open for a few moments, just to let the steam escape (the steam ruins the color of the berries); then set the bottom crust on the platter, cover thickly with berries an inch and a half deep; lay the top crust on the fruit, dust thickly with powdered sugar, and if any berry juice is left in the bowl, pour it round the cake, not over it, and you will have a delicious short-cake.

SEED CAKES.

One cup of butter, two cups of sugar, one cup of milk, three eggs, two teaspoonfuls of caraway seeds, two teaspoonfuls cream of tartar, one teaspoonful soda, and flour enough to roll them smooth. Half this recipe makes a good many.

WATERMELON CAKE.

White part: Two cups of pulverized sugar, two-thirds of a cup of butter, two-thirds of a cup of sweet milk, three cups of flour, whites of five eggs, one tablespoonful of baking powder.

Red part: One cup of red sugar, one-third of a cup of butter, one-third of a cup of sweet milk, two cups of flour, one tablespoonful of baking powder, yolks of five eggs, half a pound of raisins.

Put the red part in the center of the pan, and the white part on the outside.

WEDDING CAKE.

One pound of fine sugar, one pound of butter, one-half pound of citron chopped fine, one pound of flour, one pound of currants, twelve eggs, one and one-quarter pounds of raisins seeded and chopped, one tablespoonful of cinnamon, two tablespoonfuls of nutmeg, two tablespoonfuls of cloves, wine-glass of best brandy; stir to a cream the butter and sugar; add the beaten yolks of the eggs, and stir all very well before putting in half the flour; then add spices, next the whipped whites stirred in alternately with the rest of flour; last, the fruit and brandy; bake three hours in a slow oven.

WHITE CAKE.

One cup of butter, three cups of sugar, beaten to a cream; four cups of flour, and half cup corn starch, added alternately, with a cup of sweet milk; two teaspoonfuls baking powder; flavor to taste; lastly, the whites of twelve eggs beaten to a stiff froth.

WHITE POUND CAKE.

One pound sugar, one-half pound butter, beaten to a cream; one pound of flour, two teaspoonfuls of baking powder, whites of sixteen eggs, beaten to a stiff froth, and added last; put into a moderate oven, and gradually increase the heat; cover with frosting while warm.

TEA, COFFEE, CHOCOLATE.

TEA.

People must consult their own taste as to kind of tea. Mixed is the best to use with ice. Allow one teaspoonful for each person. Use boiling water, but do not boil the tea, and use while fresh. Tea is best made in an earthen tea pot—never in tin. Iced tea should be made several hours before it is needed, and then set upon ice. When ready to use it, sweeten, and drink without milk or cream. Use cracked ice to put into the glass.

VIENNA COFFEE.

Leach or filter the coffee through a French filterer, or any of the many coffee pots that filter instead of boiling the coffee; allow one tablespoonful of ground coffee to each person, and one extra for the pot. Put one quart of cream into a milk-boiler, or, if you have none, into a pitcher in a pail of boiling water; put it where the water will keep boiling, beat the white of an egg to a froth, then add to the egg three tablespoonfuls of cold milk, mix the egg and cold milk thoroughly together; when hot, remove the cream from the fire, and add the egg and cold milk; stir it all together briskly for a minute or two, and then ser

COFFEE.

Make a flannel bag, hem the top, and run through it a small wire, by which the bag may be suspended in the pot, so that the bottom of the bag comes within two inches of the bottom of the pot. Grind the coffee fine and put into the bag, then pour the proper quantity of water through the bag into the pot; let the water be boiling when poured in; then set the pot back where it can simmer gently fifteen minutes, and you have good coffee, without egg-shells or cold water to settle it. Coffee that needs settling is not properly made. The flannel bag should be made of flannel so fine that the coffee will not sift through.

CHOCOLATE.

1. Take one and one-half quarts of good milk, and one-half pint of cream, to one-fourth of a pound of grated chocolate; let the milk and cream come to a scald. After mixing the chocolate with a little cold milk, stir it into the scalding milk and let it simmer for fifteen minutes, adding one-fourth of a cup of sugar, and stirring occasionally.

2. Scrape two sticks of chocolate, and boil in half a cup of water. Stir to a smooth paste. Sweeten a pint of milk with loaf sugar, and, when boiling, pour on to the chocolate and let it boil together a few seconds, stirring it well. Serve immediately. Some persons prefer a little water instead of all milk. Sweeten a little cream and whip to a froth, and place on the top of each cup.

MOCK CREAM FOR TEA OR COFFEE.

To a pint of milk, take the yolk of one egg; put on the fire and let it come to a scald. It is improved by adding a little cream when it is cool.

FRESH FRUITS.

TO CRYSTALLIZE FRUIT.

Pick out the finest of any kind of fruit, leave in the stones; beat the whites of three eggs to a stiff froth; lay the fruit in the beaten egg, with the stem upward; drain them and beat the part that drips off again; select them out, one by one, and dip them into a cup of finely-powdered sugar; cover a pan with a sheet of fine paper, place the fruit on it, and set it in a cool oven; when the icing on the fruit becomes firm, pile them on a dish, and set them in a cold place.

PINE-APPLES.

Slice on a slaw-cutter, or very thin with a knife; mix with very finely-powdered sugar. Set on ice till ready to serve.

ORANGES.

Slice, mix with powdered sugar, and strew grated cocoa-nut over the top. Are also nice served whole, the skins quartered and turned down. Form in a pyramid with bananas and white grapes.

MELONS.

Melons are much nicer if kept on ice until time for serving. Cut off a slice at each end of the water-melon, then cut through the center; stand on end on a platter. Cantaloupe melons should have the seeds removed before **sending to the table.** Eat with a spoonful of strained honey in each **half of melon,**

BANANAS AND CREAM.

Peel, slice, and heap up in a glass dessert-dish, and serve raw, with fine sugar and cream.

JELLIES, JAMS, PRESERVES, ETC.

GENERAL HINTS.

A flannel **bag is the** best for straining jelly. If possible, avoid putting jelly in any stage in a metal vessel. For every pint of strained juice, allow a pound of sugar. Granulated sugar is the best.

In all cases it is best to boil the juice fifteen minutes before adding the sugar, **thus insuring the** necessary evaporation, and avoiding the liability to burn it.

It is well also **to beat the** sugar before it is added, as, in so doing, the boiling process **will not be** interrupted.

All jelly should be made over a **moderate fire,** and be carefully watched and skimmed.

In making **preserves, there must be no economy of time and** care, and the fruit **must be fresh.**

Boil without covering, **and very gently.**

Jellies and jams must not be covered and put away **until cold.**

Marmalades require constant stirring.

In making jams, boil the fruit fifteen minutes before **adding the sugar.** Mash the fruit before cooking.

JELLIED APPLES.

Peel and core, whole, small-sized apples; put them into water enough to cover, **with some lemons, and** boil until tender, and then take out; make a syrup of one-half pound of sugar to one pound of fruit, and put apples and lemons, sliced, into the syrup, and boil very gently until clear, **and** then skim out into a deep dish; to the syrup add an **ounce of** isinglass **or gelatine** dissolved in a little **water,** and let it boil a moment; garnish **the apples** with the **lemon slices, and** strain the syrup over them.

APPLE JELLY.

1. Peel two dozen golden **pippins** or Margills, **boil them with one** quart **of** water and half **an ounce of** isinglass; **when the isinglass is** dissolved, and the apples reduced to a pulp, strain; add the juice of a lemon **and the** grated rind **with a** pound and a quarter of loaf sugar; boil together twenty minutes, and strain. It is served at the table for sweetening apple pies.

2. Quarter the apples and cover them with water; cook and strain them, and to a pint of juice put three-fourths of a pound of sugar; boil twenty minutes, and flavor with lemon or vanilla.

CRAB APPLE JELLY.

1. Procure the Siberian crab, pick out those that are perfectly firm; wash in water, and pour over them just enough water to cover; let them cook until soft, then strain through a jelly-bag; add one pound of sugar to one pint of juice; let boil twenty minutes.

2. Take good, sound crab apples; cut in half; take out stems and blossoms; put in preserving kettle, and pour in cold water till the crab apples are entirely covered; then place it over a slow fire, and allow it to come to the boiling point, or until the apples are quite soft; strain them through a colander (not the pulp, but simply the juice) into an earthen vessel, and let it stand over-night; in the morning strain with care through a flannel jelly-bag, and measure; place it again in the preserving kettle, and allow it to come slowly to boiling point; let it boil for fifteen minutes, and meanwhile skim with care; for every pint of this juice when strained, allow one pound of granulated sugar; place the sugar in a warm oven in shallow pans or plates, and heat; take care not to have it warm enough to melt; when the juice has boiled fifteen minutes pour in the warm sugar, and let all boil together about five minutes more; then take from the fire and pour into jelly-glasses or bowls.

CURRANT JELLY.

1. Mash the currants without heating, having removed them from the stems; strain through a flannel bag; measure by pints, and place over the fire, in preserving kettle; let it boil fifteen minutes, carefully skimming; then for every pint of juice add a pound of heated sugar, and boil ten minutes longer, put in glasses or bowls, and seal.

2. This recipe has three advantages: First, it never fails, as the old plan is sure to do five times out of eight; secondly, it requires but half the usual quantity of sugar, and so retains the grateful acidity and peculiar flavor of the fruit; thirdly, it is by far less troublesome than the usual method. Weigh the currants without taking the trouble to remove the stems; do not wash them, but carefully remove leaves and whatever may adhere to them; to each pound of fruit allow half the weight of granulated or pure loaf sugar; put a few currants into a porcelain-lined kettle, and press them with a potato-masher, or anything convenient, in order to secure sufficient liquid to prevent burning, then add the remainder of the fruit, and boil freely for twenty minutes; stirring occasionally to prevent burning; take out and strain carefully through a three-cornered bag of strong close texture, putting the liquid into either earthen or wooden vessels—never in tin, as the action of the acid on tin materially affects both color and flavor; when strained, return the liquid to the kettle, without the trouble of measuring, and let it boil thoroughly for a moment or so, and then add the sugar; the moment the sugar is entirely dissolved, the jelly is done, and must be immediately dished, or placed in glasses; it will jelly upon the side of the cup as it is taken up, leaving no doubt as to the result. Gather the fruit early, as soon as fully ripe, since the pulp softens, and the juice is less rich if allowed to remain long after ripening. In our climate, the first week in July is usually considered the time to make currant jelly. Never gather currants or other soft or small seed fruit

immediately after a rain for preserving purposes, as they are greatly impoverished by the moisture absorbed. In preserving all fruits of this class, if they are boiled until tender or transparent in a small quantity of water, and the sugar is added afterward, the hardness of the seeds, so objectionable in small fruits, will thus be avoided. A delicious jam may be made of blackberries, currants, and raspberries, or with currants with a few raspberries to flavor, by observing the above suggestion, and adding sugar, pound for pound, and boiling about twenty minutes.

CURRANT JELLY WITHOUT COOKING.

Press the juice from the currants, and strain it; to every pint put a pound of fine white sugar; mix them together until the sugar is dissolved; then put it in jars; seal them, and expose to a hot sun for two or three days.

GRAPE JELLY.

Grapes to be used before they are ripe—when just turning. Stem the grapes, and slightly cook them; then strain and take a pint of sugar to a pint of juice. It makes the jelly of a light-red color, and much finer flavored than ripe grapes

APPLE JAM.

Ten pounds of best cooking apples, pare and slice; seven pounds of loaf sugar, the juice of three lemons, rind of one lemon, boil together slowly, stir, and mash well; when they become clear, put into molds. The apples should be put in water, to preserve their color.

APPLE PRESERVES.

Take three-quarters of a pound of sugar to a pound of apples, make a syrup of the sugar and water, in which root ginger has been boiled until strongly flavored; add a few slices of lemon, and when the syrup is clear add the apples, a few at a time, and cook until transparent; pour the syrup over the apples when cold.

CHERRY JAM.

To each pound of cherries allow three-quarters of a pound of sugar; stone them, and as you do so throw the sugar gradually into the dish with them; cover them, and let them set over night; next day boil slowly until the cherries and sugar form a smooth, thick mass; put up in jars.

DAMSON PRESERVES.

To four pounds of damsons use three pounds of sugar; prick each damson with a needle; dissolve the sugar with one-half pint of water, and put it on the fire; when it simmers put in as many damsons as will lie on the top; when they open take them out and lay them on a dish, and put others in, and so on until all have been in; then put them all in the kettle together and let them stew until done; put them in jars, and seal them.

GREEN GAGE PRESERVES.

When the fruit is ripe wipe them clean, and to one pound of fruit put one-quarter pound of sugar, which will make a fine syrup; boil the fruit until it is perfectly done in this syrup; then make a fresh syrup of one pound of fruit to one pound of sugar; moisten the sugar with water; when the syrup boils put in the fruit and leave for fifteen minutes; then put the fruit in jars; boil the syrup until thick, and when only milk-warm pour it over the fruit; tie the jars tightly, and keep in a warm place.

CITRON PRESERVES.

Pare, core, and slice, or cut into fancy shapes; allow one pound of sugar to one pound of fruit; flavor with lemon and ginger root; slice the lemon and boil in water until clear; save the water, and put the lemon in cold water until needed; put the ginger root into water, and boil until the water is sufficiently flavored, and then remove; put the sugar into the ginger water and boil and skim very thoroughly; then put in the citron and juice of the lemons, and boil until transparent, when almost done add the lemon slices; skim out the citron carefully, and pour the syrup over them.

GRAPE PRESERVES.

Press with the fingers the pulp from the fruit; put the pulp on the fire and boil; then press the whole through a colander or sieve to remove the seeds; put juice, pulp, and skins together, and to every pint add a pound of sugar, and boil until thick.

NONPARIEL PRESERVES.

Take cucumbers, as near uniform size as possible, about half grown, and lay in strong brine for six or seven days; wash and soak them twenty-four hours in clear water, changing it three or four times; take a metal kettle and line it with grape leaves, lay in the cucumbers with some alum sprinkled in, and cover with clear water and vine leaves; then cover the kettle close, and green them as for pickles, but not boil them; when greened put them in ice water; after they have become perfectly cold slit them open on one side, and with a small knife take out the seeds; then stuff them with a mixture of chopped citron and raisins, then sew up; weigh them, and for every pound of cucumbers allow a pound of sugar and a pint of water; let the water and sugar boil, and after thoroughly skimming it drop in the cucumbers; let them boil slowly for half an hour, and then take them out and put in the sun on a shallow dish, and allow the syrup to boil down, after which add some few slices of ginger root, put back the cucumbers and let all boil again about five minutes; take out, put in glass jars, and seal cold. These sweetmeats improve with age.

PINEAPPLE PRESERVES.

Pare and core and cut in small slices on a slaw-cutter; to a pound of pineapple put one pound of sugar; let it boil twenty minutes; put in jars, and cover with egg-papers.

PINEAPPLE JAM.

Pare, core, and grate fine on a grater; then proceed the same as for pineapple preserves.

PLUM BUTTER.

One peck of plums, one-half bushel of sweet apples; cook the apples and plums in separate kettles until quite soft, only putting in enough water to prevent sticking to the bottom of the kettle; when soft put through a colander, and then to each pound of mixture allow three-fourths of a pound of white sugar; let it cook for a short time, and bottle.

PEAR PRESERVES.

Preserve as directed for quince preserves, and flavor with ginger root and lemon, or with a few cloves stuck into the fruit.

PEACH PRESERVES.

Pare the fruit carefully, and remove the pits; boil the pits in water until all the flavor is extracted, allowing one-half a pint for each pound of fruit; add more as it evaporates; add the sugar; skim carefully, and when clear add the peaches, a few at a time; cook gently for twelve minutes, and then skim out carefully, and add more until all are done; then pour the syrup over the whole; the next day drain off the syrup, and boil a few minutes, and pour again over the fruit; repeat this for three or four days in succession until the fruit is clear.

PLUM PRESERVES.

Wash and prick the plums and lay in a stone jar; allow a pound of sugar to a pound of fruit; make a rich syrup, and pour, while hot, over the plums, and cover closely; drain off and boil the syrup for four successive days, and put altogether in the kettle and boil for half an hour.

QUINCE PRESERVES.

Pare, core, and quarter the fruit; boil in clear water enough to cover until they are tender; make a syrup with two pounds of sugar and a pint of water; when boiling hot, add the quinces; allow three-quarters of a pound of sugar to a pound of fruit; use parings and cores for jelly.

STRAWBERRY OR RASPBERRY JAM.

To one pound of berries, allow one and one-quarter pounds of sugar; heat an earthen bowl hot on the stove, then remove it from the stove and put into it the berries and sugar, and beat them hard with a wooden spoon for as much as an hour and a half; do not cook at all; put in jars with egg papers.

RASPBERRY JAM.

Allow one pound of sugar to a pound of berries, and one pint of currant juice to five pounds of berries, adding one extra pound of sugar for each pint of currant juice; mix the berries and sugar in layers, then mash the berries with potato-masher; add currant juice, and let boil one-half hour; put in tumblers, cover with egg-papers, while hot; make blackberry, strawberry, and currant jam the same way, omitting the currant juice.

TO PRESERVE WATERMELON RINDS.

1. Soak the fruit in salt water three days, in fresh water three days, boil in alum water; soak in fresh water over a day and night, changing the water several times; boil in ginger water; to one pound of fruit, one and one-fourth pounds of sugar, and put in ginger and mace; flavor with oil of lemon.

2. After cutting your rind properly, boil it in clean water, with vine leaves between each layer; a piece of alum, the size of a hickory nut, is sufficient for a kettleful; after boiling it, put it into ice-water to cool; then repeat this a second time, each time putting it to cool; each time boiling one hour; prepare the syrup with one and one-fourth pounds of sugar to each pound of fruit; green ginger boiled in the water you make your syrup with, flavors it, or three lemons to six pounds of fruit; if the syrup thickens too fast, add a little water. The rind should be boiled in the water untill clear and green.

APPLE MARMALADE.

Twelve pounds of apples, three pounds of brown sugar, three lemons; boil slowly; mash well.

ORANGE MARMALADE.

Separate the pulp from the skin; boil the skins until very tender, then chop fine; separate as much as possible the white part from the yellow—using only the yellow—then to every pound of pulp and skins add one pound of sugar, and boil twenty minutes.

2. Allow three-fourths of a pound of sugar to a pound of fruit; peel and quarter the oranges; remove carefully the inner skin from the peels, and boil in a large quantity of water for two hours, changing the water, and renewing with hot; then cut into fine shreds; press the inside of oranges through a sieve; put into the preserving kettle with a little water, and after it has boiled a few moments, add the sugar and shredded peel, and boil twenty minutes; the rind and juice of lemons in the proportion of one to five is an improvement.

PEACH MARMALADE.

Use three-fourths of a pound of sugar to a pound of fruit; boil the pits until the water is well flavored; peel and quarter the peaches, and add to the water boiling, half an hour before adding the sugar; stir constantly; boil an hour after adding the sugar.

QUINCE MARMALADE.

Ten pounds of ripe, yellow quinces, wash clean, pare, and core them, and cut them into small pieces. To each pound of quinces, allow half a pound of white sugar; put the parings and cores into a kettle, with enough water to cover them; boil slowly until quite soft; then having put the quinces with the sugar into a porcelain kettle, strain over them, through a cloth, the liquid from the parings, and cover; boil the whole over a clear fire until it becomes quite smooth and thick, keeping it covered except when you are skimming it, and watching and stirring closely to prevent sticking at the bottom; when cold, put in glass jars.

CREAMATED APPLES.

Choose apples that will cook nicely, that is, will cook without breaking into pieces; pare and core them whole; make a syrup with a pound of sugar and a pint of water; put in the apples and boil gently until about three-fourths done; skim them out, and place them for a few minutes in a quick oven; boil down the syrup, and when the apples are taken from the oven and are still hot, fill the center with marmalade, and roll each apple in the syrup; put them on a dish in the form of a dome, or as you may desire, and pour over them a meringue of eggs and sugar, and set into the oven to brown.

JELLIED ORANGES.

Boil small oranges in water until they can be easily pierced with a straw, and then cut in quarters; allow half a pound of sugar to a pound of fruit, and make a clear syrup; put in the fruit and cook over a slow fire until the fruit is clear; then stir in an ounce of isinglass and let it boil again; first take out the oranges and strain the jelly over them.

PIE PLANT.

Cut in pieces, put into a baking-dish in layers, with an equal weight of sugar; cover closely and bake.

APPLE BUTTER.

Fill a very large kettle with cider, and boil it until reduced to one-half of the original quantity; then have ready some fine, juicy apples, pared, cored, and quartered, and put as many into the kettle as can be kept moist by the cider; stir it frequently, and when the apples are stewed quite soft take them out with a skimmer that has holes in it, and put them into a tub; then add more apples to the cider, and stew them soft in the same manner, stirring them nearly all the time with a stick; have at hand some more boiled cider to thin the apple butter, in case you should find it too thick in the bottle; at night leave the apples to cool in a tub, covered with cloths, and finish the next day by boiling the apples and cider till the consistence is that of soft marmalade, and the color a very dark brown; twenty minutes or one-half hour before you finally take from the fire, add powdered cinnamon, cloves, and nutmeg to your taste; if the spice is boiled too long it will lose its flavor; when cold put into stone jars, and cover closely; it must not be boiled in a brass or metal kettle, on account of the verdigris which the acid will collect in it, and which will render the apple butter extremely unwholesome, not to say poisonous.

2. One-half bushel of pippin apples, one gallon of sweet, fresh cider; cook thoroughly, and put through a colander; place on the fire, and add six pounds of white sugar; stir constantly while cooking, to prevent burning; in the course of two or three hours take a little out in a dish, and if it has a watery appearance it should be cooked longer, or until quite thick.

LEMON BUTTER.

The grated rind and juice of three lemons, three-fourths of a pound of sugar, one-half pound of butter, five eggs; beat eggs and sugar well; then add the juice, rind, and butter; mix well, and set over a kettle of boiling water till it is as thick as honey; stir it occasionally while cooking.

PEACH BUTTER.

To one bushel of peaches allow from eight to ten pounds of granulated sugar; pare and halve the peaches, put into the kettle, and stir constantly, to prevent sticking to the kettle, until perfectly smooth and rather thick; a part of the peach stones thrown in and cooked with the peaches give it a nice flavor, and they can be afterward skimmed out; add the sugar a short time before taking from the fire; put in jars, and cover tight; peaches for butter should be neither too mealy nor too juicy.

CANNED FRUIT, VEGETABLES, ETC.

All fruits should be fresh and ripe; granulated sugar should always be used, and also a porcelain kettle. Put the bottles in a pan or kettle of cold water, place on the stove until the water is boiling before filling with the fruit. Do not use an iron spoon. In preserving allow a pound of sugar to one pound of fruit; these can be put in jars with egg-papers. In canning fruit great care should be taken to have the jars perfectly air tight. Keep in cool, dark place.

CHERRIES.

Take Musilla cherries, wash and remove the pits; allow a pound of sugar to one pound of fruit; make a syrup of sugar with the juice and sufficient water to cover the cherries; boil from five to ten minutes; turn into bottles and seal. Some prefer one pint of sugar to one quart of pitted cherries.

BLACK RASPBERRIES AND BLACKBERRIES.

To one quart of berries allow one pint of sugar; boil fifteen minutes, and put in air-tight jars.

GREEN GAGE PLUMS.

After stemming and washing the fruit, fill the jars full, placing them in a boiler of cold water, just enough not to have the water boil over the top of the jars into the fruit; after boiling one-half hour, or until the fruit begins to be tender, lift out the jars, and turn off the juice that may accumulate into a porcelain kettle, and sufficient sugar to make a rich syrup; when it boils fill up the jars, let them stand in the boiling water ten or fifteen minutes longer; then lift out, one at a time, and seal. All kinds of plums are nice put up in the same manner.

GRAPES.

Stew, wash, and weigh the fruit. For preserves add one pound of sugar to a pound of fruit; for canning, one-half pound of sugar to a pound of fruit, and remove the pulp; put the skins and pulp into separate dishes, cook the pulp and strain through a sieve; then add the skins and sugar. For canning cook fifteen minutes; for preserving, a little longer.

TO CAN PEACHES.

Pare and halve the peaches; pack them in tin cans as close as they can possibly be put; make a syrup of six pounds of sugar to one gallon of cold water; let this stand until well dissolved; then pour the cold syrup over the peaches until the cans are even full, after which solder perfectly tight, place the cans in a boiler, cover well with cold water, set it on the fire and let the water boil five minutes, then take the cans out and turn them upside down; one gallon syrup will do one dozen cans.

RICH CANNED PEACHES.

Pare and stone peaches, about enough for two jars at a time; if many are pared they will become dark colored standing; rinse in cold water, then cook in a rich syrup of sugar and water about fifteen or twenty minutes, or until they are clear; put into your jars all that are not broken; fill up with the hot syrup, about as thick as ordinary molasses, and seal. Same syrup will do to cook two or three more jars. After the syrup becomes dark this, with the broken peaches, can be used for marmalade or peach butter. Same rule can be used for pears, plums, and all light fruit that you desire rich.

CANNED PEACHES.

Peel and quarter choice peaches—to peel, place in a wire basket, dip into boiling water a moment, and then into cold water, and strip off the skins—have a porcelain kettle with boiling water, and another with syrup made with granulated sugar; drop the peaches into boiling water —some previously boil the pits in the water for their flavor—and let them cook until tender, and then lift out carefully into a can, pouring over them all the syrup the can will hold, and seal immediately. Cook only peaches enough to fill one can at a time. Plums are canned in the same manner.

QUINCES.

Select fair, nice apple quinces (the inferior ones can be used for jelly or marmalade), pare and cut in quarters, removing the core; for each pound of them, take three-quarters of a pound of sugar, a quart of cold water; dissolve the sugar in the water over a moderate fire; let it boil, then remove from the fire; when cool, put in the quinces. If there is not more than enough water to cover them, more should be added so the syrup will be thin. If too rich, the quinces will be hard and shrink. Boil them gently until a broom straw will go through them easily. Keep them covered while boiling, that they may be light-colored. Put in bottles and seal.

STRAWBERRIES.

Procure fresh, large strawberries, when in their prime, but not so ripe as to be very soft; hull and weigh them; take an equal weight of sugar, make a syrup, and, when boiling hot, put in the berries. A small quantity should be done at once. If crowded they will become mashed. Let them boil about twenty minutes or a half an hour; turn into tumblers or small jars, and seal with egg papers while hot.

CANNED STRAWBERRIES.

Fill glass jars with fresh strawberries, sprinkled with sugar, allowing a little over one-quarter of a pound of sugar to one pound of berries; set the jars in a boiler, with a little hay laid in the bottom to prevent the jars from breaking, filled with cold water to within an inch or two of the tops of the jars; let them *boil* fifteen minutes; then move back, and wrap the hand in a towel, and take out the jars; fill the jars to the top before sealing, using one or more jars for the purpose.

CORN.

Fill the cans with the uncooked corn (freshly gathered) cut from the cob, and seal them hermetically; surround them with straw to prevent them striking against each other, and put them into a boiler over the fire, with enough cold water to cover them; heat the water gradually, and when they have boiled an hour and a half, puncture the tops of the cans to allow the escape of gases, then seal them immediately while they are still hot; continue to boil them for two hours and a half.

CANNED TOMATOES.

Pour hot water over the tomatoes to remove the skins, and then slice; put into a porcelain kettle and cook for a few minutes; have the cans filled with hot water on the hearth; when the tomatoes are sufficiently cooked, empty the cans and fill them with tomatoes, and seal immediately.

STRING BEANS.

Remove the strings at the sides, and cut into pieces about an inch long, put them into boiling water and scald, then can them.

PICKLES.

CUCUMBERS.

1. Take small cucumbers, put them in a large stone jar; to a four gallon jar full put water enough to cover; one quart of salt, and alum the size of a walnut; turn off the brine, and scald every day, putting it on boiling hot, for nine days; then wash and soak over night, if too salt; put into jars or bottles; add whole cinnamon, cloves, mace, allspice, and peppers (green peppers preferred); scald the vinegar, and pour on hot.

2. **Make a brine of** salt and water, put in the cucumbers; and let them **remain nine** days, pouring off the brine and scalding it every **second day; on** the ninth day, take some cider vinegar, which, if very **strong, dilute** with one-third water; have it boiling hot, and pour over **the pickles,** having first covered them with vine or cabbage leaves; then take cider vinegar, and **sweeten,** say, from one and one-half pounds to two and a half pounds of sugar to one gallon of vinegar; have ready the spices, and put all into the vinegar; while **heating, turn** off the first vinegar, and pour this over **them;** exclude **them entirely from** the **air.** If liked, add grated horse-radish.

CUCUMBER PICKLES.

Lay the cucumbers **in** good brine for twenty-four hours, then take them out and scald them in equal parts of vinegar and water, (a brass kettle is best) in alternate layers of pickles and grape-vine leaves, then put **them in a jar, and pour the** hot vinegar and water over them; **let** them stand over night; then take the **vinegar** and water and pour over again for three successive **days; at the end of** that time, pour off the **old vinegar and cover the pickles** with fresh vinegar, and add small red **peppers to taste.**

PICKLED PEPPERS.

Cut the stems out in a round circle with a sharp penknife, and preserve them; fill each pepper with a mixture of fine-chopped cabbage, horse-radish, mustard seed, and salt; wash the peppers in cold water, then fill, replace the piece cut **out, tie with coarse** thread, pack **in stone** jars, and fill up with **cold, sharp vinegar.** They will be ready for use in two weeks.

PICKLING CAULIFLOWER.

Take good white heads, break them into small pieces, and boil for **ten minutes in strong salt and** water; skim out the pieces, which should **be so tender that a** splint of broom corn can be run through the stems; **lay them on** a towel to drain off the water, and when thoroughly **cold,** put them into a pickle-jar with a few whole cloves, allspice, pepper, and sticks of cinnamon tied up in a cloth; boil and skim thoroughly, then pour **it directly over** the cauliflower.

RADISH-POD PICKLES.

Gather when **young and** tender, put them into **brine over night,** then **boil this brine, and** pour it over the pods in jars, covering **closely to keep the steam in;** when the brine is cold, repeat this, **and** do so until **the pods are** green; then drain them, and pour **over** them boiling hot **vinegar,** with mace, ginger, long peppers, and horse-radish in it; **when nearly** cold, pour off the vinegar, boil it once more, and again **pour** over the pods; when **cold, tie** down, and set away.

FRENCH PICKLES—DELICIOUS.

One colander **of** sliced green tomatoes, one quart **of** sliced onions, **one** colander of cucumbers, pared and sliced, two good handfuls of **salt;** let all stand twenty-four hours, then drain **through a sieve;** one-half ounce of celery seed, one-half ounce of allspice, one teacupful of black pepper, one tablespoonful turmeric, one pound of brown sugar, two tablespoonfuls of mustard, **one gallon** of vinegar.

PICKLED ONIONS.

Select small white onions, put them over the fire in cold water, with a handful of salt; when the water becomes scalding hot, take them out and peel off the skins; lay them in a cloth to dry, then put them in a jar; boil half an ounce of allspice and half an ounce of cloves in a quart of vinegar; take out the spice, and pour the vinegar over the onions while it is hot; tie up the jar when the vinegar is cold, and keep it in a dry place.

SPANISH PICKLED ONIONS.

Cut onions into slices; put a layer of them in a jar, sprinkle with salt and cayenne pepper, then add a layer of onions, and season as before; proceed in this way until the jar is full, and pour cold vinegar over all till covered. Will be fit to use in a month.

CHOW CHOW.

Take six cucumbers just before they ripen, peel them, cut in strips, and remove the seed; four white onions, six good-sized green tomatoes, and half a head of cabbage; chop all fine, let them stand in salt water over night, then pour off the water, and add vinegar and spices to suit the taste.

ENGLISH CHOW CHOW.

One-quarter of a peck of green beans, one quart of small onions, one quart of green sliced tomatoes, two dozen small cucumbers, one dozen small green peppers, one dozen chopped red peppers, one cauliflower, two ounces of white mustard seed, the same quantity of black mustard seed, one-half pound of yellow ground mustard, one-fourth of a teacupful of sweet oil, one tablespoonful of turmeric powder, one teaspoonful of celery seed; scald the beans, onions, peppers, cauliflower, tomatoes, and cucumbers in vinegar, and drain through a colander; then place in a jar; put on the fire fresh vinegar sufficient to cover the pickle, and put into it all the seed and two-thirds of the ground mustard; let it boil some minutes, then mix the remainder of the mustard, the turmeric, and oil together; stir in, and let it boil up once, and pour over the pickle.

RED CABBAGE AND CAULIFLOWER.

Pull the loose leaves, quarter the cabbage, put them in a large jar with alternate layers of salt and cabbage, and let them stand for several days; then scald some vinegar, with pepper-corns, mace and cinnamon in proportion of an ounce each to a gallon of vinegar; add a small piece of alum, and turn this over the cabbage in the brine, which should remain with it; cloves and allspice are good, but turn the cabbage darker; the vinegar should be scalded three or four times, and poured over the cabbage, to make it tender. Cauliflower is pickled in the same way.

PICKLED CABBAGE.

Take the outside leaves off a red cabbage, cut in thin slices, place in a jar, pour boiling spiced vinegar over it; when cold, cover tightly; in ten days it will be fit for use.

TOMATO CHOW CHOW.

One-half bushel of green tomatoes, one dozen onions, one-half dozen green peppers, all chopped fine; sprinkle over the mess one pint of salt, let it stand over night, then drain off the brine; cover it with good vinegar, let cook one hour slowly, then drain, and pack in jars; take two pounds of sugar, two tablespoonfuls of cinnamon, one of allspice, one of cloves, one of pepper, one-half cup of ground mustard, one pint of grated horse radish, and vinegar enough to mix them; when boiling hot, pour over the mess packed in a jar, and cover tight; then it is ready for use, and will keep for years.

CHOPPED TOMATOES.

To one gallon of tomatoes, chopped fine, take one teacup of salt, sprinkle, and let stand over night; drain through a colander, then add one tablespoonful of ground cloves, one of allspice, two of cinnamon, three of ground mustard, two of black pepper, four of green pepper, chopped fine, one head of cabbage, cover with cold vinegar; three or four onions, if liked.

STUFFED PEPPERS.

Put the peppers in salt and water a few days; then remove the seeds; chop cabbage, and sprinkle with salt; in a few hours, drain the water from the cabbage, and season with mustard or celery seed, or a mixture of each; fill the peppers with the cabbage and seed, and sew them up; cover with hot vinegar.

HAYES PICKLES.

One peck green tomatoes, sliced, six large onions, sliced; mix these, and throw over them a teacup of salt, and let them stand twelve hours; then drain thoroughly, and boil in one quart of vinegar mixed with two quarts of water, for twenty minutes; then take two pounds of brown sugar, half pound white mustard seed, two tablespoonfuls ground cloves, cinnamon, ginger, mustard, and allspice, with four quarts of vinegar; put all together, and boil twenty minutes.

HIGDOM.

One-half bushel of green tomatoes, two large heads of cabbage, one-half dozen green cucumbers, one dozen onions, one dozen green peppers, chopped fine, and prepared as piccalilli, all except the chopped pepper, which is put in after the scalding; use ground cinnamon, allspice, and cloves, a little black mustard seed, and celery seed, one gallon of vinegar, and four pounds of granulated sugar, scalded in the vinegar.

PICCALILLI.

1. One-half bushel of green tomatoes, one-half peck of onions; slice, sprinkle salt through them, and let stand over night; in the

morning drain off the water; put over the fire with enough weak vinegar to cover; let simmer slowly until a little tender, but not cooked to pieces; drain in a colander, and put a layer of the pickle in a jar; sprinkle over black mustard seed, ground pepper, cinnamon, cloves, allspice, and a little sugar; continue in this way till the jar is filled; sprinkle plenty of spice over the top, pour over cold, strong vinegar, cover tight, and set away.

2. One peck of green tomatoes, one dozen onions, six red peppers, one-half ounce of ginger, one quarter of an ounce of mace, one tablespoonful of black pepper, one box of mustard, five cents worth of celery seed, mustard seed to taste, one pound of brown sugar; slice tomatoes, onions, and peppers, put in a jar with salt mixed well through; let stand twenty-four hours; drain off, and boil in vinegar (after adding the spices) until clear.

SWEET PICCALILLI.

Take tomatoes just turning, wash, and, without paring, slice thick; put into a crock, with salt sprinkled between the layers, and let stand over night; in the morning drain, and make a rich syrup of vinegar, sugar, and spice, cinnamon, mace, and cloves; put a few of the tomatoes into the syrup, and let them simmer slowly; take out before they are cooked to pieces, and put into a crock on the back of the stove; continue in this way with the tomatoes until all are used; if the syrup gets too thin, make fresh; pour over the tomatoes, and cover tight.

MIXED PICKLES.

One peck of green tomatoes, half a peck of onions, one pint of grated horse radish, half a pound of white mustard seed, one pound of ground mustard, half a pound of unground black pepper, three or four green peppers, one ounce each of cinnamon, cloves, and turmeric, and two or three heads of cauliflower; tie the pepper, cinnamon, and cloves in a muslin bag, place in a tin or earthen-ware dish, and boil until tender; can while hot, in glass fruit jars.

MARTINOES.

Pick from the vines before they get tough; put them in weak brine for three days, then let them drain, and pour over them boiling vinegar, spiced with cloves and cinnamon.

YELLOW PICKLE.

One-half pound of white mustard seed, one-quarter pound of black mustard seed, one ounce of turmeric, one-quarter ounce of cayenne; the above quantity for a six-gallon jar of pickle; white cauliflower cut, white cabbage sliced fine and long, one-half dozen large onions sliced fine, one-half dozen small onions whole, one-half dozen small cucumbers whole, one-half dozen large cucumbers, cut; if they can be procured, nasturtium, radish pods, string beans, and green grapes; put all in brine for twenty hours, then strain, and pour on boiling vinegar sufficient to just cover the pickle, into which has been put the above spices and turmeric; mix a pint bowl of mustard as for the table, and **add after** the pickle **has** cooled; to get the required quantity of vinegar, **measure** the brine when turned off; the **vinegar** should only just **cover the pickle.**

NASTURTIUMS.

Take those that are small and green, put them in salt and water, changing it twice in the course of a week; when you have done collecting them, turn off the brine, and **turn** on scalding vinegar, with a little **alum** in it.

SPICED APPLES.

Three pounds of apples, **pared; four** pounds of sugar, one **quart of vinegar,** one ounce of stick **cinnamon,** half an ounce of cloves; **boil the sugar, vinegar,** and spices **together; put** in the apples when **boiling, and let** them remain until **tender; take them** out, put into a jar; **boil down the** syrup until it **is thick,** and **pour it** over.

SPICED CURRANTS.

Four quarts **currants (ripe), three** and one-half pounds brown sugar, one pint vinegar, **one tablespoonful** allspice, one tablespoonful cloves, and a little nutmeg; **boil an hour,** stirring occasionally. Gooseberries and cherries may be **spiced in the same manner.**

SPICED CHERRIES.

Four **pounds of cherries,** two pounds **of sugar, one** tablespoonful of cinnamon, one of **cloves; heat** one pint **of vinegar; pour on hot, three days in succession.**

SPICED GRAPES.

1. Eight quarts of seeded grapes, two ounces of ground cloves, two of cinnamon, three and one-half pounds of sugar; boil two hours.

2. Boil **and strain** through a colander, **to** remove the skins and **seeds, six pounds** of grapes, and add to the grapes three pounds of sugar, **one pint of** vinegar, two tablespoonfuls of cinnamon, **one** each of cloves **and mace;** boil one hour.

SPICED FRUIT.

Three pounds of sugar to one pint of good **vinegar, a** teacupful of broken cinnamon, **one** tablespoonful of cloves, whole, a very little mace; this will spice about one peck of peaches; put all in a kettle and simmer slowly fifteen or twenty minutes, the fruit should be pared; when done put in small jars and cover with **egg papers.**

SPICED PEACHES.

Pare, and if very **large,** halve one peck fine Crawford peaches; to **one pint** of vinegar, **allow** three pounds of white sugar, and of this **make a** rich syrup; drop **into** the syrup a small handful of broken cinnamon, a very little cloves and mace, and a few pieces of ginger root; when boiling add as many peaches as the syrup will cover, and let them simmer about ten minutes, then take out carefully with a spoon, put into jars, then cook more peaches in the same syrup; when all are cooked, make fresh syrup and pour over them in the jars.

SPICED PEARS OR PEACHES.

Ten pounds of fruit, five pounds of sugar, one half-pint of vinegar; mace, cinnamon, and cloves tied in a bag; boil the pears until clear; then scald thoroughly in the syrup; boil it down, and pour over the pears.

SPICED PLUMS.

One peck of plums, seven pounds of sugar, spice to taste; let boil down thick; before taking from the fire, add one pint vinegar.

PICKLED CHERRIES.

Take nice, large, ripe cherries, remove the stones, take a large glass jar, and fill two-thirds full of cherries, and fill up with best vinegar; keep it well covered; no boiling or spice is necessary, as the cherry flavor will be retained, and the cherries will not shrivel.

PICKLED PEACHES.

One gallon of vinegar, four pounds of brown sugar; take clingstone peaches, rub them with a flannel, stick two or three cloves in each; put them into a glass or earthen vessel, and pour on them the liquor boiling hot; cover them, and let them stand a week or ten days; then pour off the liquor and boil it as before, after which return it boiling to the peaches, which should be covered closely. Let the vinegar and sugar, in the first place, just come to a boil.

SWEET PICKLED PEACHES.

Select ripe, but firm fruit, free from blemishes; peel them carefully; allow a pound of sugar to a pint of good cider vinegar; place cloves and cinnamon in a bag, and boil in the vinegar; when the vinegar has come to a boil, drop in the peaches (a few at a time), and let them remain till done through, but not soft or broken; then remove them carefully with a skimmer, and place them in jars; repeat this process till all are done, then fill up the jars with the remaining vinegar, and seal while warm. In the same manner may be made sweet pickled pears, plums, crab-apples, and cherries.

PICKLED PLUMS.

Wash the plums clean and put into jars, and for two quarts of plums make a rich syrup of two pounds of sugar, one pint of vinegar, with spice; put the plums in jars, and pour over them the hot syrup,

PICKLED CANTALOUPES.

Select those of rough rind and quite ripe; take out the seeds, pare, and cut them in small square pieces, and cover with good elder vinegar; let them stand twenty-four hours, then pour off part of the vinegar; to every quart of the remainder, add three pounds of sugar, and put them upon the stove and simmer slowly until a fork will go through them easily, and they look clear; then add one ounce of ground cloves and one of cinnamon; cook them ten minutes longer, and set them away to cool; after they are quite cold, cover closely, and set them in a cool, dark closet.

SWEET CANTALOUPE PICKLE.

Pare them and cover with vinegar, after cutting in pieces; pour off the vinegar, and to every pint put three-fourths of a pound of brown sugar, a little cloves, allspice, and mace; let it boil a few minutes; throw in the cantaloupe; take it out as soon as it looks clear; put in a jar, and pour the boiling mixture over them.

SWEET PICKLES.

Take ripe cucumbers, pare them, and cut out the seeds, cut in strips, and soak in weak brine twenty-four hours; then put them in vinegar and water, and soak twenty-four hours; then put them in sweetened vinegar, the same as for any sweet pickles, and cook until tender; take to a quart of vinegar three pounds of coffee sugar, a tablespoonful of ground cinnamon tied in a cloth, also a few whole cloves, and boil all together.

MUSK-MELON PICKLE.

Take the melons when not quite ripe; peel, remove the seed, and cut in shape; throw them into vinegar and water—equal proportions—and cook until tender; then drain and lay into a jar; then take vinegar enough to cover, allowing three pounds of sugar to a quart; add stick cinnamon to taste, and boil; pour over the melon boiling hot; strain off the vinegar the next day and boil again.

SWEET PICKLED WATERMELON RINDS.

Prepare the rinds and put into weak vinegar and water for twelve hours; then boil them tender in the same water; drain well, and prepare to a pint of vinegar one pound of sugar, mace, allspice, cloves, stick cinnamon; put the rinds in a jar, and pour this over them.

MOCK OLIVES.

Take green plums before they begin to ripen, and pour over them, while boiling hot, a pickle made of vinegar, salt, and mustard seed; let them stand all night, and then drain off the vinegar, and boil again, and pour over the plums.

TOMATO FIGS.

Collect a lot of ripe tomatoes, about one inch in diameter, skin and stew them in the usual manner; when done, lay them on dishes, flatten them slightly, and spread over them a light layer of pulverized white or brown sugar; expose them to a summer's sun, or place them in a drying-house; when as dry as fresh figs, pack in old fig or small boxes, with sugar between each layer; if properly managed, the difference cannot be detected from the veritable article.

SPICED GRAPES.

Ten pounds of grapes, six pounds of sugar, two tablespoonfuls cinnamon, two of allspice, and small teaspoonful ground cloves; remove the pulps and boil, then rub through a sieve or colander to remove the seeds; boil the skins till tender, and then add to the pulp, together with the sugar; spices and vinegar to taste; boil until of the desired consistency.

PICKLED PEARS.

Prepare the fruit as preferred, either pare and leave whole or quarter them; make a syrup in the proportion of three pints of sugar to one quart of vinegar, and while boiling hot put in the fruit, and cook until tender, but not broken; skim out the fruit carefully into a jar and pour the syrup over them; let them stand until the next day, and then lay them in a stone jar in layers, with whole cloves and stick cinnamon, and again pour over them the syrup, boiling hot; continue drawing off and boiling the syrup for four or five days, and then cover and set in a cool place. Apples can be pickled in the same manner.

GOOSEBERRY SAUCE.

Take nine pounds of gooseberries, nearly ripe, remove the stems, and put into a preserving kettle with four and a half pounds of sugar, and three cups of hot vinegar, and spices to taste; boil until thick.

GREEN TOMATO SAUCE.

One peck of green tomatoes, washed, and sliced very thin; sprinkle with salt, and allow them to drain twenty-four hours; in the morning press out all the water, and put into a preserving kettle in layers, with a mixture as follows: Six or seven onions cut in slices, quarter of a pound of mustard—mixed—quarter of a pound of mustard-seed, tablespoonful of cloves, nearly two tablespoonfuls black pepper, nearly two tablespoonfuls of allspice, and a tablespoonful of ginger; cover with vinegar, and boil very slowly until the tomatoes look clear.

CURRANT SAUCE.

Six pounds of currants, picked from the stems, three pounds of sugar, cup and a half of vinegar, three-quarters of an ounce of cinnamon, and spices to taste; boil slowly an hour.

SPICED CURRANTS.

Nine pounds of currants; four and a half pounds of raisins, four and a half pounds of sugar, three cups of best vinegar, three tablespoonfuls of allspice, three of cinnamon, one and a half of cloves; boil until thick.

CUCUMBER KETCHUP.

Two dozen large cucumbers, two dozen white onions, one tablespoonful black pepper, one teaspoonful red pepper, three red peppers; cut all up fine, sprinkle with salt and let drain until morning; then mix the spices in; boil the vinegar and let it cool before putting on the pickle; put in glass jars and close tight.

TOMATO KETCHUP.

To every gallon of tomatoes, put four tablespoons of salt, four of black pepper, one of cayenne pepper, three of mustard, half a tablespoonful of **ground cloves, and the** same of allspice; after having washed and **cut up the tomatoes,** boil them about twenty minutes, then strain them **and add the spice and simmer** the whole together slowly three hours, **then bottle and seal.**

CHILI SAUCE.

1. **Take five large onions, eight green peppers,** chop fine; **thirty ripe tomatoes, cut them; five tablespoonfuls sugar, three of salt, eight cups vinegar, and boil together two and a half hours, and bottle for use.**

2. **One** dozen ripe tomatoes, **four** green **peppers, one large onion, one cup of** vinegar, **one** tablespoonful of **sugar one teaspoonful of ground allspice,** two teaspoonfuls of salt, **one teaspoonful of pepper; boil half an hour, then put** in bottles while **hot, and cork tight.**

3. **Eighteen ripe tomatoes,** pared, **three green peppers, one onion, one cup of sugar, two and** one-half **cups of vinegar, two** teaspoonfuls **of salt, one teaspoonful of cinnamon, one teaspoonful of** cloves; cook the tomatoes tender, chop the onion and peppers very fine, mix all, and cook a few minutes. A few leaves of mint added to pickles is an improvement.

4. **Twenty-five pounds ripe tomatoes, peeled, ten pounds green** peppers, **four pounds onions, one pound salt, three-quarters pound** mustard, **half pound ground cloves,** quarter **pound nutmeg, one and a quarter gallons vinegar;** boil **all together, and skim well before adding the spices, then boil for about** one and a **half hours. Bottle and cork tight;** will keep for **years.**

OUDE SAUCE.

One peck of green tomatoes, **eight green peppers, and four onions chopped fine** together; to this add a cup of **salt, and let** it stand **over night, after** which drain off the water, then add a cup **of** grated horseradish, **one** cup of brown sugar, one tablespoonful of ground cloves, also **the same of** cinnamon; fill till it stands even full with cold vinegar, and **let it cook** gently all day.

CUCUMBER KETCHUP.

1. **Three dozen** large cucumbers, **three** white onions; grate **all to a pulp, drain through** a sieve several hours; add **salt,** pepper, **and good vinegar; seal** in bottles.

2. **Boil** and grate full-grown cucumbers, sprinkle with salt, and **let** stand over night; then pour out all the water, season with celery seed, and add vinegar until about **the** consistency of the cucumber when grated; bottle **for use.**

GOOSEBERRY KETCHUP

Five pounds **of** berries, **two and** one-half pounds **of** sugar; boil down until as thick **as** apple butter; add cinnamon and cloves to taste, a pinch of salt, one pint of **vinegar; strain** through a hair sieve, and bottle.

GRAPE KETCHUP.

Five pounds of grapes boiled **in a little** water, and put through a colander; three pounds of sugar, **one pint** of vinegar, one tablespoonful of ground cloves, one of cinnamon, one of pepper, one-half tablespoonful of salt; boil until a little thick; bottle and seal.

TOMATO KETCHUP.

1. One bushel of tomatoes, boiled with two or three onions until soft; press through a sieve; pour again into the kettle, and add one pint of salt, two ounces of cloves, cayenne pepper to taste, two ounces whole pepper, four ounces mace, four ounces celery seed, one-half pound allspice, cup sugar, and half a gallon vinegar; boil until reduced one-half.

2. To one gallon of ripe tomatoes add two tablespoonfuls of salt, one of pepper, two of ground mustard, one dessertspoonful of cloves, one pint of good cider vinegar, a half teacupful of sugar; boil slowly for three minutes. Do not add the spice until nearly done, as it is more liable to burn.

3. One gallon of tomatoes, one pint of vinegar, two tablespoonfuls of salt, two of black pepper, two of mustard, one of cloves, one dozen onions sliced fine; boil all together till quite thick; strain through a colander; bottle and cork tight, and keep in a cool place.

COOKERY FOR THE SICK.

BEEF TEA.—Very nice beef tea is made by cutting up tender, juicy beef into pieces about one inch square; put into a strong bottle, cork tightly, and set in a kettle of cold water. Boil it about two hours; the fluid then obtained will be the pure nutriment of the meat, and the tonic effects are powerful.

2. Cut raw beef into small pieces, cover with cold water, and set on the back of the stove where it will not boil, until all the juice is extracted from the beef. When wanted for use skim off all the fat, strain, season, and let it come to a boil.

VEAL OR MUTTON BROTH.—To each pound of meat add one quart of cold water; bring it gently to a boil; skim it, and add salt; simmer the broth about three hours. A little rice may be boiled with the meat. When cold skim off the fat.

CHICKEN BROTH.—Take part of the chicken, joint it, and cover with water; let it boil closely covered until the meat drops from the bones; then skim off the fat, strain, and season with a little salt, and if liked, add a teaspoonful of rice, and let boil until the rice is cooked.

SCRAPED BEEF.—Take a good piece of raw steak, lay it on a meat-board, and with a knife scrape into fine bits; after removing all hard and gristly parts, put it into a pan over the fire, and let it remain just long enough to become thoroughly heated through, stirring it up from the bottom occasionally. Season with a little salt. This is very nutritious, and quite palatable,

TO PREPARE AN EGG.—Beat an egg until very light, add seasoning to the taste, and then steam until thoroughly warmed through, but not hardened; this will take about two minutes. An egg prepared in this way will not distress a sensitive stomach.

MILK PORRIDGE.—Make a thin batter of white flour and cold milk, and stir it into boiling milk, with a little salt. Let it boil for a few minutes, stirring all the time.

PANADA.—Shave very thin soft parts of light bread into a bowl; put in a piece of butter the size of a large hickory-nut, grate over this some nutmeg, pour on boiling water, cover, and let stand a few minutes.

2. Break the soft part of a stale loaf in pieces, and soak in cold water for an hour, then mash; put it on the fire, with a little salt, butter, and sugar to taste, and cook slowly for an hour; add two yolks of eggs, beaten, with two tablespoonfuls of milk.

OAT-MEAL GRUEL.—Put two large spoonfuls of oat-meal, wet in cold water, into one pint of boiling water, boil it gently one-half hour, skim, and add a little salt, sugar, and nutmeg.

PORT WINE JELLY.—Melt in a little warm water one ounce of isinglass, stir into it one pint of port wine, adding two ounces of sugar, an ounce of gum arabic, and half a nutmeg, grated; mix all well, and boil ten minutes, or until everything is thoroughly dissolved; then strain, and set away to get cold.

BARLEY WATER.—Soak one pint of barley in lukewarm water for a few minutes; then drain off the water. Put the barley in three quarts of cold water, and cook slowly until the barley is quite soft, skimming occasionally. This barley water, when cold, flavor with a little jelly or lemonade.

RICE MILK.—Pick and wash the rice carefully; boil it in water until it swells and softens; when the water is partly boiled away, add some milk. It may be boiled entirely in milk, by setting the vessel in which the rice is in, in boiling water; sweeten with white sugar, and season with nutmeg. It may also be thickened with a little flour or beaten egg.

FLAXSEED TEA.—One-half pound of flaxseed, one-half pound rock candy, and three lemons, pared and sliced; pour over this two quarts of boiling water; let it stand until very cold; strain before drinking. This is good for a cough.

APPLEADE.—Cut two large apples in slices, and pour on them one pint of boiling water; strain well, and sweeten. Ice it before drinking.

BLACKBERRY SYRUP.—One quart of blackberry juice, one pound of sugar, one-half ounce of nutmeg, one-half ounce of cinnamon, one-fourth of an ounce of cloves, one-fourth of an ounce of allspice.

TOAST WATER.—Toast stale bread until quite brown, but do not burn it; put it into a large bowl, and pour over it boiling water; let it stand for an hour or so, strain, and put in a piece of ice before drinking.

TOAST.—Toast bread until a nice brown all over, taking great care not to burn; butter each slice, dip into hot water, or pour over each piece enough sweet cream to moisten it.

BLACKBERRY WINE.—To one gallon of mashed berries add one quart of boiling water, and let it stand twenty-four hours; then strain them, and to every gallon of juice add three pounds of brown sugar. Put in a jug or demijohn, and cover with a thin piece of muslin until October, then bottle it off.

WINE WHEY.—Sweeten one pint of milk to taste, and, when boiling, throw in two wine glasses of sherry; when the curd forms, strain the whey through a muslin bag into tumblers.

ARROWROOT CUSTARDS.—Boil a pint of milk, and while boiling stir into it one large spoonful of arrowroot, mixed smooth with a little cold milk; add a little salt; let it boil three or four minutes, then let it cool, and add a couple of beaten eggs, sugar, and nutmeg to the taste, and set it where it will get scalding hot, stirring all the time. As soon as it boils up, turn it into custard cups.

CRACKED WHEAT.—To one quart of hot water take one small teacup of cracked wheat and a little salt; boil slowly for half an hour, stirring occasionally to prevent burning. Serve with sugar and cream, or new milk.

RAW EGG.—Break a fresh egg into a glass, beat until very light, sweeten to taste, and add two tablespoonfuls of port wine, then beat again.

FINE HOMINY.—Put to soak one pint of hominy in two and one-half pints of boiling water over night in a tin vessel, with a tight cover; in the morning add one-half pint of sweet milk and a little salt. Place on a brisk fire in a kettle of boiling water; let boil one-half hour.

OAT-MEAL MUSH.—Sift into boiling water, with a little salt, oat-meal until about the consistency of common mush; let it boil one-half hour.

BLACKBERRY CORDIAL.—Warm and squeeze the berries; add to one pint of juice one pound of white sugar, one-half ounce of powdered cinnamon, one-fourth ounce of mace, two teaspoonfuls of cloves. Boil all together for one-fourth of an hour; strain the syrup, and to each pint add a glass of French brandy. Two or three doses of a tablespoonful or less will check any slight diarrhea. When the attack is violent, give a tablespoonful after each discharge until the complaint is in subjection. It will arrest dysentery if given in season, and is a pleasant and safe remedy.

DRIED FLOUR FOR INFANTS.—Take one teacup of flour, tie it up tightly in a close muslin bag, and put it in a pot of cold water, and boil three hours; then take it out and dry the outside. When used, grate it. One tablespoonful is enough for one teacupful of milk (which would be better with a little water); wet the flour with a little cold water, and stir into the milk; add a very little salt, and boil five minutes.

OYSTER TOAST.—Make a nice slice of toast and butter it, lay it in a hot dish; put six oysters, a teacupful of their own liquor, into a tin cup, and boil one minute. Use half milk if preferred. Season with a little butter, pepper, and salt, and pour over the toast.

EGG GRUEL.—Beat the yolk of one egg with one tablespoonful of sugar; pour one teacupful of boiling water on it; add the white of the egg beaten to a froth, with any seasoning or spice desired. To be taken warm.

MULLED JELLY.—Take one tablespoonful of currant or grape jelly; beat with it the white of one egg and a little loaf sugar; pour on it one-half pint of boiling water, and break in a slice of dry toast, or two crackers.

IRISH MOSS BLANC-MANGE.—Pick over carefully one teacupful of Irish moss; wash it first in saleratus water; then rinse it several times in fresh water. Put it in a tin pail with one quart of milk; cover closely, and set in a kettle of boiling water. Let it stand until it begins to thicken, then strain through a fine sieve, and sweeten with powdered sugar; flavor, and pour into a mold, and set in a cool place. When quite firm, turn out in a dish. Eat with sugar and cream.

CHICKEN JELLY.—Cut up a chicken, and put into a quart of cold water; let it simmer until reduced to a little less than a pint; remove from the fire, and strain as for jelly; season with a little salt. Chop the breast meat into small pieces, and mix with liquor, and then pour the whole into a mold, and set away to cool.

CANDIES.

COCOA-NUT CANDY.—Grate very fine a sound cocoa-nut, spread it on a dish, and let it dry naturally for three days, as it will not bear the heat of an oven, and too oily for use when freshly broken. Four ounces will be sufficient for a pound of sugar for most tastes, but more can be used at pleasure. To one pound of sugar take one-half pint of water, a little white of egg, and then pour over the sugar; let it stand for a short time, then place over a very clear fire, and let it boil for a few minutes, then set it one side till the scum is subsided; clear it off, and boil the sugar until very thick, then strew in the nut, stir and mix it well, and do not quit for an instant until it is finished. The pan should not be placed on the fire, but over it, as the nut is liable to burn with too fierce a heat.

ALMOND CANDY.—Proceed in the same way as for cocoa-nut candy; let the almonds be perfectly dry, and do not throw them into the sugar until they approach the candying point.

TO CANDY NUTS.—Three cups of sugar, one cup of water; boil until it hardens when dropped in water; then flavor with lemon. It must not boil after the lemon is put in. Put a nut on the end of a fine knitting-needle, take out and turn on the needle until it is cool. If the candy gets cold, set on the stove for a few minutes. Malar grapes and oranges, quartered, may be candied in the same way.

CHOCOLATE CARAMELS.—Two cups of sugar, one cup of warm water, one-half cup of grated chocolate, three-fourths of a cup of butter; let boil, without stirring, until it snaps in water.

2. One-half pound of grated chocolate, two teacups of sugar, one-half cup of milk and water, a lump of butter, one teaspoon of alum.

SUGAR CANDY.—Six cups of white sugar, one cup of vinegar, one cup of water, a tablespoonful of butter, put in at the last with one teaspoonful of soda dissolved in hot water. Boil without stirring one-half hour. Flavor to suit the taste.

CREAM CANDY.—Four cups of sugar, two cups of water, three-fourths of a cup of vinegar, one cup of cream or rich milk, a piece of butter the size of an egg, two teaspoonfuls of vanilla, a pinch of soda. Let it boil until it cracks in water; then work very white.

MAPLE CANDY.—Four cups of maple syrup; boil until it cracks in water; and just before taking from the fire put in a piece of butter the size of an egg. If preferred waxy, do not let it cook so long.

BUTTER SCOTCH.—One cup of molasses, one cup of sugar, one-half cup of butter. Boil until done.

ANTIDOTES FOR POISONS.

The following list gives some of the more common poisons, and the remedies most likely to be on hand in case of need:

ACIDS.—These cause great heat, and sensation of burning pain from the mouth down to the stomach. Remedies: Magnesia, soda, pearl-ash, or soap dissolved in water. Then use stomach-pump or emetic.

ALKALI.—Best remedy is vinegar.

AMMONIA.—Remedy: Lemon juice or vinegar.

ALCOHOL.—First cleanse out the stomach by an emetic, then dash cold water on the head, and give ammonia (spirits of hartshorn).

ARSENIC.—Remedies: In the first place evacuate the stomach; then give the white of eggs, lime water, or chalk and water, charcoal, and the preparation of iron, particularly hydrate.

LAUDANUM.—Same as opium.

BELLADONNA.—Give emetics, and then plenty of vinegar and water, or lemonade.

MORPHINE.—Same as opium.

CHARCOAL.—In poisons by carbonic gas, remove the patient to the open air, dash cold water on the head and body, and stimulate the nostrils and lungs with hartshorn, at the same time rubbing the chest briskly.

CORROSIVE SUBLIMATE.—Give white of egg, freshly mixed with water, or give wheat flour and water, or soap and water freely, or salt and water.

CREOSOTE.—White of eggs and emetics.

LEAD.—White lead and sugar of lead. Remedies: Alum, cathartics, such as castor oil and Epsom salts especially.

MUSHROOMS WHEN POISONOUS.—Give emetics, and then plenty of vinegar and water, with doses of ether, if handy.

NITRATE OF SILVER (LUNAR CAUSTIC).—Give a strong solution of common salt and then emetics.

OPIUM.—First give a strong emetic of mustard and water, then strong coffee and acid drinks; dash cold water on the head.

NUX VOMICA.—First emetics and then brandy.

OXALIC ACID (Frequently mistaken for Epsom salts).—Remedies: Chalk, magnesia, or soap and water, and other soothing drinks.

PRUSSIC ACID.—When there is time, administer chlorine in the shape of soda and lime. Hot brandy and water, hartshorn and turpentine are also useful.

SNAKE BITE, ETC.—Apply immediately strong hartshorn, and take it internally; also give sweet oil and stimulants freely; apply a ligature tightly over the part bitten, and then apply a cupping-glass.

TARTAR EMETIC.—Take large doses of tea made of galls, Peruvian bark, or white oak bark.

VERDEGRIS.—Plenty of white of eggs and water,

WHITE VITRIOL.—Give the patient plenty of milk and water.

A CURE FOR WHISKY-DRINKERS.—Sulphate of iron, five grains, magnesia, ten grains; peppermint water, eleven drachms; spirit of nutmeg, one drachm; twice a day.

MISCELLANEOUS.

WEIGHTS AND MEASURES.—Every family should be furnished with scales and weights; and it is also advisable to have wooden measures.

Two gills make half a pint.
Two pints make one quart.
Four quarts make one gallon.
Half gallon makes a quarter of a peck.
One gallon makes half a peck.
Two gallons make one peck.
Four gallons make half a bushel.
Eight gallons make one bushel.
About sixty drops of any thin liquid will fill a common-sized teaspoon.
Four tablespoons, or half a gill will fill a common-sized wineglass;
Four wine-glasses will fill half a pint measure, a common tumbler, or a large coffee-cup.
Ten eggs usually weigh one pound before they are broken. Eight large ones will weigh one pound.
A tablespoonful of salt will weigh about one ounce.
One pint of water or milk will weigh one pound.
One pint of molasses will weigh one and one-quarter pounds.

Three teaspoonfuls of baking-powder should weigh one ounce.
One quart of flour weighs one pound.
One quart of Indian meal weighs one and a quarter pounds.

REMARKS ON CARVING.—Carving is now so generally practiced by gentlemen, that ladies may, in a great measure, be considered exempt. It is, however, a very desirable accomplishment. Every lady should be competent to preside at her own table, and, as expertness is best gained by experience, it would be very advantageous to young ladies that they, before leaving the parental roof, should be permitted to occasionally do the carving and serving at table. By acquiring, properly, early habits of this kind under a mother's direction, they will be prepared to operate with confidence at their own table.

To carve with ease and elegance, it is essential to be furnished with a good and suitable carving-knife. These vary in size and form according to the purposes for which they are intended; for carving a large and fleshy joint, as a round of beef, etc., a long blade will be necessary; for lamb, etc., a smaller size will answer; and for poultry and game, a still shorter blade, sharp-pointed and somewhat curved. A new carving-knife for poultry is now in the market, which can be used as shears, and is a great help in nipping off small bones, tendons, etc. The knife should be as light as is compatible with the size and strength required; the edge very keen, and a good steel or knife-sharpener always at hand. A guard-fork is generally used for carving which requires strength, as it is a necessary security; but, for light cutting it is a needless and rather cumbersome appendage.

It is the business of the cook to see that the butcher properly divides the joint of neck and loins in all kinds of meats, as this materially facilitates the operation of carving. The seat should be sufficiently high to command the table, and render rising unnecessary. For fish, a silver fish-knife or trowel is to be preferred, as preserving the flakes more entire, which contributes greatly to the beauty of its appearance.

Although carving with ease and elegance is a necessary accomplishment, most people are lamentably deficient, not only in the art of dissecting winged game and poultry, but also in the important point of knowing the parts most esteemed. Each person, as far as possible, should be served with a portion of the best parts.

TO CLEAN PAINT.—Tea leaves may be saved from the table for a few days, and when sufficient are collected, steep, not boil, them for half an hour in a tin pan. Strain the water off through a sieve, and use this tea to wash all varnished paint. It removes spots, and gives a fresher, newer appearance than when soap and water is used. For white paint, take up a small quantity of whiting on a damp piece of old white flannel, and rub over the surface lightly, and it will leave the paint remarkably bright and new.

TO RAISE THE PILE OF VELVET.—Cover a hot smoothing-iron with a wet cloth, hold the velvet firmly over it; the vapor rising will raise the pile of the velvet with the assistance of a light whisk.

TO TAKE MILDEW FROM LINEN.—Rub the spots with soap; scrape

chalk over it, and rub it well; lay it on the grass, in the sun; as it dries, wet it a little; it will come out with two applications.

To CLEAN MARBLE.—Take two parts of common soda, one part of pumice stone, and one part of finely-powdered chalk; sift it through a fine sieve, and mix it with water; then rub it well all over the marble, and the stains will be removed; rub the marble over with salt and water.

To CLEAN TINWARE.—The best thing for cleaning tinware is common soda; dampen a cloth, dip it in soda, rub the ware briskly, after which wipe dry.

To CLEAN CUT GLASS.—Having washed cut glass articles, let them dry, and afterwards rub them with prepared chalk and a soft brush, carefully going into all the cavities.

INDELIBLE INK.—To one tablespoonful of rain water, one-half teaspoonful of vinegar and a piece of lunar caustic, three inches long; shake well together; put on to your cloth a little milk and soda (to a tablespoon of milk a piece of baking soda as large as a grain of corn); iron smooth, and write immediately.

IRON RUST.—This may be removed by salt mixed with a little lemon juice; put in the sun; if necessary use two applications.

MILDEW.—Dip the stained cloth in buttermilk, and lay in the sun.

To COOK POULTRY AND MEAT.—A writer says: "All kinds of poultry and meat can be cooked quicker by adding to the water in which they are boiled, a little vinegar or a piece of lemon. By the use of an acid there will be a considerable saving of fuel, as well as shortening of time. Its action is beneficial on old, tough meats, rendering them quite tender and easy of digestion. Tainted meats and fowls will lose their bad taste and odor if cooked in this way; and if not used too freely, no taste of it will be acquired."

To KEEP BEEF.—Dry well with clean cloth; rub ground pepper plentifully over every part of it first, then flour it well, and hang it in cool place, where the air will come to it.

To PICKLE MEAT IN ONE DAY.—Take a tub of rain or river water and put two pieces of thin wood across it, and set the beef on them, distant about an inch from the water; heap as much salt as will stand on your beef, and let it remain twenty-four hours; then take off and boil, the water having drawn the salt completely through the meat.

TESTING MILK.—A well polished knitting needle is dipped into a deep vessel of milk, and immediately withdrawn in an upright position; when, if the sample be pure, some of the fluid will be found to adhere to it, while such is not the case if water has been added to the milk.

CHEAP REFRIGERATORS.—A flower pot wrapped in a wet cloth, and placed over a butter plate, will keep the contents of the plate as hard and firm as if they were set on ice; and milk will not sour if the can containing it be wrapped in a wet cloth.

To MEND BROKEN CROCKERY.—We have used lime and the white of an egg for mending earthenware, and find it most satisfactory. It is a strong cement, easily applied, and generally at hand. Mix only enough to mend one article at a time, as it soon hardens, when it cannot be used. Powder a small quantity of the lime and mix to a paste with the white. Apply quickly to the edges, and place firmly together. It will soon become set and strong, seldom breaking in the same place again.

How to Clean a Tea or Coffee Pot.—If the inside of your tea or coffee pot is black from long use, fill it with water, throw in a piece of hard soap, set on the stove, and let it boil from half an hour to an hour. It will clean as bright as a new dollar, and cost no work.

Tinned Ware.—Tinned ware which speedily loses its brightness should be distrusted. It usually contains lead, which is dissolved by very feeble acids, and is very poisonous. Iodide of potassium is the antidote.

To Renew Black Cashmere.—Take half a pint of ammonia and enough tepid water to dip the breadths and pieces in thoroughly up and down, after which hang on the line to drip, and dry partially without wringing; then iron dry on wrong side, when it will look like new.

To Wash Black Cashmere.—Take hard soapsuds, wash your goods thoroughly, and after you have rinsed them in warm water rinse them in warm coffee, with a teaspoonful of gum arabic water to every pound of goods; take a piece of dark flannel or place a layer of flannel and then one of the goods, and so on until you have finished, then roll up tight and leave until morning, then iron on the wrong side. You can also wash soiled velvet in this way.

To Polish Shirt Fronts and Wrist Bands.—Starch the fronts and wrist bands as stiff as you can. Starch twice—that is, starch, dry, then starch again. Iron your shirt with a box iron, in the usual way, making the linen nice and firm, but without any attempt at a good finish; don't lift the plait; your shirt is now ready for polishing, but you ought to have a board same size as a common shirt board, made of hard wood, and covered with only one ply of plain cotton cloth. Put this board into the breast of your shirt, damp the front very lightly with a wet sponge, then take the polishing iron, which is flat and beveled at one end; polish gently with the beveled end, taking care not to drive the linen up into wave-like blisters. Of course this requires a little practice, but if you are careful and persevere, in a short time you will be able to give the enamel-like finish which is so much wanted.

To Clean Straw Matting.—Wash with a cloth dipped in clean salt and water. Take care to wipe dry, as this prevents its turning yellow.

Tar may be removed from either hands or clothing by rubbing well with lard, and then washing well with soap and water.

A Sure Way to Remove Tea Stains.—Mix thoroughly soft soap and salt—say a tablespoonful to a teacup of soap; rub on the spots, and spread the cloth on the grass where the sun will shine on it. Let it lay two or three days; then wash; if the stain is not all out, it will disappear in the second washing. If the spots are wet occasionally while lying on the grass it will hasten the bleaching.

HOME-MADE CAMPHOR ICE.—Melt half a teacupful of mutton tallow with a piece of camphor gum the size of a large hickory-nut; pour into a little cup or mold.

HOME-MADE HARD SOAP.—Were the good qualities of this inexpensive soap more generally known, no family would go without it. It is valuable for washing clothes, making them very clean and white, without in the least injuring them, and is excellent for flannels or calicoes. It is good also for the hands, making them soft and smooth. Take six pounds each of salsoda and lard, three pounds of stone lime, four gallons of soft water, dissolve the lime and soda in the water, stirring, settling, and pouring off, then return to the kettle, using brass or copper; add the lard, and boil until it becomes soap; then pour into a tub; when cold, cut in bars and dry.

A BEAUTIFUL WHITEWASH.—To five gallons of whitewash, made of well-burned lime, add a quarter of a pound of whiting, half a pound of loaf sugar, one quart and a half of rice flour, made into a thin and well-cooked paste, and half a pound of white glue dissolved in water; apply warm; previously scrape off all old scaly whitewash; this is like kalsomine, and gives a brilliant and lasting effect.

MOTHS.—Professor Riley says, in a scientific journal, that the early days of May should herald vigorous and exterminating warfare upon those subtle pests, clothes moths. Closets, wardrobes, etc., should be emptied, and the clothing laid open and thoroughly exposed to light and air, and well brushed before being replaced. Spirits of turpentine should be brushed in cracks, wainscots, and shelves, and camphor or tobacco placed among the garments, furs, plumes, etc., when laid aside for the summer. To secure the cloth linings of carriages from moths, sponge them on both sides with a solution of corrosive sublimate, or mercury in alcohol, made just strong enough not to leave a white mark on a black feather.

SALT AND MOTHS.—It is said, and by good authority, that after wiping up the floor, if salt is sprinkled over it while damp, moths will not try that harbor again. When making a carpet it is recommended that enough be allowed to fold under an inch or two, so that when it is put down salt can be spread between the folds, and also sprinkle salt all around the sides and corners of the room before nailing the carpet. We have never tried this, but have several good authorities who indorse it, and promise that moths will not injure carpets if this advice is followed.

CHAMOIS SKINS.—To cleanse a chamois skin wash it in cold water with plenty of soap, and rinse well in clear cold water; thus you may wash as often as you please, and still keep it soft.

POLISHING PASTE FOR TINS, BRASSES, AND COPPER.—This is composed of rotten stone, soft soap, and oil of turpentine; the stone must be powdered and sifted through a muslin or hair sieve; mix with it as much soft soap as will bring it to the stiffness of putty; to half a pound of this add two ounces of oil of turpentine; it may be made into balls; it will soon become hard, and will keep any length of time. Method of using: The articles to be polished should be perfectly free from grease and dirt; moisten a little of the paste with water, smear it over the metal, rub briskly with a dry rag or leather, and it will soon bear a beautiful polish.

A good stove polish may be made with black lead mixed with the white of an egg; put on with a brush, and polish with a dry, hard brush.

To make an excellent furniture polish: Take turpentine, linseed oil, and vinegar, in equal proportions; apply and rub with flannel.

A little soap put on the hinges or latch of a door will stop its creaking.

Salt will curdle milk; hence in preparing gravies, porridge, etc., the salt should not be added till the dish is prepared.

If your flat-irons are rough or soiled, lay some salt on a flat surface, and rub the face of the iron well over it.

Rub your griddle with fine salt before you grease it, and your cakes will not stick.

When clothes have acquired an unpleasant odor by being from the air, charcoal laid in the folds will soon remove it.

Powdered charcoal placed around roses and other flowers adds to their richness.

Camphor gum placed on shelves or in drawers will effectually drive away mice.

THE PEOPLE'S LIBRARY.

No.		Price
1.	THE GAMBLER'S WIFE. By Mrs. Grey....................	20c
2.	PUT YOURSELF IN HIS PLACE. A Story of the Great Strike. By Charles Reade............................	20c
3.	AURORA FLOYD. By Miss M. E. Braddon.................	20c
4.	HANDY ANDY. By Samuel Lover........................	20c
5.	JACOB FAITHFUL. By Captain Marryatt...................	15c
6.	IVANHOE. By Sir Walter Scott...........................	20c
7.	NIGHT AND MORNING. By Sir E. Bulwer Lytton...........	20c
8.	GWENDOLINE'S HARVEST. By James Payne...............	10c
9.	WRESTLING JOE. By Ned Buntline......................	20c
10.	THE TROUBLESOME TWINS. By Edward Harcourt.......	20c
11.	A QUEEN AMONG WOMEN...............................	10c
12.	FRITZ, THE GERMAN DETECTIVE. By Tony Pastor......	10c
13.	MONTE MADRONA. A Story of the Mines. By Will B. Schwartz................................	10c
14.	THE HAUNTED TOWER. By Mrs. Henry Wood...........	10c
15.	THE WAGES OF SIN. By Miss M. E. Braddon.............	10c
16.	VICTOR AND VANQUISHED. By Mary Cecil Hay.........	20c
17.	OTHER FOOLS AND THEIR DOINGS; or, Life Among the Freedmen...................................	15c
18.	CHRISTIE'S OLD ORGAN. By Mrs. O. F. Walton.........	10c
19.	NELLIE, THE CLOCKMAKER'S DAUGHTER.............	10c
20.	NOT FORSAKEN. By Agnes Giberne.....................	10c
21.	BEDE'S CHARITY. By Hesba Stretton....................	15c
22.	LIFE OF REV. T. DE WITT TALMAGE, D.D..............	15c
23.	THE YOUNG APPRENTICE. By Hesba Stretton...........	10c
24.	SHEER OFF. By A. L. O. E...............................	15c
25.	IN PRISON AND OUT. By Hesba Stretton................	10c
26.	HISTORY OF A THREEPENNY BIT. By J. W. Kirton.....	10c
27.	FROGGY'S LITTLE BROTHER. By Brenda..............	15c
28.	WINDOW CURTAINS. By T. S. Arthur...................	20c
29.	A THORNY PATH. By Hesba Stretton....................	10c
30.	THE POOR CLERK AND HIS CROOKED SIXPENCE. By George E. Sargent................................	10c
31.	NINETY-NINE CHOICE READINGS AND RECITATIONS. No. 1. Compiled by J. S. Ogilvie........................	10c
32.	THE LITTLE CAPTAIN. By Lynde Palmer................	10c

The above list of stories by popular and well-known authors are offered to the public with the assurance that they will give entire satisfaction. They are printed from large, new type, on a good quality of heavy paper. No effort or expense will be spared to make this in reality "The People's Library."

Each number contains a complete first-class story, from American and English authors. The People's Library is for sale by all newsdealers and booksellers in the United States. Ask your newsdealer for a copy, and try one of the stories. If you cannot get them from your bookseller, any number will be sent by mail on receipt of 12 cents for a 10-cent number, 18 cents for a 15-cent number, and 25 cents for a 20-cent number. One-cent stamps taken. Address all orders to

J. S. OGILVIE & CO., Publishers,

P. O. Box 2767.   25 Rose street, New York.

THE PEOPLE'S LIBRARY.

No.		Price
33.	THE OCTAGON; OR, THE OLD FERRY. By Mrs. M. E. Berry.	10c
34.	THE YOUNG WHALER. By W. H. G. Kingston.	10c
35.	CHATAUQUA LECTURES.	10c
36.	THE KING'S SERVANTS. By Hesba Stretton.	10c
37.	THE SECRET SORROW. By May Agnes Fleming.	20c
38.	A SHADOW ON THE THRESHOLD. By Mary Cecil Hay.	10c
39.	A LIFE'S SECRET. By Mrs. Henry Wood.	20c
40.	BUFFALO BILL. By Ned Buntline.	20c
41.	THE BLUNDERS OF A BASHFUL MAN. By the author of "A Bad Boy's Diary".	10c
42.	PERCY AND THE PROPHET. By Wilkie Collins.	10c
43.	HISTORY OF ATTEMPTED ASSASSINATION OF PRESIDENT GARFIELD.	20c
44.	THAT BEAUTIFUL WRETCH.	10c
45.	MRS. GEOFFREY. By The Duchess.	20c
46.	DORA THORNE.	20c
47.	JOSH BILLINGS' SPICE-BOX. By Josh Billings.	10c
48.	BEAUTIFUL, BUT POOR. By Julia Edwards.	10c
49.	LIKE NO OTHER LOVE. By the author of "Dora Thorne."	10c
50.	THE RUGG DOCUMENTS (First Series). By Clara Augusta.	10c
51.	NINETY-NINE CHOICE READINGS AND RECITATIONS, No. 2. Compiled by J. S. Ogilvie.	10c
52.	THE OCTOROON. By Miss M. E. Braddon.	10c
53.	THE GRASS WIDOW. By Lieut.-Col. F. E. West.	10c
54.	THE RUGG DOCUMENTS (Second Series). By Clara Augusta.	10c
55.	FATED TO MARRY. By Mrs. May Agnes Fleming.	10c
56.	CAST UPON THE WORLD. By Chas. E. Perine.	10c
57.	A DARK INHERITANCE. By Mary Cecil Hay.	10c
58.	HILARY'S FOLLY. By the author of "Dora Thorne".	10c
59.	COBWEBS AND CABLES. By Hesba Stretton.	10c
60.	THE RUGG DOCUMENTS (Third Series). By Clara Augusta	10c
61.	CHARLOTTE TEMPLE. By Mrs. Rowson.	10c
62.	A ROGUE'S LIFE. By Wilkie Collins.	10c
63.	THE BLACK SPECK. By F. W. Robinson.	10c
64.	MISSING. By Mary Cecil Hay.	10c
65.	THE RUGG DOCUMENTS (Fourth Series). By Clara Augusta.	10c
66.	A GILDED SIN. By the author of "Dora Thorne."	10c

The above list of stories by popular and well-known authors are offered to the public with the assurance that they will give entire satisfaction. They are printed from large, new type, on a good quality of heavy paper. No effort or expense will be spared to make this in reality "The People's Library."

Each number contains a complete first-class story, from American and English authors. The People's Library is for sale by all newsdealers and booksellers in the United States. Ask your newsdealer for a copy, and try one of the stories. If you cannot get them from your bookseller, any number will be sent by mail on receipt of 12 cents for a 10-cent number, 18 cents for a 15-cent number, and 25 cents for a 20-cent number. One-cent stamps taken. Address all orders to

J. S. OGILVIE & CO., Publishers,
P. O. Box 2767.   25 Rose street, New York.

THE PEOPLE'S LIBRARY.

No.		Price.
67.	BORROWED PLUMES. By Miss Jennie S. Alcott	10c
68.	THE SORROW OF A SECRET. By Mary Cecil Hay	10c
69.	EAST LYNNE. By Mrs. Henry Wood	20c
70.	THE RUGG DOCUMENTS (Fifth Series). By Clara Augusta	10c
71.	THE FATAL LILIES. By the author of "Dora Thorne."	10c
72.	THE TALE OF SIN. By Mrs. Henry Wood	10c
73.	OUR GERALDINE. By the author of "A Family History."	10c
74.	SISTER DORA. By Margaret Lonsdale	10c
75.	A STRANGE DREAM. By Rhoda Broughton	10c
76.	HIS HEART OF OAK. By the author of "Dora Thorne."	10c
77.	ROUND THE MOON. By Jules Verne	10c
78.	THE SHADOW IN THE HOUSE. By Eliza A. Dupuy	10c
79.	A GREAT ATONEMENT. By author of "An Error of Love"	10c
80.	THORNS OR GRAPES? By author of "His Victoria Cross."	10c
81.	SHE WOULD BE A LADY. By author of "Love's Devotion"	10c
82.	THE PRIVATE SECRETARY. By the author of "The Battle of Dorking."	15c
83.	THE DOCTOR'S DAUGHTER. By Mrs. Henry Wood	10c
84.	LOVE IN IDLENESS. By the author of "Loveday."	10c
85.	THE LITTLE EARL. By Ouida	10c
86.	WON FOR A WAGER. By Mary N. Holmes	10c
87.	LIL: "Fair, Fair, With Golden Hair." By the Hon. Mrs. Fetherstonhaugh	10c
88.	IN THE HOLIDAYS. By Mary Cecil Hay	10c
89.	PROPOSING TO HER. By Emma S Southworth	10c
90.	BACK TO THE OLD HOME. By Mary Cecil Hay	10c
91.	THE LITTLE WIDOW. By the author of "Bertie."	10c
92.	UNDER LIFE'S KEY, and other stories. By Mary Cecil Hay	10c
93.	JANE EYRE. By Charlotte Bronte	20c
94.	FIGHTING HER WAY. By Rose Ashleigh	20c
95.	A CUNNING WOMAN. By author of "Ladybird's Penitence"	10c
96.	INTO THE SHADE, and other stories. By Mary Cecil Hay	10c
97.	TWICE STOLEN. By the author of "Tempted by Gold."	10c
98.	THE FUGITIVES. By Mrs. Oliphant	10c
99.	HER FACE TO THE FOE. By Mary N. Holmes	10c
100.	FOR LOVE OR GOLD? By Miss Jennie S. Alcott	20c
101.	THAT AMAZING PROFESSOR	10c
102.	A HAPPY RELEASE. By the author of "Constance Dare."	10c
103.	HER DARING VENTURE. By the author of "Mildred's Mistake."	10c
104.	THE FIGURE IN THE CORNER. By Miss M. E. Braddon.	10c
105.	DARKEST BEFORE DAWN	10c
106.	LADY AUDLEY'S SECRET. By Miss M. E. Braddon	20c
107.	"CASH SEVENTEEN." By Sophy S. Burr	10c

J. S. OGILVIE & CO., Publishers,

P. O. Box 2767. 25 Rose street, New York.

THE PEOPLE'S LIBRARY.

NUMBER.	PRICE.
100—FOR LOVE OR GOLD? By Miss Jennie S. Alcott	20c
101—THAT AMAZING PROFESSOR	10c
102—A HAPPY RELEASE. By the author of "Constance Dare"	10c
103—HER DARING VENTURE. By author of "Mildred's Mistake"	10c
104—THE FIGURE IN THE CORNER. By Miss M. E. Braddon	10c
105—DARKEST BEFORE DAWN	10c
106—LADY AUDLEY'S SECRET. By Miss M. E. Braddon	20c
107—"CASH SEVENTEEN." By Sophy S. Burr	10c
108—WIFE OR WIDOW? By the author of "The Missing Diamonds."	10c
109—GILT AND GOLD. By the author of "A Wife's Honor."	10c
110—A WIFE'S ORDEAL. By Emma S. Southworth	10c
111—SOUGHT AND SAVED. By M. A. Paull	20c
112—THE MISSING DIAMONDS. By the author of "Wife or Widow?"	10c
113—BY FAITH ALONE. By Nellie F. Haynes	10c
114—THE MYSTERY OF CEDAR COURT	10c
115—MAB TARLETON'S TRIAL	10c
116—HER FIRST LOVE. By the author of "Miss Litton's Lovers"	10c
117—MRS. CAUDLE'S CURTAIN LECTURES. By Douglas Jerrold	10c
118—HEIRESS TO A MILLION	10c
119—COBWEBS AND CABLES. (Part Second). By Hesba Stretton	15c
120—LIONEL FRANKLIN'S VICTORY. By E. Van Sommer	20c
121—WAS HE SEVERE? By Mrs. Henry Wood	10c
122—BRENDA YORKE. By Mary Cecil Hay	10c
123—THE SAD FORTUNES OF THE REV. AMOS BARTON. By George Eliot	10c
124—THE HAUNTED MAN. By Charles Dickens	10c
125—OWEN'S HOBBY. By Elmer Burleigh	20c
126—LADY MARABOUT'S TROUBLES. By "Ouida"	10c
127—A CHRISTMAS CAROL. By Charles Dickens	10c
128—THAT BEAUTIFUL LADY. By the author of "Dora Thorne"	10c
129—CHRISTOWELL. By R. D Blackmore	20c
130—THE THREE COUSINS. By Mrs. May Agnes Fleming	10c
131—THE LOST BANK-NOTE. By Mrs. Henry Wood	10c
132—MACON MOORE. By Judson R. Taylor	20c
133—DICK NETHERBY. By L. B. Walford	10c
134—A GOLDEN DAWN. By the author of "Dora Thorne"	10c
135—THE FARMER'S DAUGHTERS	10c
136—MY DARLING'S RANSOM. By Richard Dowling	10c
137—WEDDED AND PARTED. By the author of "Dora Thorne"	10c
138—HIS SECRET. By Miss M. E. Braddon	10c
139—A FROZEN SEA. By Wilkie Collins	10c
140—MARJORIE'S TRIAL. By the author of "A Cunning Woman"	10c
141—RETURNED TO LIFE. By Gerald Burre	10c
142—A TERRIBLE MISTAKE. By the author of "Dora Thorne"	10c
143—THE CLOVEN FOOT. By Miss M. E. Braddon	20c
144—NUMA ROUMESTAN. By Alphonse Daudet	10c
145—YOUR MONEY OR YOUR LIFE. By Wilkie Collins	10c
146—THE CAPTAINS' ROOM. By Walter Besant and James Rice	10c
147—TOM YORKE'S LEGACY. By Edward Garrett	10c
148—A DOUBLE BOND. By Linda Villari	10c
149—HIS GREAT REVENGE	10c
150—DIED YOUNG. By Elmer E. Russell	10c
151—HIS PHANTOM BRIDE	10c
152—TWO KISSES. By the author of "Dora Thorne"	10c
153—"A BAND OF THREE." By L. T. Meade	10c
154—THE WHITE NUN. By author of "The Bondage of Brandon"	10c
155—LOVE'S SACRIFICE. By W. G. Waleen	10c

Full sets of The People's Library always on hand, and for sale by

J. S. OGILVIE & Co., Publishers.

P. O. Box 2767.   25 Rose street, New York.

Something to Read!

$10.00 WORTH FOR $1.50!

We desire to call the attention of lovers of pure fiction to the fact that we now offer, in *bound book form*, the following seven complete stories, written by

Miss M. E. Braddon,

one of the most popular and pleasing authors in the world, and which are usually sold, in book form, for from $1.25 to $1.50 EACH.

We offer the SEVEN STORIES, bound in handsome English cloth, with elegant ornamental gold side and back stamp, sent by mail, post-paid, to any address, for only $1.50! Bound in heavy paper covers, $1.00.

List of Stories we sell for $1.50:

Lady Audley's Secret
The Octoroon,
The Cloven Foot,
His Secret,
A Wavering Image,
The Wages of Sin,
Aurora Floyd.

These stories are printed on fine heavy paper, from large, new type, and we guarantee satisfaction in *every respect* to all purchasers.

Ask your bookseller for "SOMETHING TO READ," written by Miss M. E. Braddon, and published by us; or send $1.50 to us and we will send them by mail, post-paid.

THE STORIES ARE NOT SOLD SEPARATELY IN THIS FORM. We want Agents to sell them in every town and village in the whole land, to whom we offer liberal terms.

Address all orders and applications for Agency to

J. S. OGILVIE & CO., Publishers,

P. O. Box 2767.   25 Rose Street, New York.

Something to Read!

$10.00 WORTH FOR $1.50!

We desire to call the attention of lovers of pure fiction to the fact that we now offer, in *bound book form*, the following seven complete stories, written by

Mrs. Henry Wood,

one of the most popular and pleasing authors in the world, and which are usually sold, in book form, for from $1.25 to $1.50 EACH.

We offer the SEVEN STORIES, bound in handsome English cloth, with elegant ornamental gold side and back stamp, sent by mail, post-paid, to any address, for only $1.50! Bound in heavy paper covers, $1.00.

List of Stories we send for $1.50:

East Lynne;
    A Life's Secret;
        The Tale of Sin;
            Was He Severe?
                The Lost Bank-Note;
                    The Doctor's Daughter;
                        The Haunted Tower.

These stories are printed on fine heavy paper, from large, new type, and we guarantee satisfaction in every respect to all purchasers.

Ask your bookseller for "SOMETHING TO READ," published by us; or send $1.50 to us and we will send them by mail, post-paid.

THE STORIES ARE NOT SOLD SEPARATELY IN THIS FORM. We want Agents to sell them in every town and village in the whole land, to whom we offer liberal terms.

Address all orders and applications for Agency to

J. S. OGILVIE & CO., Publishers,

P. O. Box 2767.   25 Rose Street, New York.

Courtship and Marriage; or, The Mysteries of Making Love Fully Explained $0.15

Crime Against Society (A). By Rev. Leonard Woolsey Bacon. 12mo, 36 pages, price.................................. .10

A Dark Marriage Morn. 12mo. 336 pages. By Bertha M. Clay, author of "Dora Thorne." 1.50

The Diary of a Minister's Wife. Complete in Nine Parts. Price per part. .... .10

Diary of a Minister's Wife. By Almedia M. Brown. Complete edition, 12mo, 544 pages. Handsomely bound in cloth, with fine, full-page illustrations................................ 1.50

Fritz, the German Detective. By Tony Pastor. 12mo, 150 pages. Paper cover, 25 cents; cloth................... .60

From Farm Boy to Senator. By Horatio Alger, Jr. 16mo, 310 pages. Handsomely bound in cloth. Price....... 1.25

Fun for All. This book contains nearly five hundred conundrums, riddles, humorous sayings, and is just the book to have if you wish to entertain an evening company. 16mo, 64 pages. Paper cover, 15 cents; board cover............................... .25

The Garfield Memorial Picture. Handsomely printed on heavy plate paper. Size 19 x 24 inches................. .25

The Guiteau Trial Picture. Size 19 x 24 inches........ .25

Gipsy Blair, The Western Detective. By Judson R. Taylor. 12mo, 150 pages. Paper cover, 25 cents; cloth... .60

Ha! Ha! Ha! 72 pages of Fun. Paper cover........... .10

In Prison and Out. By Hesba Stretton. 12mo, 206 pages. .75

The Life and Death of James A. Garfield. 500 pp., with 10 illustrations.. 1.50

The Lord's Purse Bearer. 16mo, 225 pages. By Hesba Stretton .... .75

The Lover's Guide. A book no lover should be without. .15

Macon Moore, the Southern Detective. By Judson R. Taylor. 12mo, 150 pages. Paper cover, 25 cents; cloth... .60

Miss Slimmens' Boarding House. By the author of "A Bad Boy's Diary." 16mo, 188 pages, with nine illustrations. Paper cover, 25 cents; cloth............................... .60

Miss Slimmens' Window. 16mo, 150 pages. Paper cover, with 13 illustrations 25 cents; cloth...................... .60

Nancy Hartshorn at Chautauqua. By Mrs. Nancy Hartshorn. 16mo, 200 pages, illustrated. Paper cover, 50 cents; cloth.. 1.00

Something to Read, No. 2. Heavy paper cover, $1.00; bound in cloth.. $1.50

Contains the following seven complete stories, by Miss M. E. Braddon: Lady Audley's Secret, The Octoroon, The Cloven Foot, His Secret, A Wavering Image, The Wages of Sin, Aurora Floyd.

Something to Read, No. 3. Heavy paper cover, $1.00; bound in cloth.. 1.50

Contains the following seven complete stories by Bertha M. Clay: Dora Thorne, A Golden Heart, Hilda, Wedded and Parted, Hilary's Folly, The Cost of Her Love, A Gilded Sin.

Something to Read, No. 4. Heavy paper cover, $1.00; bound in cloth.. 1.50

Contains the following ten complete stories by Mary Cecil Hay: A Shadow on the Threshold, A Dark Inheritance, Back to the Old Home, Victor and Vanquished, The Sorrow of a Secret, In the Holidays, Under Life's Key, Into the Shade, Brenda Yorke, Missing.

Sunday-School Reward Cards. Packet No. 1. Eight handsome designs. Size 2¾ x 4¼ inches. 25 cards in packet, with Scripture text on each card, 25 cents.—Packet No. 2 contains 18 cards, 6 designs, 25 cents.—Packet No. 3 contains 30 cards, 6 designs...... .25

Tom the Bootblack. By Horatio Alger, Jr. 12mo, 263 pages... 1.25

Tony the Hero. By Horatio Alger, Jr. 12mo, 255 pages. 1.25

Trify, the Maid of Copps Cliff. By Mrs. M. L. B. Ewell, 8vo, 96 pages.. .15

Wayside Gleanings. By Evalyne T. Perine. 12mo, 260 pages... 1.00

Why I Ought to Go to Church. By Rev. Selah W. Strong. 18mo, 16 pages. Price, 3 cents each; 100 copies................. 2.50

Window Curtains. By T. S. Arthur. 12mo, 288 pages.... 1.00

The Young Apprentice. By Hesba Stretton. 12mo, 220 pages... .75

Advertising Cards. The People's Packet, No. 1. Price per packet.. .15

The intense interest among all classes of people in collecting advertising cards has created a demand for a great variety, and we call attention to our set of fifty cards, size 4¼ x 2¼ inches, no two alike, which we sell for only 15 cents. No collection is complete without this set. They are all comic, and we guarantee satisfaction.

The above publications are for sale by all newsdealers and booksellers, or they will be mailed free, to any address, on receipt of price, by the publishers. Send money by Post-Office Order or Registered Letter. Sums under One Dollar send in one-cent postage-stamps. Address all orders to

J. S. OGILVIE & CO., Publishers,

P. O. Box 2767.   31 ROSE STREET, NEW YORK.

www.ingramcontent.com/pod-product-compliance
Lightning Source LLC
Chambersburg PA
CBHW020053200426
43197CB00050B/583